DevOps with Kubernetes

Accelerating software delivery with container orchestrators

Hideto Saito
Hui-Chuan Chloe Lee
Cheng-Yang Wu

BIRMINGHAM - MUMBAI

DevOps with Kubernetes

First published: October 2017

Production reference: 1121017

Published by Packt Publishing Ltd.
Livery Place
35 Livery Street
Birmingham
B3 2PB, UK.

ISBN 978-1-78839-664-6

www.packtpub.com

Credits

Authors
Hideto Saito
Hui-Chuan Chloe Lee
Cheng-Yang Wu

Copy Editors
Laxmi Subramanian
Safis Editing

Reviewer
Guang Ya Liu

Project Coordinator
Shweta H Birwatkar

Proofreader
Safis Editing

Commissioning Editor
Gebin George

Acquisition Editor
Chandan Kumar

Indexer
Pratik Shirodkar

Content Development Editor
Dattatraya More

Graphics
Tania Dutta

Technical Editor
Jovita Alva

Production Coordinator
Shantanu Zagade

About the Authors

Hideto Saito has around 20 years of experience in the computer industry. In 1998, while working for Sun Microsystems Japan, he was impressed with Solaris OS, OPENSTEP, and Sun Ultra Enterprise 10000 (AKA StarFire). Then, he decided to pursue the UNIX and MacOS X operation systems.

In 2006, he relocated to southern California as a software engineer to develop products and services running on Linux and MacOS X. He was especially renowned for his quick Objective-C coding when he was drunk.

He is also an enthusiastic fan of Japanese anime, drama, and motor sports, and loves Japanese Otaku culture.

Hui-Chuan Chloe Lee is a DevOps and software developer. She has worked in the software industry on a wide range of projects for over 5 years. As a technology enthusiast, Chloe loves trying and learning new technologies, which makes her life happier and more fulfilled. In her free time, she enjoys reading, traveling, and spending time with the people she loves.

Cheng-Yang Wu has been tackling infrastructure and system reliability since he received his master's degree in computer science from the National Taiwan University. His laziness prompted him to master DevOps skills to maximize his efficiency at work in order to squeeze in writing code for fun. He enjoys cooking as it's just like working with software—a perfect dish always comes from balanced flavors and fine-tuned tastes.

About the Reviewer

Guang Ya Liu is a Senior Software Architect in IBM CSL (China System Lab) and now focuses on cloud computing, data center operating systems and container technology, he is also a Member of IBM Academy of Technology. He used to be a OpenStack Magnum Core Member from 2015 to 2017, and now act as Kubernetes Member and Apache Mesos Committer & PMC Member. Guang Ya is also the organizer for Mesos, Kubernetes and OpenStack Xi'an Meetup and successfully held many meetups for those open source projects in China. He also holds two US patents related to cloud and six publised IPs. Visit his GitHub here: https://github.com/gyliu513.

www.PacktPub.com

For support files and downloads related to your book, please visit `www.PacktPub.com`. Did you know that Packt offers eBook versions of every book published, with PDF and ePub files available? You can upgrade to the eBook version at `www.PacktPub.com` and as a print book customer, you are entitled to a discount on the eBook copy. Get in touch with us at `service@packtpub.com` for more details. At `www.PacktPub.com`, you can also read a collection of free technical articles, sign up for a range of free newsletters and receive exclusive discounts and offers on Packt books and eBooks.

`https://www.packtpub.com/mapt`

Get the most in-demand software skills with Mapt. Mapt gives you full access to all Packt books and video courses, as well as industry-leading tools to help you plan your personal development and advance your career.

Why subscribe?

- Fully searchable across every book published by Packt
- Copy and paste, print, and bookmark content
- On demand and accessible via a web browser

Customer Feedback

Thanks for purchasing this Packt book. At Packt, quality is at the heart of our editorial process. To help us improve, please leave us an honest review on this book's Amazon page at `https://www.amazon.com/dp/1788396642`.

If you'd like to join our team of regular reviewers, you can email us at `customerreviews@packtpub.com`. We award our regular reviewers with free eBooks and videos in exchange for their valuable feedback. Help us be relentless in improving our products!

Table of Contents

Preface

This book walks you through a journey of learning fundamental concept and useful skills for DevOps, containers and Kubernetes.

What this book covers

Chapter 1, *Introduction to DevOps*, walks you through the evolution from the past to what we call DevOps today and the tools that you should know. Demand for people with DevOps skills has been growing rapidly over the last few years. It has accelerated software development and delivery speed and has also helped business agility.

Chapter 2, *DevOps with Container*, helps you learn the fundamentals and container orchestration. With the trend of microservices, container has been a handy and essential tool for every DevOps because of its language agnostic isolation.

Chapter 3, *Getting Started with Kubernetes*, explores the key components and API objects in Kubernetes and how to deploy and manage containers in a Kubernetes cluster. Kubernetes eases the pain of container orchestration with a lot of killer features, such as container scaling, mounting storage systems, and service discovery.

Chapter 4, *Working with Storage and Resources*, describes volume management and also explains CPU and memory management in Kubernetes. Container storage management can be hard in a cluster.

Chapter 5, *Network and Security*, explains how to allow inbound connection to access Kubernetes services and how default networking works in Kubernetes. External access to our services is necessary for business needs.

Chapter 6, *Monitoring and Logging*, shows you how to monitor a resource's usage at application, container, and node level using Prometheus. This chapter also shows how to collect logs from your applications, as well as Kubernetes with Elasticsearch, Fluentd, and Kibana stack. Ensuring a service is up and healthy is one of the major responsibilities of DevOps.

Chapter 7, *Continuous Delivery*, explains how to build a Continuous Delivery pipeline with GitHub/DockerHub/TravisCI. It also explains how to manage updates, eliminate the potential impact when doing rolling updates, and prevent possible failure. Continuous Delivery is an approach to speed up your time-to-market.

Chapter 8, *Cluster Administration*, describes how to solve the preceding problems with the Kubernetes namespace and ResourceQuota and how to do access control in Kubernetes. Setting up administrative boundaries and access control to Kubernetes cluster are crucial to DevOps.

Chapter 9, *Kubernetes on AWS*, explains AWS components and shows how to provision Kubernetes on AWS. AWS is the most popular public cloud. It brings the infrastructure agility and flexibility to our world.

Chapter 10, *Kubernetes on GCP*, helps you understand the difference between GCP and AWS, and the benefit of running containerized applications in hosted service from Kubernetes' perspective. Google Container Engine in GCP is a managed environment for Kubernetes.

Chapter 11, *What's Next?*, introduces other similar technologies, such as Docker Swarm mode, Amazon ECS, and Apache Mesos and you'll have an understanding of which the best approach is for your business. Kubernetes is open. This chapter will teach you how to get in touch with Kubernetes community to learn ideas from others.

What you need for this book

This book will guide you through the methodology of software development and delivery with Docker container and Kubernetes using macOS and public cloud (AWS and GCP). You will need to install minikube, AWSCLI, and the Cloud SDK to run the code samples present in this book.

Who this book is for

This book is intended for DevOps professionals with some software development experience who are willing to scale, automate, and shorten software delivery to the market.

Conventions

In this book, you will find a number of text styles that distinguish between different kinds of information. Here are some examples of these styles and an explanation of their meaning.

Code words in text, database table names, folder names, filenames, file extensions, pathnames, dummy URLs, user input, and Twitter handles are shown as follows: "Mount the downloaded `WebStorm-10*.dmg` disk image file as another disk in your system."

Any command-line input or output is written as follows:

```
$ sudo yum -y -q install nginx
$ sudo /etc/init.d/nginx start
Starting nginx:
```

New terms and **important words** are shown in bold. Words that you see on the screen, for example, in menus or dialog boxes, appear in the text like this: "The shortcuts in this book are based on the **Mac OS X 10.5+** scheme."

Warnings or important notes appear like this.

Tips and tricks appear like this.

Reader feedback

Feedback from our readers is always welcome. Let us know what you think about this book-what you liked or disliked. Reader feedback is important for us as it helps us develop titles that you will really get the most out of.

To send us general feedback, simply email feedback@packtpub.com, and mention the book's title in the subject of your message. If there is a topic that you have expertise in and you are interested in either writing or contributing to a book, see our author guide at www.packtpub.com/authors.

Customer support

Now that you are the proud owner of a Packt book, we have a number of things to help you to get the most from your purchase.

Downloading the example code

You can download the example code files for this book from your account at `http://www.packtpub.com`. If you purchased this book elsewhere, you can visit `http://www.packtpub.com/support` and register to have the files emailed directly to you. You can download the code files by following these steps:

1. Log in or register to our website using your email address and password.
2. Hover the mouse pointer on the **SUPPORT** tab at the top.
3. Click on **Code Downloads & Errata**.
4. Enter the name of the book in the **Search** box.
5. Select the book for which you're looking to download the code files.
6. Choose from the drop-down menu where you purchased this book from.
7. Click on **Code Download**.

Once the file is downloaded, please make sure that you unzip or extract the folder using the latest version of:

- WinRAR / 7-Zip for Windows
- Zipeg / iZip / UnRarX for Mac
- 7-Zip / PeaZip for Linux

The code bundle for the book is also hosted on GitHub at `https://github.com/PacktPublishing/DevOpswithKubernetes`. We also have other code bundles from our rich catalog of books and videos available at `https://github.com/PacktPublishing/`. Check them out!

Downloading the color images of this book

We also provide you with a PDF file that has color images of the screenshots/diagrams used in this book. The color images will help you better understand the changes in the output. You can download this file from `https://www.packtpub.com/sites/default/files/downloads/DevOpswithKubernetes_ColorImages.pdf`.

Errata

Although we have taken every care to ensure the accuracy of our content, mistakes do happen. If you find a mistake in one of our books-maybe a mistake in the text or the code-we would be grateful if you could report this to us. By doing so, you can save other readers from frustration and help us improve subsequent versions of this book. If you find any errata, please report them by visiting http://www.packtpub.com/submit-errata, selecting your book, clicking on the **Errata Submission Form** link, and entering the details of your errata. Once your errata are verified, your submission will be accepted and the errata will be uploaded to our website or added to any list of existing errata under the Errata section of that title.

To view the previously submitted errata, go to https://www.packtpub.com/books/content/support and enter the name of the book in the search field. The required information will appear under the **Errata** section.

Piracy

Piracy of copyrighted material on the internet is an ongoing problem across all media. At Packt, we take the protection of our copyright and licenses very seriously. If you come across any illegal copies of our works in any form on the internet, please provide us with the location address or website name immediately so that we can pursue a remedy. Please contact us at copyright@packtpub.com with a link to the suspected pirated material.

We appreciate your help in protecting our authors and our ability to bring you valuable content.

Questions

If you have a problem with any aspect of this book, you can contact us at questions@packtpub.com, and we will do our best to address the problem.

1
Introduction to DevOps

Software delivery cycle has been getting shorter and shorter, while on the other hand, application size has been getting bigger and bigger. Software developers and IT operators are under the pressure to find a solution to this. There is a new role, called **DevOps**, which is dedicated to support software building and delivery.

This chapter covers the following topics:

- How has software delivery methodology changed?
- What is microservice, and why do people adopt this architecture?
- How does DevOps support to build and deliver the application to the user?

Software delivery challenges

Building a computer application and delivering it to the customer has been discussed and has evolved over time. It is related to **Software Development Life Cycle (SDLC)**; there are several types of processes, methodologies, and histories. In this section, we will describe its evolution.

Waterfall and physical delivery

Back in the 1990s, software delivery was adopted by a **physical** method, such as a floppy disk or a CD-ROM. Therefore, SDLC was a very long-term schedule, because it was not easy to (re)deliver to the customer.

At that moment, a major software development methodology was a **waterfall model**, which has requirements/design/implementation/verification/maintenance phases as shown in the following diagram:

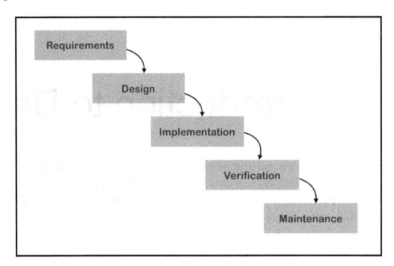

In this case, we can't go back to the previous phase. For example, after starting or finishing the **Implementation** phase, it is not acceptable to go back to the **Design** phase (to find a technical expandability issue, for example). This is because it will impact the overall schedule and cost. The project tends to proceed and complete to release, then it goes to the next release cycle including a new design.

It perfectly matches the physical software delivery because it needs to coordinate with logistics management that press and deliver the floppy/CD-ROM to the user. Waterfall model and physical delivery used to take a year to several years.

Agile and electrical delivery

A few years later, the internet became widely accepted, and then software delivery method also changed from physical to **electrical**, such as online download. Therefore, many software companies (also known as dot-com companies) tried to figure out how to shorten the SDLC process in order to deliver the software that can beat the competitors.

Many developers started to adopt new methodologies such as incremental, iterative, or **agile** models and then deliver to the customer faster. Even if new bugs are found, it is now easier to update and deliver to the customer as a patch by electrical delivery. Microsoft Windows update was also introduced since Windows 98.

In this case, the software developer writes only a small logic or module, instead of the entire application in one shot. Then, it delivers to the QA, and then the developer continues to add a new module and finally delivers it to the QA again.

When the desired modules or functions are ready, it will be released as shown in the following diagram:

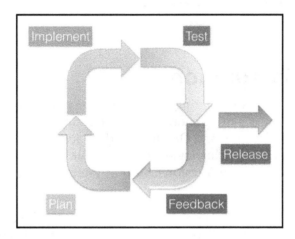

This model makes the SDLC cycle and the software delivery faster and also easy to be adjust during the process, because the cycle is from a few weeks to a few months which is small enough to make a quick adjustment.

Although this model is currently favoured by the majority, at that moment, application software delivery meant software binary, such as EXE program which is designed to be installed and run on the customer's PC. On the other hand, the infrastructure (such as server and network) is very static and set up beforehand. Therefore, SDLC doesn't tend to include these infrastructures in the scope yet.

Software delivery on the cloud

A few years later, smartphones (such as iPhone) and wireless technology (such as Wi-Fi and 4G network) became widely accepted, and software application also changed from binary to the online service. The web browser is the interface of the application software, which need not be installed anymore. On the other hand, infrastructure becomes dynamic, since the application requirement keeps changing and the capacity needs to grow as well.

Virtualization technology and **Software Defined Network** (**SDN**) make the server machine dynamic. Now, cloud services such as **Amazon Web Services** (**AWS**) and **Google Cloud Platform** (**GCP**) can be easy to create and manage dynamic infrastructures.

Now, infrastructure is one of the important components and being within a scope of Software Development Delivery Cycle, because the application is installed and runs on the server side, rather than a client PC. Therefore, software and service delivery cycle takes between a few days to a few weeks.

Continuous Integration

As discussed previously, the surrounding software delivery environment keeps changing; however, the delivery cycle is getting shorter and shorter. In order to achieve rapid delivery with higher quality, the developer and QA start to adopt some automation technologies. One of the popular automation technologies is **Continuous Integration** (**CI**). CI contains some combination of tools, such as **Version Control Systems** (**VCS**), **build server**, and **testing automation tools**.

VCS helps the developer to maintain program source code onto the central server. It prevents overwriting or conflict with other developers' code and also preserves the history. Therefore, it makes it easier to keep the source code consistent and deliver to the next cycle.

The same as VCS, there is a centralized build servers that connects VCS to retrieve the source code periodically or automatically when the developer updates the code to VCS, and then trigger a new build. If the build fails, it notifies the developer in a timely manner. Therefore, it helps the developer when someone commits the broken code into the VCS.

Testing automation tools are also integrated with build server that invoke the unit test program after the build succeeds, then notifies the result to the developer and QA. It helps to identify when somebody writes a buggy code and stores to VCS.

The entire flow of CI is as shown in the following diagram:

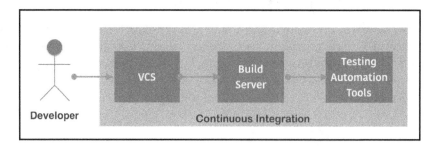

CI helps both the developer and the QA not only to increase the quality, but also to shorten archiving an application or module package cycle. In an age of electrical delivery to the customer, CI is more than enough. However, because delivery to the customer means to deploy to the server.

Continuous Delivery

CI plus deployment automation is the ideal process for the server application to provide a service to customers. However, there are some technical challenges that need to be resolved. How to deliver a software to the server? How to gracefully shutdown the existing application? How to replace and rollback the application? How to upgrade or replace if the system library also needs to change? How to modify the user and group settings in OS if needed? and so on.

Because the infrastructure includes the server and network, it all depends on an environment such as Dev/QA/staging/production. Each environment has different server configuration and IP address.

Continuous Delivery (**CD**) is a practice that could be achieved; it is a combination of CI tool, configuration management tool, and orchestration tool:

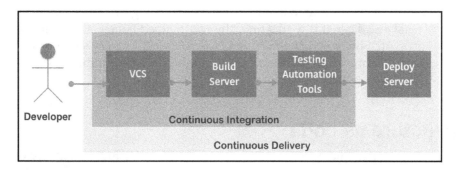

Configuration management

The configuration management tool helps to configure an OS including the user, group, and system libraries, and also manages multiple servers that keep consistent with the desired state or configuration if we replace the server.

It is not a scripting language, because scripting language performs to execute a command based on the script line by line. If we execute the script twice, it may cause some error, for example, attempt to create the same user twice. On the other hand, configuration management looks at the **state**, so if user is created already, the configuration management tool doesn't do anything. But if we delete a user accidentally or intentionally, the configuration management tool will create the user again.

It also supports to deploy or install your application to the server. Because if you tell the configuration management tool to download your application, then set it up and run the application, it tries to do so.

In addition, if you tell the configuration management tool to shut down your application, then download and replace to a new package if available, and then restart the application, it keeps up to date with the latest version.

Of course, some of the users want to update the application only when it is required, such as blue-green deployments. The configuration management tool allows you to trigger to execute manually too.

Blue-green deployments is a technique that prepares the two sets of application stack, then only one environment (example: blue) is servicing to the production. Then when you need to deploy a new version of application, deploy to the other side (example: green) then perform the final test. Then if it works fine, change the load balancer or router setting to switch the network flow from blue to green. Then green becomes a production, while blue becomes dormant and waiting for the next version deployment.

Infrastructure as code

The configuration management tool supports not only OS or Virtual Machine, but also cloud infrastructure. If you need to create and configure a network, storage, and Virtual Machine on the cloud, it requires some of the cloud operations.

But the configuration management tool helps to automate the setupcloud infrastructure by configuration file, as shown in the following diagram:

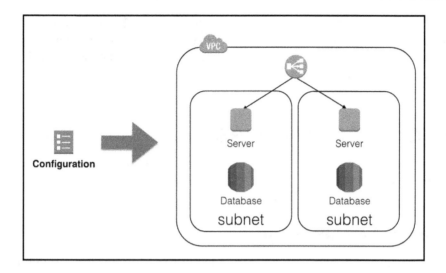

Configuration management has some advantage against maintaining an operation manual **Standard Operation Procedure** (**SOP**). For example, maintaining a configuration file using **VCS** such as Git, you can trace the history of how the environment setting has changed.

It is also easy to duplicate the environment. For example, you need an additional environment on cloud. If you follow the traditional approach, (that is, to read the SOP document to operate the cloud), it always has a potential human error and operation error. On the other hand, we can execute the configuration management tool that creates an environment on cloud quickly and automatically.

 Infrastructure as code may or may not be included in the CD process, because infrastructure replacement or update cost is higher than just replacing an application binary on the server.

Orchestration

The orchestration tool is also categorized as one of the configuration management tools. However its more intelligent and dynamic when configuring and allocating the cloud resources. For example, orchestration tool manages several server resources and networks, and then when the administrator wants to increase the application instances, orchestration tool can determine an available server and then deploy and configure the application and network automatically.

Although orchestration tool is beyond the SDLC, it helps Continuous Delivery when it needs to scale the application and refactor the infrastructure resource.

Overall, the SDLC has been evolved to achieve rapid delivery by several processes, tools, and methodologies. Eventually, software (service) delivery takes anywhere from a few hours to a day. While at the same time, software architecture and design has also evolved to achieve large and rich applications.

Trend of microservices

Software architecture and design also keep evolving, based on the target environment and volume of the application's size.

Modular programming

When the application size is getting bigger, developers tried to divide by several modules. Each module should be independent and reusable, and should be maintained by different developer teams. Then, when we start to implement an application, the application just initializes and uses these modules to build a larger application efficiently.

The following example shows what kind of library Nginx (https://www.nginx.com) uses on CentOS 7. It indicates that Nginx uses OpenSSL, POSIX thread library, PCRE the regular expression library, zlib the compression library, GNU C library, and so on. So, Nginx didn't reinvent to implement SSL encryption, regular expression, and so on:

```
$ /usr/bin/ldd /usr/sbin/nginx
  linux-vdso.so.1 =>  (0x00007ffd96d79000)
  libdl.so.2 => /lib64/libdl.so.2 (0x00007fd96d61c000)
  libpthread.so.0 => /lib64/libpthread.so.0
  (0x00007fd96d400000)
  libcrypt.so.1 => /lib64/libcrypt.so.1
  (0x00007fd96d1c8000)
  libpcre.so.1 => /lib64/libpcre.so.1 (0x00007fd96cf67000)
  libssl.so.10 => /lib64/libssl.so.10 (0x00007fd96ccf9000)
  libcrypto.so.10 => /lib64/libcrypto.so.10
  (0x00007fd96c90e000)
  libz.so.1 => /lib64/libz.so.1 (0x00007fd96c6f8000)
  libprofiler.so.0 => /lib64/libprofiler.so.0
  (0x00007fd96c4e4000)
   libc.so.6 => /lib64/libc.so.6 (0x00007fd96c122000)
   . . .
```

The `ldd` command is included in the `glibc-common` package on CentOS.

Package management

Java language and several lightweight programming languages such as Python, Ruby, and JavaScript have their own module or package management tool. For example, Maven (`http://maven.apache.org`) for Java, pip (`https://pip.pypa.io`) for Python, RubyGems (`https://rubygems.org`) for Ruby and npm (`https://www.npmjs.com`) for JavaScript.

Package management tool allows you to register your module or package to the centralized or private repository, and also allows to download the necessary packages. The following screenshot shows Maven repository for AWS SDK:

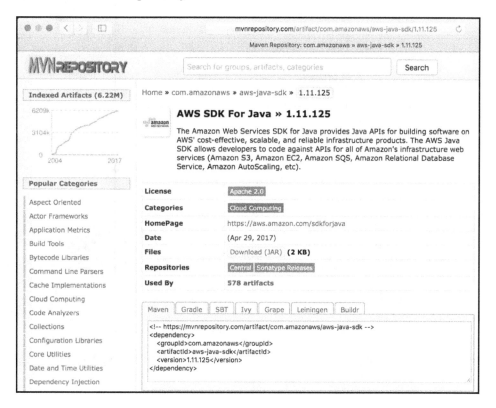

When you add some particular dependencies to your application, Maven downloads the necessary packages. The following screenshot is the result you get when you add `aws-java-sdk` dependency to your application:

Modular programming helps you to increase software development speed and reduce it to reinvent the wheel, so it is the most popular way to develop a software application now.

However, applications need more and more combination of modules, packages, and frameworks, as and when we keep adding a feature and logic. This makes the application more complex and larger, especially server-side applications. This is because it usually needs to connect to a database such as RDBMS, as well as an authentication server such as LDAP, and then return the result to the user by HTML with the appropriate design.

Therefore, developers have adopted some software design patterns in order to develop an application with a bunch of modules within an application.

MVC design pattern

One of the popular application design patterns is **Model View and Controller** (MVC). It defines three layers. **View** layer is in charge of **user interface (UI) input output (I/O)**. **Model** layer is in charge of data query and persistency such as load and store to database. Then, the **Controller** layer is in charge of business logic that is halfway between **View** and **Model**:

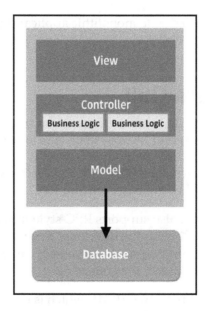

There are some frameworks that help developers to make MVC easier, such as Struts (https://struts.apache.org/), SpringMVC (https://projects.spring.io/spring-framework/), Ruby on Rails (http://rubyonrails.org/), and Django (https://www.djangoproject.com/). MVC is one of the successful software design pattern that is used for the foundation of modern web applications and services.

MVC defines a border line between every layer which allows many developers to jointly develop the same application. However, it causes side effects. That is, the size of the source code within the application keeps getting bigger. This is because database code (**Model**), presentation code (**View**), and business logic (**Controller**) are all within the same VCS repository. It eventually makes impact on the software development cycle, which gets slower again! It is called **monolithic**, which contains a lot of code that builds a giant exe/war program.

Monolithic application

There is no clear measurement of monolithic application definition, but it used to have more than 50 modules or packages, more than 50 database tables, and then it needs more than 30 minutes to build. When it needs to add or modify one module, it affects a lot of code, therefore developers try to minimize the application code change. This hesitation causes worse effects such that sometimes the application even dies because no one wants to maintain the code anymore.

Therefore, the developer starts to divide monolithic applications in to small pieces of application and connect via the network.

Remote Procedure Call

Actually, dividing an application in to small pieces and connecting via the network has been attempted back in the 1990s. Sun Microsystems introduced **Sun RPC** (**Remote Procedure Call**). It allows you to use the module remotely. One of popular Sun RPC implementers is **Network File System** (**NFS**). CPU OS versions are independent across NFS client and NFS server, because they are based on Sun RPC.

The programming language itself also supports RPC-style functionality. UNIX and C language have the `rpcgen` tool. It helps the developer to generate a stub code, which is in charge of network communication code, so the developer can use the C function style and be relieved from difficult network layer programming.

Java has **Java Remote Method Invocation** (**RMI**) which is similar to Sun RPC, but for Java, **RMI compiler** (**rmic**) generates the stub code that connects remote Java processes to invoke the method and get a result back. The following diagram shows Java RMI procedure flow:

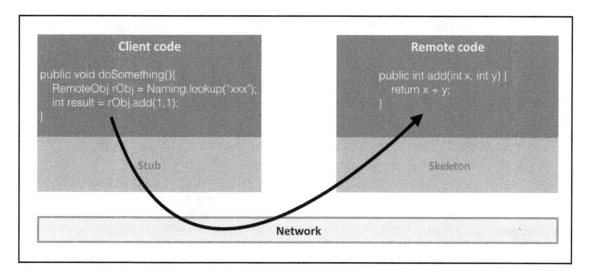

Objective C also has **distributed object** and .NET has **remoting**, so most of the modern programming languages have the capability of Remote Procedure Call out of the box.

These Remote Procedure Call designs have the benefit to divide an application into multiple processes (programs). Individual programs can have separate source code repositories. It works well although machine resource (CPU, memory) was limited during 1990s and 2000s.

However, it was designed and intended to use the same programming language and also designed for client/server model architecture, instead of a distributed architecture. In addition, there was less security consideration; therefore, it is not recommended to use over a public network.

In the 2000s, there was an initiative **web services** that used **SOAP** (HTTP/SSL) as data transport, using XML as data presentation and service definition **Web Services Description Language** (**WSDL**), then used **Universal Description, Discovery, and Integration** (**UDDI**) as the service registry to look up a web services application. However, as the machine resources were not rich and due to the complexity of web services programming and maintainability, it is not widely accepted by developers.

RESTful design

Go to 2010s, now machine power and even the smartphone have plenty of CPU resource, in addition to network bandwidth of a few hundred Mbps everywhere. So, the developer starts to utilize these resources to make application code and system structure as easy as possible making the software development cycle quicker.

Based on hardware resources, it is a natural decision to use HTTP/SSL as RPC transport, but from having experience with web services difficulty, the developer makes it simple as follows:

- By making HTTP and SSL/TLS a standard transport
- By using HTTP method for **Create/Load/Upload/Delete** (**CLUD**) operation, such as GET/POST/PUT/DELETE
- By using URI as the resource identifier such as: user ID 123 as /user/123/
- By using JSON as the standard data presentation

It is called **RESTful** design, and that has been widely accepted by many developers and become de facto standard of distributed applications. RESTful application allows any programming language as it is HTTP-based, so the RESTful server is Java and client Python is very natural.

It brings freedom and opportunities to the developer that its easy to perform code refactoring, upgrade a library and even switch to another programming language. It also encourages the developer to build a distributed modular design by multiple RESTful applications, which is called microservices.

If you have multiple RESTful applications, there is a concern on how to manage multiple source code on VCS and how to deploy multiple RESTful servers. However, Continuous Integration, and Continuous Delivery automation makes a lower bar to build and deploy a multiple RESTful server application easier.

Therefore, microservices design is getting popular for web application developers.

Microservices

Although the name is micro, it is actually heavy enough compared to the applications from 1990s or 2000s. It uses full stack of HTTP/SSL server and contains entire MVC layers. The microservices design should care about the following topics:

- **Stateless**: This doesn't store user session to the system, which helps to scale out easier.
- **No shared datastore**: The microservice should own the datastore such as database. It shouldn't share with the other application. It helps to encapsulate the backend database that is easy to refactor and update the database scheme within a single microservice.

- **Versioning and compatibility**: The microservice may change and update the API but should define a version and it should have backward compatibility. This helps to decouple between other microservices and applications.
- **Integrate CI/CD**: The microservice should adopt CI and CD process to eliminate management effort.

There are some frameworks that can help to build the microservice application such as Spring Boot (`https://projects.spring.io/spring-boot/`) and Flask (`http://flask.pocoo.org`). However, there are a lot of HTTP-based frameworks, so the developer can feel free to try and choose any preferred framework or even programming language. This is the beauty of the microservice design.

The following diagram is a comparison between monolithic application design and microservices design. It indicates that microservice (also MVC) design is the same as monolithic, which contains interface layer, business logic layer, model layer, and datastore.

But the difference is that the application (service) is constructed by multiple microservices and that different applications can share the same microservice underneath:

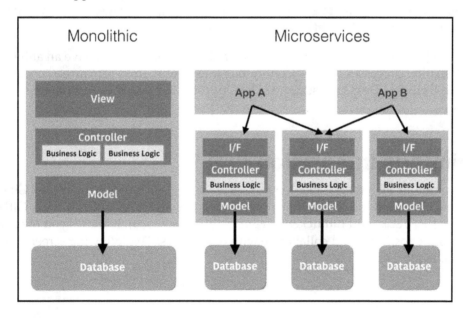

The developer can add the necessary microservice and modify an existing microservice with the rapid software delivery method that won't affect an existing application (service) anymore.

It is a breakthrough to an entire software development environment and methodology that is getting widely accepted by many developers now.

Although Continuous Integration and Continuous Delivery automation process helps to develop and deploy multiple microservices, the number of resources and complexity, such as Virtual Machine, OS, library, and disk volume and network can't compare with monolithic applications.

Therefore, there are some tools and roles that can support these large automation environments on the cloud.

Automation and tools

As discussed previously, automation is the best practice to achieve rapid software delivery and solves the complexity to manage many microservices. However, automation tools are not an ordinary IT/infrastructure applications such as **Active Directory**, **BIND** (DNS), and **Sendmail** (MTA). In order to achieve automation, there is an engineer who should have both developer skill set to write a code, especially scripting language, and infrastructure operator skill set such as VM, network, and storage.

DevOps is a clipped compound of *development* and *operations* that can have an ability to make automation processes such as Continuous Integration, Infrastructure as code, and Continuous Delivery. DevOps uses some DevOps tools to make these automation processes.

Continuous Integration tool

One of the popular VCS tools is Git (`https://git-scm.com`). The developer uses Git to check-in and check-out the code all the time. There are some hosting Git service: GitHub (`https://github.com`) and Bitbucket (`https://bitbucket.org`). It allows you to create and save your Git repositories and collaborate with other users. The following screenshot is a sample pull request on GitHub:

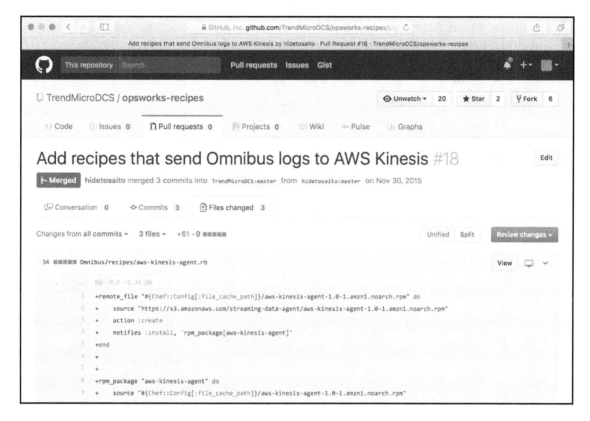

The build server has a lot of variation. Jenkins (`https://jenkins.io`) is one of well-established applications, which is the same as TeamCity (`https://www.jetbrains.com/teamcity/`). In addition to build server, you also have hosted services, the **Software as a Service (SaaS)** such as Codeship (`https://codeship.com`) and Travis CI (`https://travis-ci.org`). SaaS has the strength to integrate with other SaaS tools.

Build server is capable of invoking an external command such as a unit test program; therefore, build server is a key tool within CI pipeline.

The following screenshot is a sample build using Codeship; it checks out the code from GitHub and invokes Maven to build (`mvn compile`) and unit testing (`mvn test`):

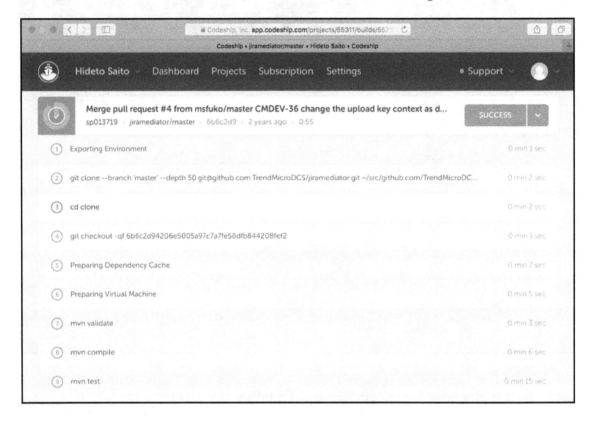

Continuous Delivery tool

There are a variety of configuration management tools such as Puppet (`https://puppet.com`), Chef (`https://www.chef.io`), and Ansible (`https://www.ansible.com`), which are the most popular in configuration management.

AWS OpsWorks (`https://aws.amazon.com/opsworks/`) provides a managed Chef platform. The following screenshot is a Chef recipe (configuration) of installation of Amazon CloudWatch Log agent using AWS OpsWorks. It automates to install CloudWatch Log agent when launching an EC2 instance:

AWS CloudFormation (https://aws.amazon.com/cloudformation/) helps to achieve infrastructure as code. It supports the automation for AWS operation, for example, to perform the following functions:

1. Creating a VPC.
2. Creating a subnet on VPC.
3. Creating an internet gateway on VPC.
4. Creating a routing table to associate a subnet to the internet gateway.
5. Creating a security group.
6. Creating a VM instance.
7. Associating a security group to a VM instance.

The configuration of CloudFormation is written by JSON as shown in the following screenshot:

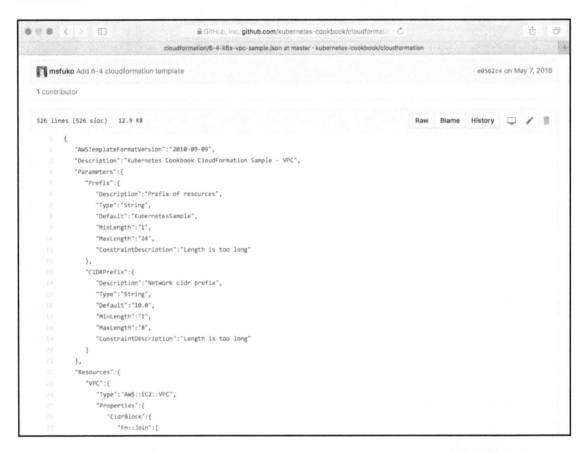

It supports parameterize, so it is easy to create an additional environment with different parameters (for example, VPC and CIDR) using a JSON file with the same configuration. In addition, it supports the update operation. So, if there is a need to change a part of the infrastructure, there's no need to recreate. CloudFormation can identify a delta of configuration and perform only the necessary infrastructure operations on behalf of you.

AWS CodeDeploy (https://aws.amazon.com/codedeploy/) is also a useful automation tool. But focus on software deployment. It allows the user to define. The following are some actions onto the YAML file:

1. Where to download and install.
2. How to stop the application.
3. How to install the application.
4. After installation, how to start and configure an application.

The following screenshot is an example of AWS CodeDeploy configuration file appspec.yml:

```
appspec.yml (~/Downloads/SampleApp_Linux) - VIM
 1 version: 0.0
 2 os: linux
 3 files:
 4   - source: /index.html
 5     destination: /var/www/html/
 6 hooks:
 7   BeforeInstall:
 8     - location: scripts/install_dependencies
 9       timeout: 300
10       runas: root
11     - location: scripts/start_server
12       timeout: 300
13       runas: root
14   ApplicationStop:
15     - location: scripts/stop_server
16       timeout: 300
17       runas: root
18
~
~
~
```

Monitoring and logging tool

Once you start to manage some microservices using a cloud infrastructure, there are some monitoring tools that help you to manage your servers.

Amazon CloudWatch is the built-in monitoring tool on AWS. No agent installation is needed; it automatically gathers some metrics from AWS instances and visualizes for DevOps. It also supports to set an alert based on the criteria that you set. The following screenshot is an Amazon CloudWatch metrics for EC2 instance:

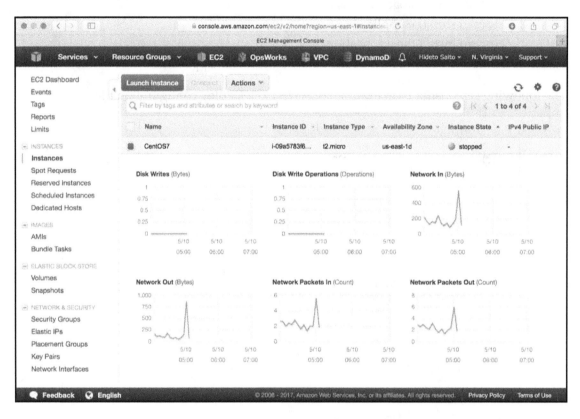

Amazon CloudWatch also supports to gather an application log. It requires installing an agent on EC2 instance; however, centralized log management is useful when you need to start managing multiple microservice instances.

ELK is a popular combination of stack that stands for Elasticsearch (https://www.elastic.co/products/elasticsearch), Logstash (https://www.elastic.co/products/logstash), and Kibana (https://www.elastic.co/products/kibana). Logstash helps to aggregate the application log and transform to JSON format and then send to Elasticsearch.

Elasticsearch is a distributed JSON database. Kibana can visualize the data, which is stored on Elasticsearch. The following example is a Kibana, which shows Nginx access log:

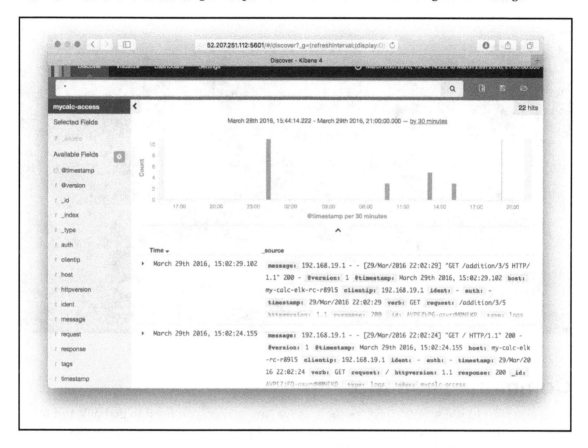

Grafana (https://grafana.com) is another popular visualization tool. It used to be connected with time series database such as Graphite (https://graphiteapp.org) or InfluxDB (https://www.influxdata.com). Time series database is designed to store the data, which is flat and de-normalized numeric data such as CPU usage and network traffic. Unlike RDBMS, time series database has some optimization to save the data space and faster query for numeric data history. Most of DevOps monitoring tools are using time series database in the backend.

The following example is a Grafana that shows **Message Queue Server** statistics:

Communication tool

Once you start to use several DevOps tools as we saw earlier, you need to go back and forth to visit several consoles to check whether CI and CD pipelines work properly or not. For example, consider the following points:

1. Merge the source code to GitHub.
2. Trigger the new build on Jenkins.
3. Trigger AWS CodeDeploy to deploy the new version of the application.

These events need to be tracked by time sequence, and if there are some troubles, DevOps needs to discuss it with the developer and QA to handle the cases. However, there are some over-communication needs, because DevOps needs to capture the event one by one and then explain, probably via e-mail. It is not efficient and in the meantime the issue is still going on.

There are some communication tools that help to integrate these DevOps tools and anyone can join to look at the event and comment to each other. Slack (`https://slack.com`) and HipChat (`https://www.hipchat.com`) are the most popular communication tools.

These tools support to integrate to SaaS services so that DevOps can see the event on the single chat room. The following screenshot is a Slack chat room that integrates with Jenkins:

Public cloud

CI CD and automation work can be achieved easily when used with cloud technology. Especially public cloud API helps DevOps to come up with many CI CD tools. Public cloud such as Amazon Web Services (`https://aws.amazon.com`) and Google Cloud Platform (`https://cloud.google.com`) provides some APIs to DevOps to control the cloud infrastructure. DevOps can be a relief from capacity and resource limitation, just pay as you go whenever the resource is needed.

Public cloud will keep growing the same way as software development cycle and architecture design; these are best friends and the important key to achieve your application/service to success.

The following screenshot is a web console for Amazon Web Services:

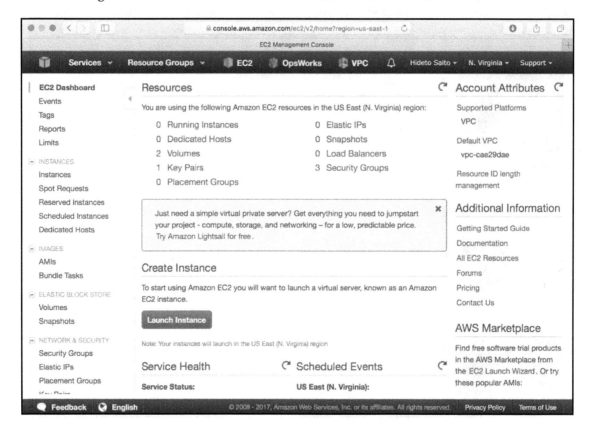

Google Cloud Platform also has a web console as shown here:

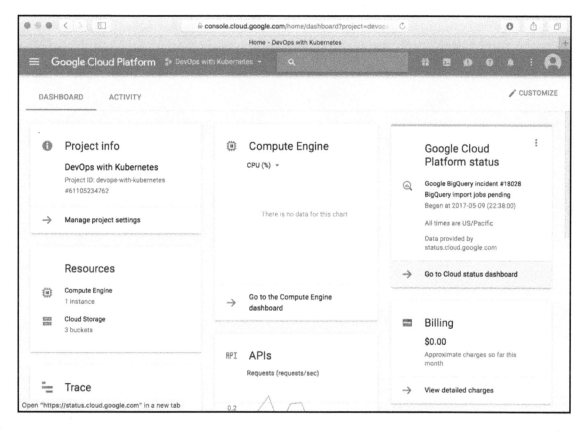

Both cloud services have a free trial period that DevOps engineer can use to try and understand the benefits of cloud infrastructure.

Summary

In this chapter, we have discussed the history of software development methodology, programming evolution and DevOps tools. These methodologies and tools support quicker software delivery cycle. Microservice design also helps continuous software update. However, microservice makes complexity of environment management.

The next chapter will describe the Docker container technology, which helps to compose microservice application and manage it in a more efficient and automated way.

2
DevOps with Container

We are already familiar with a lot of DevOps tools that help us automate tasks and manage configuration at different stages of application delivery, but challenges still exist as applications become more micro and diverse. In this chapter, we will add another swiss army knife to our tool belt, namely Container. In doing so, we will seek to acquire the following skills:

- Container concepts and fundamentals
- Running Docker applications
- Building Docker applications with `Dockerfile`
- Orchestrating multiple containers with Docker Compose

Understanding container

The key feature of container is isolation. In this section, we will elaborate how container achieves it and why it matters in the software development life cycle to help establish a proper understanding of this powerful tool.

Resource isolation

When an application launches, it consumes CPU time, occupies memory space, links to its dependent libraries, and may write to disk, transmit packets, and access other devices. Everything it uses up is a resource, and is shared by all the programs on the same host. The idea of container is to isolate resources and programs to separate boxes.

You may have heard such terms as para-virtualization, **Virtual Machines** (**VMs**), BSD jails, and Solaris containers, which can also isolate the resources of a host. However, since their designs differ, they are fundamentally distinct but provide a similar isolation concept. For example, the implementation of a VM is for virtualizing the hardware layer with a hypervisor. If you want to run an application on a Virtual Machine, you have to install a full operating system first. In other words, the resources are isolated between guest operating systems on the same hypervisor. In contrast, container is built on top of Linux primitives, which means it can only run in an operating system with those capabilities. BSD jails and Solaris containers also work in a similar fashion on other operating systems. The isolation relationship of container and VMs is illustrated in the following diagram. Container isolates an application at the OS-layer, while VM-based separation is achieved by the operating system.

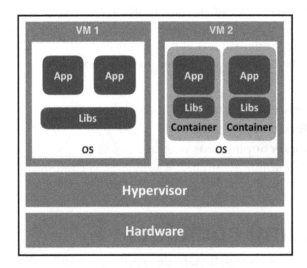

Linux container concept

Container comprises several building blocks, the two most important being **namespaces** and **cgroups** (**control groups**). Both of them are Linux kernel features. Namespaces provide logical partitions of certain kinds of system resources, such as mounting point (mnt), process ID (PID), network (net), and so on. To explain the concept of isolation, let's look at some simple examples on the pid namespace. The following examples are all from Ubuntu 16.04.2 and util-linux 2.27.1.

When we type `ps axf`, we will see a long list of running processes:

```
$ ps axf
  PID TTY       STAT    TIME COMMAND
    2 ?         S       0:00 [kthreadd]
    3 ?         S       0:42  \_ [ksoftirqd/0]
    5 ?         S<      0:00  \_ [kworker/0:0H]
    7 ?         S       8:14  \_ [rcu_sched]
    8 ?         S       0:00  \_ [rcu_bh]
```

 `ps` is a utility to report current processes on the system. `ps axf` is to list all processes in forest.

Now let's enter a new `pid` namespace with `unshare`, which is able to disassociate a process resource part-by-part to a new namespace, and check the processes again:

```
$ sudo unshare --fork --pid --mount-proc=/proc /bin/sh
$ ps axf
  PID TTY       STAT    TIME COMMAND
    1 pts/0     S       0:00 /bin/sh
    2 pts/0     R+      0:00 ps axf
```

You will find the `pid` of the shell process at the new namespace becoming 1, with all other processes disappearing. That is to say, you have created a `pid` container. Let's switch to another session outside the namespace, and list the processes again:

```
$ ps axf // from another terminal
  PID TTY    COMMAND
  ...
25744 pts/0 \_ unshare --fork --pid --mount-proc=/proc
/bin/sh
25745 pts/0    \_ /bin/sh
 3305 ?       /sbin/rpcbind -f -w
 6894 ?       /usr/sbin/ntpd -p /var/run/ntpd.pid -g -u
113:116
  ...
```

You can still see the other processes and your shell process within the new namespace.

With the `pid` namespace isolation, processes in different namespaces cannot see each other. Nonetheless, if one process eats up a considerable amount of system resources, such as memory, it could cause the system to run out of memory and become unstable. In other words, an isolated process could still disrupt other processes or even crash a whole system if we don't impose resource usage restrictions on it.

The following diagram illustrates the `PID` namespaces and how an **out-of-memory (OOM)** event can affect other processes outside a child namespace. The bubbles are the process in the system, and the numbers are their PID. Processes in the child namespace have their own PID. Initially, there is still free memory available in the system. Later, the processes in the child namespace exhaust the whole memory in the system. The kernel then starts the OOM killer to release memory, and the victims may be processes outside the child namespace:

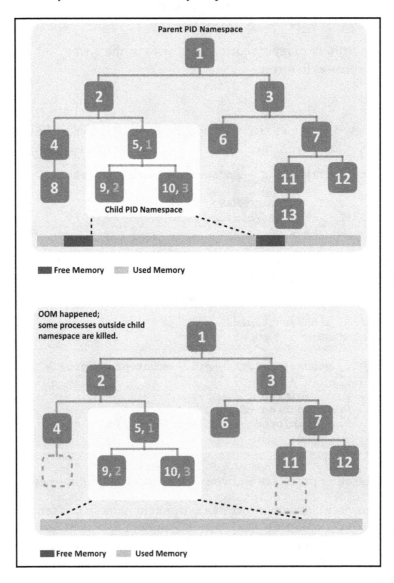

In light of this, `cgroups` is utilized here to limit resource usage. Like namespaces, it can set constraint on different kinds of system resources. Let's continue from our `pid` namespace, stress the CPU with `yes > /dev/null`, and monitor it with `top`:

```
$ yes > /dev/null & top
$ PID USER  PR  NI    VIRT    RES    SHR S  %CPU %MEM
TIME+ COMMAND
   3 root  20   0    6012    656    584 R 100.0  0.0
   0:15.15 yes
   1 root  20   0    4508    708    632 S   0.0  0.0
   0:00.00 sh
   4 root  20   0   40388   3664   3204 R   0.0  0.1
   0:00.00 top
```

Our CPU load reaches 100% as expected. Now let's limit it with the CPU cgroup. Cgroups are organized as directories under `/sys/fs/cgroup/` (switch to the host session first):

```
$ ls /sys/fs/cgroup
blkio          cpuset     memory              perf_event
cpu            devices    net_cls             pids
cpuacct        freezer    net_cls,net_prio    systemd
cpu,cpuacct    hugetlb    net_prio
```

Each of the directories represents the resources they control. It's pretty easy to create a cgroup and control processes with it: just create a directory under the resource type with any name, and append the process IDs you'd like to control to `tasks`. Here we want to throttle the CPU usage of our `yes` process, so create a new directory under `cpu` and find out the PID of the `yes` process:

```
$ ps x | grep yes
11809 pts/2    R      12:37 yes
$ mkdir /sys/fs/cgroup/cpu/box && \
  echo 11809 > /sys/fs/cgroup/cpu/box/tasks
```

We've just added `yes` into the newly created CPU group `box`, but the policy remains unset, and processes still run without restriction. Set a limit by writing the desired number into the corresponding file and check the CPU usage again:

```
$ echo 50000 > /sys/fs/cgroup/cpu/box/cpu.cfs_quota_us
$ PID USER  PR  NI    VIRT    RES    SHR S  %CPU %MEM
 TIME+ COMMAND
   3 root  20   0    6012    656    584 R  50.2  0.0
   0:32.05 yes
   1 root  20   0    4508   1700   1608 S   0.0  0.0
   0:00.00 sh
   4 root  20   0   40388   3664   3204 R   0.0  0.1
   0:00.00 top
```

The CPU usage is dramatically reduced, meaning that our CPU throttle works.

These two examples elucidate how Linux container isolates system resources. By putting more confinements in an application, we can definitely build a fully isolated box, including filesystem and networks, without encapsulating an operating system within it.

Containerized delivery

To deploy applications, the configuration management tool is often used. It's true that it works well with its modular and code-based configuration design until the application stacks grow complex and diverse. Maintaining a large configuration manifest base is complicated. When we want to change one package, we'll have to deal with entangled and fragile dependencies between the system and application packages. It's not uncommon that some applications break inadvertently after upgrading an unrelated package. Moreover, upgrading the configuration management tool itself is also a challenging task.

In order to overcome such a conundrum, immutable deployments with pre-baked VM images are introduced. That is, whenever we have any update on the system or application packages, we'll build a full VM image against the change and deploy it accordingly. It solves a certain degree of package problems because we are now able to customize runtimes for applications that cannot share the same environments. Nevertheless, doing immutable deployment with VM images is costly. From another point of view, provisioning a VM for the sake of isolating applications rather than insufficient resources results in inefficient resource utilization, not to mention the overhead of booting, distributing, and running a bloating VM image. If we want to eliminate such inefficiency by sharing VM to multiple applications, we'll soon realize that we will run into further trouble, namely, resource management.

Container, here, is a jigsaw piece that snugly fits the deployment needs. A manifest of a container can be managed within VCS, and built into a blob image; no doubt the image can be deployed immutably as well. This enables developers to abstract from actual resources, and infrastructure engineers can escape from their dependency hell. Besides, since we only need to pack up the application itself and its dependent libraries, its image size would be significantly smaller than a VM's. Consequently, distributing a container image is more economical than a VM's. Additionally, we have already known that running a process inside a container is basically identical to running it on its Linux host and as such almost no overhead will be produced. To summarize, container is lightweight, self-contained, and immutable. This also gives a clear border to distinguish responsibilities between applications and infrastructure.

Getting started with container

There are many mature container engines such as Docker (`https://www.docker.com`) and rkt (`https://coreos.com/rkt`) that have already implemented features for production usages, so you don't need to start building one from scratch. Besides, the **Open Container Initiative** (`https://www.opencontainers.org`), an organization formed by container industry leaders, has framed some container specifications. Any implementation of those standards, regardless of the underlying platform, should have similar properties as OCI aims to provide, with seamless experience of containers across a variety of operating systems. In this book, we will use the Docker (community edition) container engine to fabricate our containerized applications.

Installing Docker for Ubuntu

Docker requires a 64-bit version of Yakkety 16.10, Xenial 16.04LTS, and Trusty 14.04LTS. You can install Docker with `apt-get install docker.io`, but it usually updates more slowly than the Docker official repository. Here are the installation steps from Docker (`https://docs.docker.com/engine/installation/linux/docker-ce/ubuntu/#install-docker-ce`):

1. Make sure you have the packages to allow `apt` repositories; get them if not:

   ```
   $ sudo apt-get install apt-transport-https ca-certificates curl
   software-properties-common
   ```

2. Add Docker's `gpg` key and verify if its fingerprint matches `9DC8 5822 9FC7 DD38 854A E2D8 8D81 803C 0EBF CD88`:

   ```
   $ curl -fsSL https://download.docker.com/linux/ubuntu/gpg | sudo
   apt-key add -
   $ sudo apt-key fingerprint 0EBFCD88
   ```

3. Set up the repository of `amd64` arch:

   ```
   $ sudo add-apt-repository "deb [arch=amd64]
   https://download.docker.com/linux/ubuntu $(lsb_release -cs) stable"
   ```

4. Update the package index and install Docker CE:

   ```
   $ sudo apt-get update
   $ sudo apt-get install docker-ce
   ```

Installing Docker for CentOS

CentOS 7 64-bit is required to run Docker. Similarly, you can get the Docker package from CentOS's repository via `sudo yum install docker`. Again, the installation steps from Docker official guide (`https://docs.docker.com/engine/installation/linux/docker-ce/centos/#install-using-the-repository`) are as follows:

1. Install the utility to enable `yum` to use the extra repository:

    ```
    $ sudo yum install -y yum-utils
    ```

2. Set up Docker's repository:

    ```
    $ sudo yum-config-manager --add-repo
    https://download.docker.com/linux/centos/docker-ce.repo
    ```

3. Update the repository and verify if the fingerprint matches:

    ```
     060A 61C5 1B55 8A7F 742B 77AA C52F EB6B 621E 9F35:
    ```

    ```
    $ sudo yum makecache fast
    ```

4. Install Docker CE and start it:

    ```
    $ sudo yum install docker-ce
    $ sudo systemctl start docker
    ```

Installing Docker for macOS

Docker wraps a micro Linux moby with the hypervisor framework to build a native application on macOS, which means we don't need third-party virtualization tools to develop Docker in Mac. To benefit from the Hypervisor framework, you must upgrade your macOS to 10.10.3 or above.

Download the Docker package and install it:

```
https://download.docker.com/mac/stable/Docker.dmg
```

> Likewise, Docker for Windows requires no third-party tools. Check here for the installation guide:
> `https://docs.docker.com/docker-for-windows/install`

Now you are in Docker. Try creating and running your first Docker container; run it with `sudo` if you are on Linux:

```
$ docker run alpine ls
bin dev etc home lib media mnt proc root run sbin srv sys tmp usr var
```

You will see that you're under a `root` directory instead of your current one. Let's check the processes list again:

```
$ docker run alpine ps aux
PID   USER      TIME    COMMAND
1 root          0:00 ps aux
```

It is isolated, as expected. You are all ready to work with container.

 Alpine is a Linux distribution. Since it's really small in size, many people use it as their base image to build their application container.

Container life cycle

Using containers is not as intuitive as the tools that we are used to work with. In this section, we will go through Docker usages from the most fundamental ideas to the extent that we are able to benefit from containers.

Docker basics

When `docker run alpine ls` is executed, what Docker did behind the scenes is:

1. Find the image `alpine` locally. If not found, Docker will try to find and pull it from the public Docker registry to the local image storage.
2. Extract the image and create a container accordingly.
3. Execute the entry point defined in the image with commands, which are the arguments after the image name. In this example, it is `ls`. The entry point by default is `/bin/sh -c` on the Linux-based Docker.
4. When the entry point process is exited, the container then exits.

An image is an immutable bundle of codes, libraries, configurations, and everything needed to run an application. A container is an instance of an image, which would actually be executed during runtime. You can use the `docker inspect IMAGE` and `docker inspect CONTAINER` commands to see the difference.

Sometimes when we need to enter a container for checking the image or updating something inside, we'll use the option `-i` and `-t` (`--interactive` and `--tty`). Besides, option `-d` (`--detach`) enables you to run a container in detached mode. If you would like to interact with a detached container, `exec` and `attach` commands can do us a favor. The `exec` command allows us run a process in a running container, and `attach` works, as per its literal meaning. The following example demonstrates how to use them:

```
$ docker run alpine /bin/sh -c "while :;do echo
   'meow~';sleep 1;done"
meow~
meow~
...
```

Your Terminal should be flooded with meow~ now. Switch to another Terminal and run `docker ps`, a command to get the status of containers, to find out the name and ID of the meowing container. Both the name and ID here are generated by Docker, and you can access a container with either of them. As a matter of convenience, the name can be assigned upon `create` or `run` with the `--name` flag:

```
$ docker ps
CONTAINER ID      IMAGE      (omitted)      NAMES
d51972e5fc8c      alpine        ...         zen_kalam
$ docker exec -it d51972e5fc8c /bin/sh
/ # ps
PID   USER      TIME    COMMAND
  1 root        0:00 /bin/sh -c while :;do echo
   'meow~';sleep 1;done
 27 root        0:00 /bin/sh
 34 root        0:00 sleep 1
 35 root        0:00 ps
/ # kill -s 2 1
$ // container terminated
```

Once we get in the container and inspect its processes, we will see two shells: one is meowing and another one is where we are. Kill it with `kill -s 2 1` inside the container and we'll see the whole container stopped as the entry point is exited. Finally, let's list the stopped containers with `docker ps -a`, and clean them up with `docker rm CONTAINER_NAME` or `docker rm CONTAINER_ID`. Since Docker 1.13, the `docker system prune` command has been introduced, which helps us clean up stopped containers and occupied resources with ease.

Layer, image, container, and volume

We know that an image is immutable; a container is ephemeral, and we know how to run an image as a container. Nevertheless, there's still a missing step on packing an image.

An image is a read-only stack that consists of one or more layers, and a layer is a collection of files and directories in the filesystem. To improve the disk size usage, layers are not locked to only one image but shared among images; which means that Docker simply stores only one copy of a base image locally regardless of how many images are derived from it. You can utilize the `docker history [image]` command to understand how an image is built. For example, there's only one layer in an Alpine Linux image if you type `docker history alpine`.

Whenever a container is created, it adds a writable layer on top of the base image. Docker adopts the **copy-on-write** (**COW**) strategy on the layer. That is to say, a container reads against the layers of the base image where the target files are stored, and copies the file to its own writable layer if the file is modified. Such an approach prevents containers created from the same image intervening with each other. The `docker diff [CONTAINER]` command shows the difference between the container and its base image in terms of filesystem states. For example, if `/etc/hosts` in the base image is modified, Docker copies the file to the writable layer, and it will also be the only one file in the output of `docker diff`.

The following diagram illustrates the hierarchical structure of Docker's images:

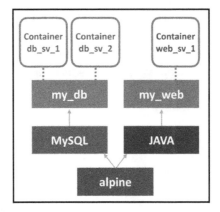

It's important to note that data in the writable layer is deleted along with its container. To persist data, you commit the container layer with the `docker commit [CONTAINER]` command as a new image, or mount data volumes into a container.

A data volume allows a container's reading and writing to bypass Docker's filesystem, and it can be on a host's directory or other storages, such as Ceph or GlusterFS. Therefore, any disk I/O against the volume can operate at native speeds depending on the underlying storage. Since the data is persistent outside a container, it can be reused and shared by multiple containers. Mounting a volume is done by specifying the `-v(--volume)` flag at `docker run` or `docker create`. The following example mounts a volume under `/chest` in the container, and leaves a file there. Afterwards, we use `docker inspect` to locate the data volume:

```
$ docker run --name demo -v /chest alpine touch /chest/coins
$ docker inspect demo
...
"Mounts": [
  {
    "Type": "volume",
     "Name":(hash-digits),
     "Source":"/var/lib/docker/volumes/(hash-
      digits)/_data",
      "Destination": "/chest",
      "Driver": "local",
      "Mode": "",
        ...
$ ls /var/lib/docker/volumes/(hash-digits)/_data
     coins
```

The default `tty` path of moby Linux provided by Docker CE on macOS is under:
`~/Library/Containers/com.docker.docker/Data/com.docker.driver.amd64-linux/tty`.
You can attach to it with `screen`.

One use case of data volumes is sharing data between containers. To do so, we first create a container and mount volumes on it, and then mount one or more containers and reference the volume with `--volumes-from` flag. The following examples create a container with a data volume, `/share-vol`. Container A can put a file into it, and container B can read it as well:

```
$ docker create --name box -v /share-vol alpine nop
c53e3e498ab05b19a12d554fad4545310e6de6950240cf7a28f42780f382c649
$ docker run --name A --volumes-from box alpine touch /share-vol/wine
$ docker run --name B --volumes-from box alpine ls /share-vol
wine
```

In addition, data volumes can be mounted under a given host path, and of course the data inside is persistent:

```
$ docker run --name hi -v $(pwd)/host/dir:/data alpine touch /data/hi
$ docker rm hi
$ ls $(pwd)/host/dir
hi
```

Distributing images

Registry is a service that stores, manages, and distributes images. Public services, such as Docker Hub (`https://hub.docker.com`) and Quay (`https://quay.io`), converge all kinds of pre-built images of popular tools, such as Ubuntu and Nginx, and custom images from other developers. The Alpine Linux we have used many times is actually pulled from Docker Hub (`https://hub.docker.com/_/alpine`). Absolutely, you can upload your tool onto such services and share with everyone as well.

If you need a private registry, but for some reason you don't want to subscribe to paid plans of registry service providers, you can always set up one on your own with registry (`https://hub.docker.com/_/registry`).

Before provisioning a container, Docker will try to locate the specified image in a rule indicated in the image name. An image name consists of three sections `[registry/]name[:tag]`, and it's resolved with the following rules:

- If the `registry` field is left out, search for the name on Docker Hub
- If the `registry` field is a registry server, search the name for it
- You can have more than one slash in a name
- The tag defaults to `latest` if it's omitted

For example, an image name such as `gcr.io/google-containers/guestbook:v3` instructs Docker to download `v3` of `google-containers/guestbook` from `gcr.io`. Likewise, if you want to push an image to a registry, tag your image in the same manner and push it. To list the images you currently own in the local disk, use `docker images`, and remove an image with `docker rmi [IMAGE]`. The following example shows how to work between different registries: Download an `nginx` image from Docker Hub, tag it to a private registry path, and push it accordingly. Notice that though the default tag is `latest`, you have to tag and push it explicitly.

```
$ docker pull nginx
Using default tag: latest
latest: Pulling from library/nginx
ff3d52d8f55f: Pull complete
...
Status: Downloaded newer image for nginx:latest
$ docker tag nginx localhost:5000/comps/prod/nginx:1.14
$ docker push localhost:5000/comps/prod/nginx:1.14
The push refers to a repository [localhost:5000/comps/prod/nginx]
...
8781ec54ba04: Pushed
1.14: digest: sha256:(64-digits-hash) size: 948
$ docker tag nginx localhost:5000/comps/prod/nginx
$ docker push localhost:5000/comps/prod/nginx
The push refers to a repository [localhost:5000/comps/prod/nginx]
...
8781ec54ba04: Layer already exists
latest: digest: sha256:(64-digits-hash) size: 948
```

Most registry services ask for authentications if you are going to push images. The `docker login` is designed for this purpose. Sometimes you may receive an `image not found error` when attempting to pull an image, even though the image path is valid. It's very likely that you are unauthorized with the registry that keeps the image. To resolve this problem, log in first:

```
$ docker pull localhost:5000/comps/prod/nginx
Pulling repository localhost:5000/comps/prod/nginx
Error: image comps/prod/nginx:latest not found
$ docker login -u letme -p in localhost:5000
Login Succeeded
$ docker pull localhost:5000/comps/prod/nginx
Pulling repository localhost:5000/comps/prod/nginx
...
latest: digest: sha256:(64-digits-hash) size: 948
```

In addition to distributed images via the registry service, there are options to dump images as a TAR archive, and import them back into the local repository:

- `docker commit [CONTAINER]`: Commits the changes of the container layer into a new image
- `docker save --output [filename] IMAGE1 IMAGE2 ...`: Saves one or more images to a TAR archive
- `docker load -i [filename]`: Loads a `tarball` image into the local repository
- `docker export --output [filename] [CONTAINER]`: Exports a container's filesystem as a TAR archive
- `docker import --output [filename] IMAGE1 IMAGE2`: Imports a filesystem `tarball`

The `commit` command with `save` and `export` looks pretty much the same. The main difference is that a saved image preserves files in-between layers even if they are to be deleted eventually; on the other hand, an exported image squashes all intermediate layers into one final layer. Another difference is that a saved image keeps metadata such as layer histories, but those are not available at the exported one. As a result, the exported image is usually smaller in size.

The following diagram depicts the relationship of states between container and images. The captions on the arrows are the corresponding sub-commands of Docker:

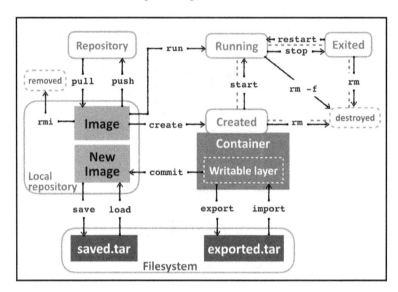

Connect containers

Docker provides three kinds of networks to manage communications within containers and between the hosts, namely `bridge`, `host`, and `none`.

```
$ docker network ls
NETWORK ID          NAME                DRIVER              SCOPE
1224183f2080        bridge              bridge              local
801dec6d5e30        host                host                local
f938cd2d644d        none                null                local
```

By default, every container is connected to the bridge network upon creation. In this mode, every container is allocated a virtual interface as well as a private IP address, and the traffic going through the interface is bridged to the host's `docker0` interface. Also, other containers within the same bridge network can connect to each other via their IP address. Let's run one container that is feeding a short message over port 5000, and observe its configuration. The `--expose` flag opens the given ports to the world outside a container:

```
$ docker run --name greeter -d --expose 5000 alpine \
/bin/sh -c "echo Welcome stranger! | nc -lp 5000"
2069cbdf37210461bc42c2c40d96e56bd99e075c7fb92326af1ec47e64d6b344
$ docker exec greeter ifconfig
```

```
eth0      Link encap:Ethernet  HWaddr 02:42:AC:11:00:02
inet addr:172.17.0.2  Bcast:0.0.0.0  Mask:255.255.0.0
...
```

Here the container `greeter` is allocated with IP `172.17.0.2`. Now run another container connecting to it with this IP address:

```
$ docker run alpine telnet 172.17.0.2 5000
Welcome stranger!
Connection closed by foreign host
```

The `docker network inspect bridge` command gives configuration details, such as subnet segments and the gateway information.

On top of that, you can group some containers into one user-defined bridge network. It's also the recommended way to connect multiple containers on a single host. The user-defined bridge network slightly differs from the default one, the major difference being that you can access a container from other containers with its name rather than IP address. Creating a network is done by `docker network create [NW-NAME]`, and attaching containers to it is done by the flag `--network [NW-NAME]` at the time of creation. The network name of a container defaults to its name, but it can be given another alias name with the `--network-alias` flag as well:

```
$ docker network create room
b0cdd64d375b203b24b5142da41701ad9ab168b53ad6559e6705d6f82564baea
$ docker run -d --network room \
--network-alias dad --name sleeper alpine sleep 60
b5290bcca85b830935a1d0252ca1bf05d03438ddd226751eea922c72aba66417
$ docker run --network room alpine ping -c 1 sleeper
PING sleeper (172.18.0.2): 56 data bytes
...
$ docker run --network room alpine ping -c 1 dad
PING dad (172.18.0.2): 56 data bytes
...
```

The host network works literally according to its name; every connected container shares the host's network, but it loses the isolation property at the same time. The none network is a completely separated box. Regardless of ingress or egress, traffic is isolated inside as there is no network interface attached to the container. Here we attach a container that listens on port `5000` to the host network, and communicates with it locally:

```
$ docker run -d --expose 5000 --network host alpine \
/bin/sh -c "echo im a container | nc -lp 5000"
ca73774caba1401b91b4b1ca04d7d5363b6c281a05a32828e293b84795d85b54
```

```
$ telnet localhost 5000
im a container
Connection closed by foreign host
```

If you are using Docker CE for macOS, the host means the moby Linux on top of the hypervisor framework.

The interaction between the host and three network modes are shown in the following diagram. Containers in the host and bridge networks are attached with proper network interfaces and communicate with containers within the same network as well as the outside world, but the none network is kept away from the host interfaces.

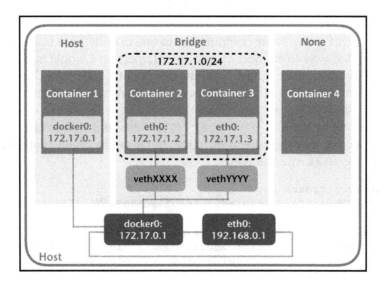

Other than sharing the host network, the flag -p(--publish) [host]:[container], on creating a container, also allows you to map a host port to a container. This flag implies --expose, as you'll need to open a container's port in any case. The following command launches a simple HTTP server at port 80. You can view it with a browser as well.

```
$ docker run -p 80:5000 alpine /bin/sh -c \
"while :; do echo -e 'HTTP/1.1 200 OK\n\ngood day'|nc -lp 5000; done"
$ curl localhost
good day
```

Working with Dockerfile

When assembling an image, whether by a Docker commit or export, optimizing the outcome in a managed way is a challenge, let alone integrating with a CI/CD pipeline. On the other hand, `Dockerfile` represents the building task in the form of as-a-code, which significantly reduces the complexities of building a task for us. In this section, we will describe how to map Docker commands into a `Dockerfile` and go a step further to optimizing it.

Writing your first Dockerfile

A `Dockerfile` consists of a series of text instructions to guide the Docker daemon to form a Docker image. Generally, a `Dockerfile` is and must be starting with the directive `FROM`, and follows zero or more instructions. For example, we may have an image built from the following one liner:

```
docker commit $(    \
docker start $(  \
docker create alpine /bin/sh -c    \
"echo My custom build > /etc/motd" \
  ))
```

It roughly equates to the following `Dockerfile`:

```
./Dockerfile:
---
FROM alpine
RUN echo "My custom build" > /etc/motd
---
```

Obviously, building with a `Dockerfile` is more concise and clear.

The `docker build [OPTIONS] [CONTEXT]` command is the only one command associated with building tasks. A context can be a local path, URL, or `stdin`; which denotes the location of the `Dockerfile`. Once a build is triggered, the `Dockerfile`, alongside everything under the context, will be sent to the Docker daemon beforehand, and then the daemon will start to execute instructions in the `Dockerfile` sequentially. Every execution of instructions results in a new cache layer, and the ensuing instruction is executed at the new cache layer in the cascade. Since the context will be sent to somewhere that is not guaranteed to be a local path, it's a good practice to put the `Dockerfile`, codes, the necessary files, and a `.dockerignore` file in an empty folder to make sure the resultant image encloses only the desired files.

The `.dockerignore` file is a list indicating which files under the same directory can be ignored during the building time, and it typically looks like the following file:

```
./.dockerignore:
---
# ignore .dockerignore, .git
.dockerignore
.git
# exclude all *.tmp files and vim swp file recursively
**/*.tmp
**/[._]*.s[a-w][a-z]
...
---
```

Generally, `docker build` will try to find a file named `Dockerfile` under the `context` to start a build; but sometimes we may like to give it another name for some reason. The `-f`(`--file`) flag is for this purpose. Also, another useful flag, `-t`(`--tag`), is able to give an image of one or more repository tags after an image is built. Say we want to build a `Dockerfile` named `builder.dck` under `./deploy` and label it with the current date and the latest tag, the command will be:

```
$ docker build -f deploy/builder.dck \
-t my-reg.com/prod/teabreak:$(date +"%g%m%d") \
-t my-reg.com/prod/teabreak:latest .
```

Dockerfile syntax

The building blocks of a `Dockerfile` are a dozen or more directives; most of them are a counterpart of the functions of `docker run/create` flags. Here we list the most essential ones:

- `FROM <IMAGE>[:TAG|[@DIGEST]`: This is to tell the Docker daemon which image the current `Dockerfile` is based on. It's also the one and only instruction that must be in a `Dockerfile`, which means that you can have a `Dockerfile` that contains only one line. Like all the other image-relevant commands, the tag defaults to the latest if unspecified.

- RUN:

```
RUN <commands>
RUN ["executable", "params", "more params"]
```

The RUN instruction runs one line of a command at the current cache layer, and commits out the outcome. The main discrepancy between the two forms is in how the command is executed. The first one is called **shell form**, which actually executes commands in the form of /bin/sh -c <commands>; the other form is called **exec form**, and it treats the command with exec directly.

Using the shell form is similar to writing shell scripts, thus concatenating multiple commands by shell operators and line continuation, condition tests, or variable substitutions are totally valid. But bear in mind that commands are not processed by bash but sh.

The exec form is parsed as a JSON array, which means that you have to wrap texts with double quotes and escape reserved characters. Besides, as the command is not processed by any shell, the shell variables in the array will not be evaluated. On the other hand, if the shell doesn't exist in the base image, you can still use the exec form to invoke executables.

- CMD:

```
CMD ["executable", "params", "more params"]
CMD ["param1","param2"]
CMD command param1 param2 ...:
```

The CMD sets default commands for the built image; it doesn't run the command during build time. If arguments are supplied at Docker run, the CMD configurations here are overridden. The syntax rule of CMD is almost identical to RUN; the first form is the exec form, and the third one is the shell form, which is the prepend a /bin/sh -c as well. There is another directive in which ENTRYPOINT interacts with CMD; three forms of CMD actually would be a prepend with ENTRYPOINT when a container starts. There can be many CMD directives in a Dockerfile, but only the last one will take effect.

- ENTRYPOINT:

```
ENTRYPOINT ["executable", "param1", "param2"]
ENTRYPOINT command param1 param2
```

These two forms are, respectively, the exec form and the shell form, and the syntax rules are the same as RUN. The entry point is the default executable for an image. That is to say, when a container spins up, it runs the executable configured by the ENTRYPOINT. When the ENTRYPOINT is combined with CMD and docker run arguments, writing in a different form would lead to very diverse behavior. Here are the organized rules of their combinations:

- If the ENTRYPOINT is in shell form, then the CMD and Docker run arguments would be ignored. The command will become:

```
/bin/sh -c entry_cmd entry_params ...
```

- If the ENTRYPOINT is in exec form and the Docker run arguments are specified, then the CMD commands are overridden. The runtime command would be:

```
entry_cmd entry_params run_arguments
```

- If the ENTRYPOINT is in exec form and only CMD is configured, the runtime command would become the following for the three forms:

```
entry_cmd entry_parms CMD_exec CMD_parms
entry_cmd entry_parms CMD_parms
entry_cmd entry_parms /bin/sh -c CMD_cmd
CMD_parms
```

- ENV:

```
ENV key value
ENV key1=value1 key2=value2 ...
```

The ENV instruction sets environment variables for the consequent instructions and the built image. The first form sets the key to the string after the first space, including special characters. The second form allows us to set multiple variables in a line, separated with spaces. If there are spaces in a value, either enclose it with double quotes or escape the space character. Moreover, the key defined with ENV also takes effect on variables in the same documents. See the following examples to observe the behavior of ENV:

```
FROM alpine
ENV key wD # aw
ENV k2=v2 k3=v\ 3 \
    k4="v 4"
```

```
ENV k_${k2}=$k3 k5=\"K\=da\"
RUN echo key=$key ;\
    echo k2=$k2 k3=$k3 k4=$k4 ;\
    echo k_\${k2}=k_${k2}=$k3 k5=$k5
```

And the output during the Docker build would be:

```
...
---> Running in 738709ef01ad
key=wD # aw
k2=v2 k3=v 3 k4=v 4
k_${k2}=k_v2=v 3 k5="K=da"
...
```

- LABEL key1=value1 key2=value2 ...: The usage of LABEL resembles ENV, but a label is stored only in the metadata section of the images and is used by other host programs instead of programs in a container. It deprecates the maintainer instruction in the following form:

  LABEL maintainer=johndoe@example.com

  And we can filter objects with labels if a command has the -f (--filter) flag. For example, docker images --filter label=maintainer=johndoe@example.com queries out the images labeled with the preceding maintainer.

- EXPOSE <port> [<port> ...]: This instruction is identical to the --expose flag at docker run/create, exposing ports at the container created by the resulting image.

- USER <name|uid>[:<group|gid>]: The USER instruction switches the user to run the subsequent instructions. However, it cannot work properly if the user doesn't exist in the image. Otherwise, you have to run adduser before using the USER directive.

- `WORKDIR <path>`: This instruction sets the working directory to a certain path. The path would be created automatically if the path doesn't exist. It works like `cd` in a `Dockerfile`, as it takes both relative and absolute paths and can be used multiple times. If an absolute path is followed by a relative path, the result would be relative to the previous path:

```
WORKDIR /usr
WORKDIR src
WORKDIR app
RUN pwd
---> Running in 73aff3ae46ac
/usr/src/app
---> 4a415e366388
```

Also, environment variables set with `ENV` take effect on the path.

- `COPY`:

```
COPY <src-in-context> ... <dest-in-container>
COPY ["<src-in-context>",... "<dest-in-container>"]
```

This directive copies the source to a file or a directory in the building container. The source could be files or directories, as could be the destination. The source must be within the context path, as only files under the context path will be sent to the Docker daemon. Additionally, `COPY` makes use of `.dockerignore` to filter files that would be copied into the building container. The second form is for a use case where the path contains spaces.

- `ADD`:

```
ADD <src > ... <dest >
ADD ["<src>",... "<dest >"]
```

`ADD` is quite analogous to `COPY` in terms of functionality: moving files into an image. More than copying files, `<src>` can also be URL or a compressed file. If `<src>` is a URL, `ADD` will download it and copy it into the image. If `<src>` is inferred as a compressed file, it will be extracted into `<dest>` path.

- `VOLUME`:

```
VOLUME mount_point_1 mount_point_2
VOLUME ["mount point 1", "mount point 2"]
```

The VOLUME instruction creates data volumes at the given mount points. Once it has been declared during build time, any change in the data volume at consequent directives would not persist. Besides, mounting host directories in a `Dockerfile` or `docker build` isn't doable because of portability issues: there's no guarantee that the specified path would exist in the host. The effect of both syntax forms is identical; they only differ in syntax parsing; The second form is a JSON array, so characters such as `"\"` should be escaped.

- `ONBUILD [Other directives]`: ONBUILD allows you to postpone some instructions to later builds in the derived image. For example, we may have the following two Dockerfiles:

```
--- baseimg ---
FROM alpine
RUN apk add --no-update git make
WORKDIR /usr/src/app
ONBUILD COPY . /usr/src/app/
ONBUILD RUN git submodule init && \
         git submodule update && \
         make
--- appimg ---
FROM baseimg
EXPOSE 80
CMD ["/usr/src/app/entry"]
```

The instruction then would be evaluated in the following order on `docker build`:

```
$ docker build -t baseimg -f baseimg .
---
FROM alpine
RUN apk add --no-update git make
WORKDIR /usr/src/app
---
$ docker build -t appimg -f appimg .
---
COPY . /usr/src/app/
RUN git submodule init    && \
    git submodule update && \
    make
EXPOSE 80
CMD ["/usr/src/app/entry"]
```

Organizing a Dockerfile

Even though writing a `Dockerfile` is the same as composing a building script, there are some more factors we should consider to build efficient, secure, and stable images. Moreover, a `Dockerfile` itself is also a document, and keeping its readability eases management efforts.

Say we have an application stack that consists of application codes, a database, and cache, we'll probably start from a `Dockerfile`, such as the following:

```
---
FROM ubuntu
ADD . /app
RUN apt-get update
RUN apt-get upgrade -y
RUN apt-get install -y redis-server python python-pip mysql-server
ADD db/my.cnf /etc/mysql/my.cnf
ADD db/redis.conf /etc/redis/redis.conf
RUN pip install -r /app/requirements.txt
RUN cd /app ; python setup.py
CMD /app/start-all-service.sh
```

The first suggestion is making a container dedicated to one thing and one thing only. So, we'll remove the installation and configuration at both `mysql` and `redis` in this `Dockerfile` at the beginning. Next, the code is moved into the container with `ADD`, which means we will very likely move the whole code repository into the container. Usually there are lots of files that are not directly relevant to the application, including VCS files, CI server configurations, or even build caches, and we probably wouldn't like to pack them into an image. Thus, using a `.dockerignore` to filter out those files is suggested as well. Incidentally, due to the `ADD` instruction, we could do more than just add files into a build container. Using `COPY` is preferred in general, unless there is a real need not to do so. Now our `Dockerfile` is simpler, as shown in the following code:

```
FROM ubuntu
COPY . /app
RUN apt-get update
RUN apt-get upgrade -y
RUN apt-get install -y python python-pip
RUN pip install -r /app/requirements.txt
RUN cd /app ; python setup.py
CMD python app.py
```

While building an image, the Docker engine will try to reuse the cache layer as much as possible, which notably reduces the build time. In our `Dockerfile`, we have to go through whole updating and dependency installation processes as long as there's any update in our repository. To benefit from building caches, we'll re-order the directives based on a rule of thumb: run less frequent instructions first.

Additionally, as we've described before, any change to the container filesystem results in a new image layer. Even though we deleted certain files in the consequent layer, those files are still occupied image sizes as they are still being kept at intermediate layers. Therefore, our next step is to minimize the image layers by simply compacting multiple RUN instructions. Moreover, to keep the readability of the `Dockerfile`, we tend to format the compacted RUN with the line continuation character, "\".

In addition to working with the building mechanisms of Docker, we'd also like to write a maintainable `Dockerfile` to make it more clear, predictable, and stable. Here are some suggestions:

- Use WORKDIR instead of inline cd, and use absolute path for WORKDIR
- Explicitly expose the required ports
- Specify a tag for the base image
- Use the exec form to launch an application

The first three suggestions are pretty straightforward, aimed at eliminating ambiguity. The last one is about how an application is terminated. When a stop request from the Docker daemon is sent to a running container, the main process (PID 1) will receive a stop signal (SIGTERM). If the process is not stopped after a certain period of time, the Docker daemon will send another signal (SIGKILL) to kill the container. The exec form and shell form differ here. In the shell form, the PID 1 process is "/bin/sh -c", not the application. Further, different shells don't handle signals in the same way. Some forward the stop signal to child processes while some do not. The shell at Alpine Linux doesn't forward them. As a result, to stop and clean up our application properly, using the exec form is encouraged. Combining those principles, we have the following `Dockerfile`:

```
FROM ubuntu:16.04
RUN apt-get update && apt-get upgrade -y  \
&& apt-get install -y python python-pip
ENTRYPOINT ["python"]
CMD ["entry.py"]
EXPOSE 5000
WORKDIR /app
COPY requirements.txt .
RUN pip install -r requirements.txt
COPY . /app
```

There are still other practices to make a `Dockerfile` better, including starting from a dedicated and smaller base image such as Alpine-based ones rather than generic purpose distributions, using users other than `root` for security, and removing unnecessary files in the `RUN` in which they are joined.

Multi-containers orchestration

As we pack more and more applications into isolated boxes, we'll soon realize that we need a tool that is able to help us tackle many containers simultaneously. In this section, we'll move a step up from spinning up simply one single container to orchestrating containers in a band.

Piling up containers

Modern systems are usually built as a stack made up of multiple components that are distributed over networks, such as application servers, caches, databases, message queues, and so on. Meanwhile, a component itself is also a self-contained system with many sub-components. What's more, the trend of microservices introduces additional degrees of complexity into such entangled relationships between systems. From this fact, even though container technology gives us a certain degree of relief regarding deployment tasks, launching a system is still difficult.

Say we have a simple application called kiosk, which connects to a Redis to manage how many tickets we currently have. Once a ticket is sold, it publishes an event through a Redis channel. The recorder subscribes the Redis channel and writes a timestamp log into a MySQL database upon receiving any event.

For the **kiosk** and the **recorder**, you can find the code as well as the Dockerfiles here: `https://github.com/DevOps-with-Kubernetes/examples/tree/master/chapter2`. The architecture is as follows:

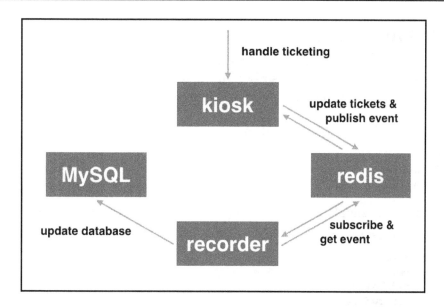

We know how to start those containers separately, and connect them to each other. Based on what we have discussed before, we would first create a bridge network, and run the containers inside:

```
$ docker network create kiosk
$ docker run -d -p 5000:5000 \
                -e REDIS_HOST=lcredis --network=kiosk kiosk-example
$ docker run -d --network-alias lcredis --network=kiosk redis
$ docker run -d -e REDIS_HOST=lcredis -e MYSQL_HOST=lmysql \
-e MYSQL_ROOT_PASSWORD=$MYPS -e MYSQL_USER=root \
--network=kiosk recorder-example
$ docker run -d --network-alias lmysql -e MYSQL_ROOT_PASSWORD=$MYPS \
  --network=kiosk mysql:5.7
```

Everything works well so far. However, if next time we want to launch the same stack again, our applications are very likely to start up prior to the databases, and they might fail if any incoming connection requests any change against the databases. In other words, we have to consider the startup order in our startup scripts. Additionally, scripts are also inept with problems such as how to deal with a random components crash, how to manage variables, how to scale out certain components, and so on.

Docker Compose overview

Docker Compose is the very tool that enables us to run multiple containers with ease, and it's a built-in tool in the Docker CE distribution. All it does is read `docker-compose.yml` (or `.yaml`) to run defined containers. A `docker-compose` file is a YAML-based template, and it typically looks like this:

```
version: '3'
services:
  hello-world:
    image: hello-world
```

Launching it is pretty simple: save the template to `docker-compose.yml` and use the `docker-compose up` command to start it:

```
$ docker-compose up
Creating network "cwd_default" with the default driver
Creating cwd_hello-world_1
Attaching to cwd_hello-world_1
hello-world_1  |
hello-world_1  | Hello from Docker!
hello-world_1  | This message shows that your installation appears to be
working correctly.
...
cwd_hello-world_1 exited with code 0
```

Let's see what `docker-compose` did behind the `up` command.

Docker Compose is basically a medley of Docker functions for multiple containers. For example, the counterpart of `docker build` is `docker-compose build`; the previous one builds a Docker image, and so the later one builds Docker images listed in the `docker-compose.yml`. But there's one thing that needs to be pointed out: the `docker-compose run` command is not the correspondent of `docker run`; it's running a specific container from the configuration in the `docker-compose.yml`. In fact, the closest command to `docker run` is `docker-compose up`.

The `docker-compose.yml` file consists of configurations of volumes, networks, and services. Besides, there should be a version definition to indicate which version of the `docker-compose` format is used. With such an understanding of the template structure, what the previous `hello-world` example does is quite clear; it creates a service called `hello-world` and it is created by the image `hello-world:latest`.

Since there is no network defined, `docker-compose` would create a new network with a default driver and connect services to the same network as shown in lines 1 to 3 of the example's output.

Additionally, the network name of a container would be the service's name. You may notice that the name displayed in the console slightly differs from its original one in the `docker-compose.yml`. It's because Docker Compose tries to avoid name conflicts between containers. As a result, Docker Compose runs the container with the name it generated, and makes a network-alias with the service name. In this example, both "`hello-world`" and "`cwd_hello-world_1`" are resolvable to other containers within the same network.

Composing containers

As Docker Compose is the same as Docker in many aspects, it's more efficient to understand how to write a `docker-compose.yml` with examples than start from `docker-compose` syntaxes. Here let's go back to the `kiosk-example` earlier and start with a `version` definition and four `services`:

```
version: '3'
services:
  kiosk-example:
  recorder-example:
  lcredis:
  lmysql:
```

The `docker run` arguments for the `kiosk-example` are pretty simple, including a publishing port and an environment variable. On the Docker Compose side, we fill the source image, publishing port, and environment variables accordingly. Because Docker Compose is able to handle `docker build`, it would build images if those images cannot be found locally. We are very likely to want to leverage it to further decrease the effort of image management:

```
kiosk-example:
  image: kiosk-example
  build: ./kiosk
  ports:
  - "5000:5000"
  environment:
    REDIS_HOST: lcredis
```

Converting the Docker run of the `recorder-example` and `redis` in the same manner, we have a template like this:

```yaml
version: '3'
services:
  kiosk-example:
    image: kiosk-example
    build: ./kiosk
    ports:
    - "5000:5000"
    environment:
      REDIS_HOST: lcredis
  recorder-example:
    image: recorder-example
    build: ./recorder
    environment:
      REDIS_HOST: lcredis
      MYSQL_HOST: lmysql
      MYSQL_USER: root
      MYSQL_ROOT_PASSWORD: mysqlpass
  lcredis:
    image: redis
    ports:
    - "6379"
```

For the MySQL part, it requires a data volume to keep its data as well as configurations. Therefore, in addition to the `lmysql` section, we add `volumes` at the level of `services` and an empty map `mysql-vol` to claim a data volume:

```yaml
  lmysql:
    image: mysql:5.7
    environment:
      MYSQL_ROOT_PASSWORD: mysqlpass
    volumes:
    - mysql-vol:/var/lib/mysql
    ports:
    - "3306"
    ---
volumes:
  mysql-vol:
```

Combining all of preceding configurations, we have the final template, as follows:

```yaml
docker-compose.yml
---
version: '3'
services:
  kiosk-example:
```

```
    image: kiosk-example
    build: ./kiosk
    ports:
    - "5000:5000"
    environment:
      REDIS_HOST: lcredis
  recorder-example:
    image: recorder-example
    build: ./recorder
    environment:
      REDIS_HOST: lcredis
      MYSQL_HOST: lmysql
      MYSQL_USER: root
      MYSQL_ROOT_PASSWORD: mysqlpass
  lcredis:
    image: redis
    ports:
    - "6379"
  lmysql:
    image: mysql:5.7
    environment:
      MYSQL_ROOT_PASSWORD: mysqlpass
    volumes:
    - mysql-vol:/var/lib/mysql
    ports:
    - "3306"
volumes:
  mysql-vol:
```

This file is put in the root folder of a project. The corresponding file tree is shown here:

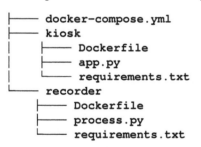

```
├─── docker-compose.yml
├─── kiosk
│    ├─── Dockerfile
│    ├─── app.py
│    └─── requirements.txt
└─── recorder
     ├─── Dockerfile
     ├─── process.py
     └─── requirements.txt
```

Lastly, run `docker-compose up` to check if everything is fine. And we can check if our kiosk is up by sending a `GET /tickets` request.

Writing a template for Docker Compose is nothing more than this. We are now able to run an application in the stack with ease.

Summary

Starting from the very primitive elements of Linux container to Docker tool stacks, we went through every aspect of containerizing an application, including packing and running a Docker container, writing a `Dockerfile` for code-based immutable deployment, and manipulating multi-containers with Docker Compose. However, our abilities gained in this chapter only allow us to run and connect containers within the same host, which limits the possibility to build larger applications. As such, in the next chapter, we'll meet Kubernetes, unleashing the power of Container beyond the limits of scale.

3
Getting Started with Kubernetes

We've learned the benefits that containers can bring us, but what if we need to scale out our services for business needs? Is there a way to build services across multiple machines without dealing with cumbersome network and storage settings? Also, is there any other easy way to manage and roll out our microservices by different service cycle? That's how Kubernetes comes into play. In this chapter, we'll learn:

- Kubernetes concept
- Kubernetes components
- Kubernetes resources and their configuration file
- How to launch the kiosk application by Kubernetes

Understanding Kubernetes

Kubernetes is a platform for managing application containers across multiple hosts. It provides lots of management features for container-oriented applications, such as auto scaling, rolling deployment, compute resource, and volume management. Same as the nature of containers, it's designed to run anywhere, so we're able to run it on a bare metal, in our data center, on the public cloud, or even hybrid cloud.

Kubernetes considers most of the operational needs for application containers. The highlights are:

- Container deployment
- Persistent storage
- Container health monitoring
- Compute resource management
- Auto-scaling
- High availability by cluster federation

Kubernetes is a perfect match for microservices. With Kubernetes, we can create a `Deployment` to rollout, rollover, or roll back selected containers (`Chapter 7`, *Continous Delivery*). Containers are considered as ephemeral. We can mount the volume into a container to preserve the data in a single host world. In the cluster world, a container might be scheduled to run on any host. How do we make the volume mounting work as permanent storage seamlessly? Kubernetes **Volumes** and **Persistent Volumes** are introduced to solve that problem (`Chapter 4`, *Working with Storage and Resources*). The lifetime of containers might be short. They may be killed or stopped anytime when they exceed the limit of resource, how do we ensure our services always serve a certain number of containers? **ReplicationController** or **ReplicaSet** in Kubernetes will ensure a certain number of group of containers are up. Kubernetes even supports **liveness probe** to help you define your application health. For better resource management, we can also define the maximum capacity on Kubernetes nodes and the resource limit for each group of containers (a.k.a **pod**). Kubernetes scheduler will then select a node that fulfills the resource criteria to run the containers. We'll learn this in `Chapter 4`, *Working with Storage and Resources*. Kubernetes provides an optional horizontal pod auto-scaling feature. With this feature, we could scale a pod horizontally by resource or custom metrics. For those advanced readers, Kubernetes is designed with high availability (**HA**). We are able to create multiple master nodes from preventing single point of failure.

Kubernetes components

Kubernetes includes two major players:

- **Masters**: The Master is the heart of Kubernetes, which controls and schedules all the activities in the cluster
- **Nodes**: Nodes are the workers that run our containers

Master components

The master includes the API server, Controller Manager, scheduler, and etcd. All the components can run on different hosts with clustering. However, from a learning perspective, we'll make all the components run on the same node.

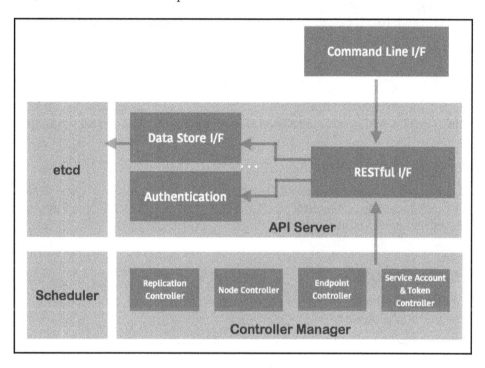

Master components

API server (kube-apiserver)

The API server provides an HTTP/HTTPS server, which provides a RESTful API for all the components in the Kubernetes master. For example, we could GET resource status, such as pod, POST to create a new resource and also watch a resource. API server reads and updates etcd, which is Kubernetes' backend data store.

Controller Manager (kube-controller-manager)

The Controller Manager controls lots of different things in the cluster. Replication Controller Manager ensures all the ReplicationControllers run on the desired container amount. Node Controller Manager responds when the nodes go down, it will then evict the pods. Endpoint Controller is used to associate the relationship between services and pods. Service Account and Token Controller are used to control default account and API access tokens.

etcd

etcd is an open source distributed key-value store (`https://coreos.com/etcd`). Kubernetes stores all the RESTful API objects here. etcd is responsible for storing and replicating data.

Scheduler (kube-scheduler)

Scheduler decides which node is suitable for pods to run on, according to the resource capacity or the balance of the resource utilization on the node. It also considers spreading the pods in the same set to different nodes.

Node components

Node components need to be provisioned and run on every node, which report the runtime status of the pod to the master.

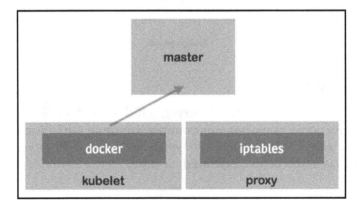

Node components

Kubelet

Kubelet is a major process in the nodes, which reports node activities back to kube-apiserver periodically, such as pod health, node health, and liveness probe. As the preceding graph shows, it runs containers via container runtimes, such as Docker or rkt.

Proxy (kube-proxy)

Proxy handles the routing between pod load balancer (a.k.a. **service**) and pods, it also provides the routing from outside to service. There are two proxy modes, userspace and iptables. Userspace mode creates large overhead by switching kernel space and user space. Iptables mode, on the other hand, is the latest default proxy mode. It changes iptables **NAT** in Linux to achieve routing TCP and UDP packets across all containers.

Docker

As described in `Chapter 2`, *DevOps with Container*, Docker is a container implementation. Kubernetes uses Docker as a default container engine.

Interaction between Kubernetes master and nodes

In the following graph, the client uses **kubectl** to send requests to the API server; API server responds to the request, pushes and pulls the object information from etcd. Scheduler determines which node should be assigned to do the tasks (for example, run pods). **Controller Manager** monitors the running tasks and responds if any undesired state occurs. On the other hand, the **API server** fetches the logs from pods by kubelet, and is also a hub between other master components.

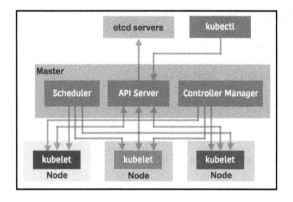

Interaction between master and nodes

Getting started with Kubernetes

In this section, we will learn how to set up a small single-node cluster at the start. Then we'll get to learn how to interact with Kubernetes via its command-line tool--kubectl. We will go through all the important Kubernetes API objects and their expression in YAML format, which is the input to kubectl, then kubectl will send the request to the API server accordingly.

Preparing the environment

The easiest way to start is running minikube (`https://github.com/kubernetes/minikube`), which is a tool to run Kubernetes on a single node locally. It supports to run on Windows, Linux, and macOS. In the following example, we'll run on macOS. Minikube will launch a VM with Kubernetes installed. Then we'll be able to interact with it via kubectl.

Note that minikube is not suitable for production or any heavy load environment. There are some limitations by its single node nature. We'll learn how to run a real cluster in `Chapter 9`, *Kubernetes on AWS* and `Chapter 10`, *Kubernetes on GCP* instead.

Before installing minikube, we'll have to install Homebrew (`https://brew.sh/`) and VirtualBox (`https://www.virtualbox.org/`) first. Homebrew is a useful package manager in macOS. We can easily install Homebrew via the `/usr/bin/ruby -e "$(curl -fsSL https://raw.githubusercontent.com/Homebrew/install/master/install)"` command, and download VirtualBox from the Oracle website and click to install it.

Then it's time to start! We can install minikube via `brew cask install minikube`:

```
// install minikube
# brew cask install minikube
==> Tapping caskroom/cask
==> Linking Binary 'minikube-darwin-amd64' to '/usr/local/bin/minikube'.
...
minikube was successfully installed!
```

After minikube is installed, we now can start the cluster:

```
// start the cluster
# minikube start
Starting local Kubernetes v1.6.4 cluster...
Starting VM...
Moving files into cluster...
Setting up certs...
Starting cluster components...
```

```
Connecting to cluster...
Setting up kubeconfig...
Kubectl is now configured to use the cluster.
```

This will launch a Kubernetes cluster locally. At the time of writing, the latest version is `v.1.6.4` minikube. Proceed to start a VM named minikube in VirtualBox. Then it will be setting up `kubeconfig`, which is a configuration file to define the context and authentication settings of the cluster.

With `kubeconfig`, we're able to switch to different clusters via the `kubectl` command. We could use the `kubectl config view` command to see current settings in `kubeconfig`:

```
apiVersion: v1
# cluster and certificate information
clusters:
- cluster:
    certificate-authority-data: REDACTED
    server: https://35.186.182.157
  name: gke_devops_cluster
- cluster:
    certificate-authority: /Users/chloelee/.minikube/ca.crt
    server: https://192.168.99.100:8443
  name: minikube
# context is the combination of cluster, user and namespace
contexts:
- context:
    cluster: gke_devops_cluster
    user: gke_devops_cluster
  name: gke_devops_cluster
- context:
    cluster: minikube
    user: minikube
  name: minikube
current-context: minikube
kind: Config
preferences: {}
# user information
users:
- name: gke_devops_cluster
user:
  auth-provider:
   config:
    access-token: xxxx
    cmd-args: config config-helper --format=json
    cmd-path: /Users/chloelee/Downloads/google-cloud-sdk/bin/gcloud
    expiry: 2017-06-08T03:51:11Z
    expiry-key: '{.credential.token_expiry}'
```

```
        token-key: '{.credential.access_token}'
      name: gcp
  # namespace info
  - name: minikube
  user:
    client-certificate: /Users/chloelee/.minikube/apiserver.crt
    client-key: /Users/chloelee/.minikube/apiserver.key
```

Here we know we're currently using minikube context with the same name of cluster and user. Context is a combination of authentication information and cluster connection information. You could use `kubectl config use-context $context` to force switch the context if you have more than one context.

In the end, we'll need to enable `kube-dns` addon in minikube. `kube-dns` is a DNS service in Kuberentes:

```
// enable kube-dns addon
# minikube addons enable kube-dns
kube-dns was successfully enabled
```

kubectl

`kubectl` is the command to control Kubernetes cluster manager. The most general usage is to check the version of cluster:

```
// check Kubernetes version
# kubectl version
Client Version: version.Info{Major:"1", Minor:"6", GitVersion:"v1.6.2",
GitCommit:"477efc3cbe6a7effca06bd1452fa356e2201e1ee", GitTreeState:"clean",
BuildDate:"2017-04-19T20:33:11Z", GoVersion:"go1.7.5", Compiler:"gc",
Platform:"darwin/amd64"}
Server Version: version.Info{Major:"1", Minor:"6", GitVersion:"v1.6.4",
GitCommit:"d6f433224538d4f9ca2f7ae19b252e6fcb66a3ae", GitTreeState:"clean",
BuildDate:"2017-05-30T22:03:41Z", GoVersion:"go1.7.3", Compiler:"gc",
Platform:"linux/amd64"}
```

We then know our server version is up to date, which is the latest at the time of writing—version 1.6.4. The general syntax of `kubectl` is:

```
kubectl [command] [type] [name] [flags]
```

The `command` indicates the operation you want to perform. If you just type `kubectl help` in the Terminal, it will show the supported commands. `type` means the resource type. We'll learn major resource types in the next section. `name` is how we name our resources. It's always good practice to have clear and informational naming along the way. For the `flags`, if you type `kubectl options`, it will show all the flags you could pass on.

`kubectl` comes in handy and we could always add `--help` to get more detailed information for the specific command. For example:

```
// show detailed info for logs command
kubectl logs --help
Print the logs for a container in a pod or specified resource. If the pod
has only one container, the container name is
optional.

Aliases:
logs, log

Examples:
  # Return snapshot logs from pod nginx with only one container
  kubectl logs nginx

  # Return snapshot logs for the pods defined by label
  app=nginx
  kubectl logs -lapp=nginx

  # Return snapshot of previous terminated ruby container logs
  from pod web-1
  kubectl logs -p -c ruby web-1
...
```

We then get the full supported option in the `kubectl logs` command.

Kubernetes resources

Kubernetes objects are the entries in the cluster, which are stored in etcd. They represent the desired state of your cluster. When we create an object, we send the request to API Server by kubectl or RESTful API. API Server will store the state into etcd and interact with other master components to ensure the object exists. Kubernetes uses namespace to isolate the objects virtually, according to different teams, usages, projects, or environments. Every object has its own name and unique ID. Kubernetes also supports labels and annotation to let us tag our objects. Labels especially could be used to group the objects together.

Kubernetes objects

Object spec describes the desired state of Kubernetes objects. Most of the time, we write an object spec, and send the spec to the API Server via kubectl. Kubernetes will try to fulfill that desired state and update object status.

Object spec could be written in YAML (`http://www.yaml.org/`) or JSON (`http://www.json.org/`). YAML is more common in the Kubernetes world. We'll use YAML format to write object specs in the rest of this book. The following code block shows a YAML-formatted spec fragment:

```
apiVersion: Kubernetes API version
kind: object type
metadata:
  spec metadata, i.e. namespace, name, labels and annotations
spec:
  the spec of Kubernetes object
```

Namespace

Kubernetes namespace is considered to be an isolation as multiple virtual clusters. Objects in different namespaces are invisible to each other. This is useful when different teams or projects are sharing the same cluster. Most of the resources are under a namespace (a.k.a. namespaced resources); however, some generic resources, such as nodes or namespace itself, don't belong to any namespace. Kubernetes has three namespaces by default:

- default
- kube-system
- kube-public

Without explicitly assigning namespace to the namespaced resource, it will be located in the namespace under current context. If we never add a new namespace, a default namespace will be used.

Kube-system namespaces are used by the objects created by the Kubernetes system, such as addon, which are the pods or services that implement cluster features, such as dashboard. Kube-public namespaces are newly introduced in Kubernetes 1.6, which is used by a beta controller manager (BootstrapSigner `https://kubernetes.io/docs/admin/bootstrap-tokens`), putting the signed cluster location information into the `kube-public` namespace, so this information could be visible to authenticated/unauthenticated users.

In the following sections, all the namespaced resources will be located in a default namespace. Namespace is also very important for resource management and role. We'll introduce more in `Chapter 8`, *Cluster Administration*.

Name

Every object in Kubernetes owns its own name. Object name in one resource is uniquely identified within the same namespace. Kubernetes uses object name as part of a resource URL to API Server, so it must be the combination of lower case of alphanumeric characters, dash and dot, less than 254 characters. Besides object name, Kubernetes also assigns a unique ID (UID) to every object to distinguish historical occurrences of similar entities.

Label and selector

Labels are a set of key/pair values, used to attach to objects. Labels are designed to specify meaningful, identifying information for the object. Common usage is micro-service name, tier, environment, and software version. Users could define meaningful labels that could be used with selector later. Labels syntax in object spec is:

```
labels:
  $key1: $value1
  $key2: $value2
```

Along with label, label selector is used to filter the set of objects. Separated by commas, multiple requirements will be joined by the AND logical operator. There are two ways to filter:

- Equality-based requirement
- Set-based requirement

Equality-based requirement supports the operator of =, ==, and !=. For example, if selector is `chapter=2,version!=0.1`, the result will be **object C**. If requirement is `version=0.1`, the result will be **object A** and **object B**. If we write the requirement in supported object spec, it'll be as follows:

```
selector:
  $key1: $value1
```

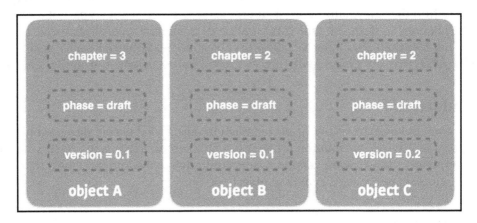

Selector example

Set-based requirement supports `in`, `notin`, and `exists` (for key only). For example, if requirement is `chapter in (3, 4),version`, then object A will be returned. If requirement is `version notin (0.2), !author_info`, the result will be **object A** and **object B**. The following is an example if we write to the object spec that supports set-based requirement:

```
selector:
  matchLabels:
    $key1: $value1
  matchExpressions:
{key: $key2, operator: In, values: [$value1, $value2]}
```

The requirements of `matchLabels` and `matchExpressions` are combined together. It means the filtered objects need to be true on both requirements.

We will learn along the way in this chapter with ReplicationController, Service, ReplicaSet, and Deployment.

Annotation

Annotation is a set of user-specified key/value pairs, used for specifying non-identifying metadata. With annotation acts such as normal tagging, for example, a user could add timestamp, commit hash, or build number to annotation. Some of the kubectl commands support the `--record` option to record the commands that make the changes to the objects to the annotation. Another use case of annotation is storing the configuration, such as Kubernetes Deployments (`https://kubernetes.io/docs/concepts/workloads/controllers/deployment`) or Critical Add-On pods (`https://coreos.com/kubernetes/docs/latest/deploy-addons.html`). Annotation syntax is as follows in the metadata section:

```
annotations:
  $key1: $value1
  $key2: $value2
```

 Namespace, name, label, and annotation are located in the metadata section of object spec. Selector is located in the spec section of selector-supported resources, such as ReplicationController, service, ReplicaSet, and Deployment.

Pods

Pod is the smallest deployable unit in Kubernetes. It can contain one or more containers. Most of the time, we just need one container per pod. In some special cases, more than one container is included in the same pod, such as Sidecar containers (`http://blog.kubernetes.io/2015/06/the-distributed-system-toolkit-patterns.html`). The containers in the same pod run in a shared context, on the same node, sharing the network namespace and shared volumes. Pod is also designed as mortal. When a pod dies for some reasons, such as getting killed by Kubernetes controller when lacking resources, it won't recover by itself. Instead, Kubernetes uses controllers to create and manage the desired state of pods for us.

We could use `kubectl explain <resource>` to get the detailed description for the resource by command line. It will show up the fields that the resource supports:

```
// get detailed info for `pods`
# kubectl explain pods
DESCRIPTION:
Pod is a collection of containers that can run on a host. This resource is
created by clients and scheduled onto hosts.

FIELDS:
   metadata  <Object>
```

```
      Standard object's metadata. More info:
      http://releases.k8s.io/HEAD/docs/devel/api-
      conventions.md#metadata

  spec   <Object>
      Specification of the desired behavior of the pod.
      More info:
      http://releases.k8s.io/HEAD/docs/devel/api-
      conventions.md#spec-and-status

  status   <Object>
      Most recently observed status of the pod. This data
      may not be up to date.
      Populated by the system. Read-only. More info:
      http://releases.k8s.io/HEAD/docs/devel/api-
      conventions.md#spec-and-status

  apiVersion   <string>
      APIVersion defines the versioned schema of this
      representation of an
      object. Servers should convert recognized schemas to
      the latest internal
      value, and may reject unrecognized values. More info:
      http://releases.k8s.io/HEAD/docs/devel/api-
      conventions.md#resources

  kind   <string>
      Kind is a string value representing the REST resource
      this object represents. Servers may infer this from
      the endpoint the client submits
      requests to. Cannot be updated. In CamelCase. More
         info:
      http://releases.k8s.io/HEAD/docs/devel/api-
      conventions.md#types-kinds
```

In the following example, we'll show how to create two containers in a pod, and demonstrate how they access each other. Please note that it's neither a meaningful nor classic Sidecar pattern example. Those are used in very specific scenarios. The following is just an example of how we access other containers within a pod:

```
// an example for creating co-located and co-scheduled container by pod
# cat 3-2-1_pod.yaml
apiVersion: v1
kind: Pod
metadata:
  name: example
spec:
  containers:
```

```
 - name: web
   image: nginx
 - name: centos
   image: centos
   command: ["/bin/sh", "-c", "while : ;do curl http://localhost:80/;
sleep 10; done"]
```

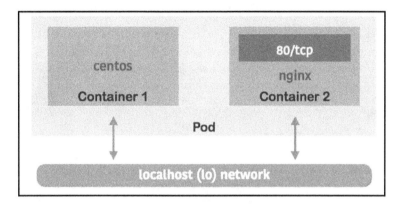

Containers inside a Pod are visible via localhost

This spec will create two containers, web and centos. Web is a nginx container (https://hub.docker.com/_/nginx/). Expose container port 80 by default, since centos shares the same context with nginx, when doing curl in http://localhost:80/, it should be able to access nginx.

Next, using the kubectl create command to launch the pod -f option lets kubectl know using the data in the file:

```
// create the resource by `kubectl create` - Create a resource by filename
or stdin
# kubectl create -f 3-2-1_pod.yaml
pod "example" created
```

Adding --record=true at the end of the kubectl command when we create the resources. Kubernetes will add the latest command while creating or updating this resource. Therefore, we won't forget which resources are created by which spec.

We could use the `kubectl get <resource>` command to get the current status of the object. In this case, we use the `kubectl get pods` command.

```
// get the current running pods
# kubectl get pods
NAME       READY      STATUS            RESTARTS   AGE
example    0/2        ContainerCreating 0          1s
```

Add `--namespace=$namespace_name` could access the object in different namespaces. The following is an example to check the pods in the `kube-system` namespace, which is used by system-type pods:
```
# kubectl get pods --namespace=kube-system
```

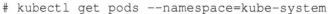

```
NAME READY STATUS RESTARTS AGE

kube-addon-manager-minikube 1/1 Running 2 3d

kube-dns-196007617-jkk4k 3/3 Running 3 3d

kubernetes-dashboard-3szrf 1/1 Running 1 3d
```

Most of the objects have their short names, which come in handy when we use `kubectl get <object>` to list their status. For example, pods could be called po, services could be called svc, and deployment could be called deploy. Type `kubectl get` to know more.

The status of our example pod is `ContainerCreating`. In this phase, Kubernetes has accepted the request, trying to schedule the pod and pulling down the image. Zero containers are currently running. After waiting a moment, we could get the status again:

```
// get the current running pods
# kubectl get pods
NAME       READY      STATUS            RESTARTS   AGE
example    2/2        Running           0          3s
```

We can see two containers are currently running. Uptime is three seconds. Using `kubectl logs <pod_name> -c <container_name>` could get `stdout` for the container, similar to `docker logs <container_name>`:

```
// get stdout for centos
# kubectl logs example -c centos
<!DOCTYPE html>
<html>
<head>
<title>Welcome to nginx!</title>
```

. . .

Centos in the pod shares the same networking with nginx via localhost! Kubernetes creates a network container along with the pod. One of the functions in the network container is to forward the traffic between containers within a pod. We'll learn more in `Chapter 5`, *Network and Security*.

 If we specify labels in pod spec, we could use the `kubectl get pods -l <requirement>` command to get the pods that are satisfying the requirements. For example, `kubectl get pods -l 'tier in (frontend, backend)'`. Additionally, if we use `kubectl pods -owide`, it will list down which pod is running on which nodes.

We could use `kubectl describe <resource> <resource_name>` to get the detailed information of a resource:

```
// get detailed information for a pod
# kubectl describe pods example
Name:       example
Namespace:  default
Node:       minikube/192.168.99.100
Start Time: Fri, 09 Jun 2017 07:08:59 -0400
Labels:     <none>
Annotations: <none>
Status:     Running
IP:         172.17.0.4
Controllers: <none>
Containers:
```

At this point, we know which node this pod is running on, in minikube we only get a single node so it won't make any difference. In the real cluster environment, knowing which node is useful for troubleshooting. We didn't associate any labels, annotations, and controllers for it:

```
web:
    Container ID:
 docker://a90e56187149155dcda23644c536c20f5e039df0c174444e 0a8c8
7e8666b102b
    Image:      nginx
    Image ID:
docker://sha256:958a7ae9e56979be256796dabd5845c704f784cd422734184999cf91f24
c2547
    Port:
    State:      Running
      Started:      Fri, 09 Jun 2017 07:09:00 -0400
    Ready:      True
```

```
    Restart Count:   0
    Environment:   <none>
    Mounts:
       /var/run/secrets/kubernetes.io/serviceaccount from
       default-token-jd1dq (ro)
    centos:
    Container ID:
docker://778965ad71dd5f075f93c90f91fd176a8add4bd35230ae0fa6c73cd1c2158f0b
       Image:      centos
       Image ID:
docker://sha256:3bee3060bfc81c061ce7069df35ce090593bda584d4ef464bc0f38086c1
1371d
       Port:
       Command:
         /bin/sh
         -c
         while : ;do curl http://localhost:80/; sleep 10;
         done
       State:      Running
        Started:      Fri, 09 Jun 2017 07:09:01 -0400
       Ready:      True
       Restart Count:  0
       Environment:   <none>
       Mounts:
            /var/run/secrets/kubernetes.io/serviceaccount from default-token-
    jd1dq (ro)
```

In the containers section, we'll see there are two containers included in this pod. Their states, images, and restart count:

```
Conditions:
   Type      Status
   Initialized     True
   Ready     True
   PodScheduled      True
```

A pod has a `PodStatus`, which including a map of array represents as `PodConditions`. The possible key for `PodConditions` are `PodScheduled`, `Ready`, `Initialized`, and `Unschedulable`. Value will be true, false, or unknown. If the pod is not created accordingly, `PodStatus` will give us a brief view of which part failed:

```
Volumes:
  default-token-jd1dq:
   Type:  Secret (a volume populated by a Secret)
   SecretName:  default-token-jd1dq
   Optional:  false
```

Pod is associated with a service account that provides an identity for processes that are running a pod. It's controlled by service account and token controller in API Server.

It will mount a read only volume to each container under `/var/run/secrets/kubernetes.io/serviceaccount` in a pod that contains a token for API access. Kubernetes creates a default service account. We could use the `kubectl get serviceaccounts` command to list them:

```
QoS Class:  BestEffort
Node-Selectors:  <none>
Tolerations:  <none>
```

We don't assign any selectors to this pod yet. QoS means Resource Quality of Service. Toleration is used to restrict how many pods that can use a node. We will learn more in `Chapter 8`, *Cluster Administration:*

```
Events:
 FirstSeen  LastSeen  Count  From        SubObjectPath     Type
 Reason      Message
 ---------  --------  -----  ----        -------------     ------
 --  ------  -------
 19m    19m    1  default-scheduler       Normal    Scheduled
 Successfully assigned example to minikube
 19m    19m    1  kubelet, minikube  spec.containers{web}
 Normal    Pulling    pulling image "nginx"
 19m    19m    1  kubelet, minikube  spec.containers{web}
 Normal    Pulled    Successfully pulled image "nginx"
 19m    19m    1  kubelet, minikube  spec.containers{web}
 Normal    Created    Created container with id
 a90e56187149155dcda23644c536c20f5e039df0c174444e0a8c87e8666b102b
 19m    19m    1  kubelet, minikube  spec.containers{web}
 Normal    Started    Started container with id
 a90e56187149155dcda23644c536c20f5e039df0c174444e0a8c87e86
 66b102b
 19m    19m    1  kubelet, minikube  spec.containers{centos}
 Normal    Pulling    pulling image "centos"
 19m    19m    1  kubelet, minikube  spec.containers{centos}
 Normal    Pulled    Successfully pulled image "centos"
 19m    19m    1  kubelet, minikube  spec.containers{centos}
 Normal    Created    Created container with id
 778965ad71dd5f075f93c90f91fd176a8add4bd35230ae0fa6c73cd1c
 2158f0b
 19m    19m    1  kubelet, minikube  spec.containers{centos}
 Normal    Started    Started container with id
 778965ad71dd5f075f93c90f91fd176a8add4bd35230ae0fa6c73cd1c
 2158f0b
```

By seeing events, we could know what the steps are for Kubernetes to run a node. First, scheduler assigns the task to a node, here it is named minikube. Then kubelet on minikube starts pulling the first image and creates a container accordingly. Then kubelet pulls down the second container and runs.

ReplicaSet (RS) and ReplicationController (RC)

A pod is not self-healing. When a pod encounters failure, it won't recover on its own. **ReplicaSet** (RS) and **ReplicationController** (RC) therefore come into play. Both ReplicaSet and ReplicationController will ensure a specified number of replica pods are always up and running in the cluster. If a pod crashes for any reason, ReplicaSet and ReplicationController will request to spin up a new Pod.

After the latest Kubernetes, ReplicationController is replaced by ReplicaSet gradually. They share the same concept, just using different requirements for the pod selector. ReplicationController uses equality-based selector requirements while ReplicaSet uses set-based selector requirements. ReplicaSet usually is not created by users, but by Kubernetes Deployments objects, while ReplicationController is created by users ourselves. In this section, we'll explain the concept for RC first by walking through examples, which is much easier to understand. Then we'll bring in ReplicaSet at the end.

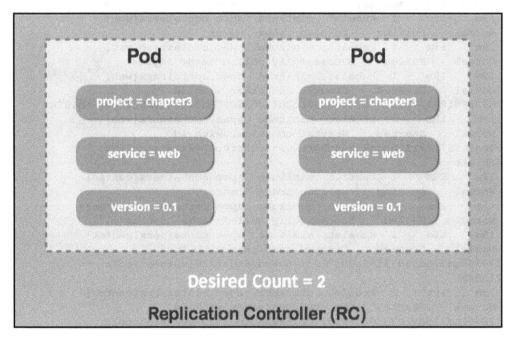

ReplicationController with desired count 2

Let's say we'd like to create a `ReplicationController` object, with desired count two. It means we will always have two pods in service. Before we write the spec for ReplicationController, we'll have to decide pod template first. Pod template is similar to the spec of pod. In ReplicationController, labels in the metadata section are required. ReplicationController uses pod selector to select which pods it manages. Labels allow ReplicationController to distinguish whether all the pods matching the selectors are all on track.

In this example, we'll create two pods with the labels `project`, `service`, and `version`, as shown in the preceding figure:

```
// an example for rc spec
# cat 3-2-2_rc.yaml
apiVersion: v1
kind: ReplicationController
metadata:
  name: nginx
spec:
  replicas: 2
  selector:
   project: chapter3
   service: web
   version: "0.1"
  template:
   metadata:
    name: nginx
    labels:
     project: chapter3
     service: web
     version: "0.1"
  spec:
    containers:
   - name: nginx
     image: nginx
     ports:
   - containerPort: 80
// create RC by above input file
# kubectl create -f 3-2-2_rc.yaml
replicationcontroller "nginx" created
```

Then we can use `kubectl` to get current RC status:

```
// get current RCs
# kubectl get rc
NAME        DESIRED    CURRENT    READY     AGE
nginx       2          2          2         5s
```

It shows we have two desired pods, we currently have two pods and two pods are ready. How many pods do we have now?

```
// get current running pod
# kubectl get pods
NAME          READY     STATUS      RESTARTS    AGE
nginx-r3bg6   1/1       Running     0           11s
nginx-sj2f0   1/1       Running     0           11s
```

It shows we have two pods up and running. As described previously, ReplicationController manages all the pods matching the selector. If we create a pod with the same label manually, in theory, it should match the pod selector of the RC we just created. Let's try it out:

```
// manually create a pod with same labels
# cat 3-2-2_rc_self_created_pod.yaml
apiVersion: v1
kind: Pod
metadata:
  name: our-nginx
  labels:
    project: chapter3
    service: web
    version: "0.1"
spec:
  containers:
  - name: nginx
    image: nginx
    ports:
    - containerPort: 80
// create a pod with same labels manually
# kubectl create -f 3-2-2_rc_self_created_pod.yaml
pod "our-nginx" created
```

Let's see if it's up and running:

```
// get pod status
# kubectl get pods
NAME          READY     STATUS        RESTARTS    AGE
nginx-r3bg6   1/1       Running       0           4m
nginx-sj2f0   1/1       Running       0           4m
our-nginx     0/1       Terminating   0           4s
```

It's scheduled, and ReplicationController catches it. The amount of pods becomes three, which exceeds our desired count. The pod is eventually killed:

```
// get pod status
# kubectl get pods
NAME            READY    STATUS      RESTARTS    AGE
nginx-r3bg6     1/1      Running     0           5m
nginx-sj2f0     1/1      Running     0           5m
```

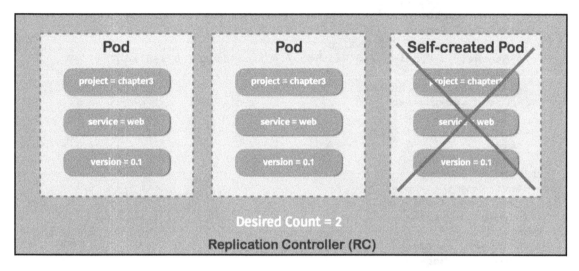

ReplicationController makes sure pods are in desired state

If we want to scale on demand, we could simply use `kubectl edit <resource>` `<resource_name>` to update the spec. Here we'll change replica count from 2 to 5:

```
// change replica count from 2 to 5, default system editor will pop out.
Change `replicas` number
# kubectl edit rc nginx
replicationcontroller "nginx" edited
```

Let's check RC information:

```
// get rc information
# kubectl get rc
NAME      DESIRED    CURRENT    READY    AGE
nginx     5          5          5        5m
```

We have five pods now. Let's check how RC works:

```
// describe RC resource `nginx`
# kubectl describe rc nginx
Name:      nginx
Namespace: default
Selector:  project=chapter3,service=web,version=0.1
Labels:    project=chapter3
           service=web
           version=0.1
Annotations: <none>
Replicas:  5 current / 5 desired
Pods Status: 5 Running / 0 Waiting / 0 Succeeded / 0 Failed
Pod Template:
  Labels:  project=chapter3
           service=web
           version=0.1
  Containers:
   nginx:
   Image:     nginx
   Port:      80/TCP
   Environment:  <none>
   Mounts:      <none>
  Volumes:      <none>
Events:
  FirstSeen  LastSeen  Count  From          SubObjectPath  Type
  Reason        Message
  ---------  --------  -----  ----          -------------  --------  ------
  -------
34s    34s    1 replication-controller        Normal    SuccessfulCreate
Created pod: nginx-r3bg6
34s    34s    1 replication-controller        Normal    SuccessfulCreate
Created pod: nginx-sj2f0
20s    20s    1 replication-controller        Normal    SuccessfulDelete
Deleted pod: our-nginx
15s    15s    1 replication-controller        Normal    SuccessfulCreate
Created pod: nginx-nlx3v
15s    15s    1 replication-controller        Normal    SuccessfulCreate
Created pod: nginx-rqt58
15s    15s    1 replication-controller        Normal    SuccessfulCreate
Created pod: nginx-qb3mr
```

By describing the command; we can learn the spec of RC, also the events. At the time we created `nginx` RC, it launched two containers by spec. Then we created another pod manually by another spec, named `our-nginx`. RC detected that pod matches its pod selector. Then the amount exceeded our desired count, so it evicted it. Then we scaled out the replicas to five. RC detected that it didn't fulfill our desired state, launching three pods to fill the gap.

If we want to delete an RC, simply use the `kubectl` command by `kubectl delete <resource> <resource_name>`. Since we have a configuration file on hand, we could also use `kubectl delete -f <configuration_file>` to delete the resources listing in the file:

```
// delete a rc
# kubectl delete rc nginx
replicationcontroller "nginx" deleted
// get pod status
# kubectl get pods
NAME            READY   STATUS        RESTARTS   AGE
nginx-r3bg6     0/1     Terminating   0          29m
```

The same concept is brought to ReplicaSet. The following is RS version of `3-2-2.rc.yaml`. Two major differences are:

- The `apiVersion` is `extensions/v1beta1` at the time of writing
- Selector requirement is changed set-based requirement, with `matchLabels` and `matchExpressions` syntax

Following the same steps with the preceding example should work exactly the same between RC and RS. This is just an example; however, we shouldn't create RS on our own, while it should be always managed by Kubernetes `deployment` object. We'll learn more in the next section:

```
// RS version of 3-2-2_rc.yaml
# cat 3-2-2_rs.yaml
apiVersion: extensions/v1beta1
kind: ReplicaSet
metadata:
  name: nginx
spec:
  replicas: 2
  selector:
   matchLabels:
     project: chapter3
   matchExpressions:
    - {key: version, operator: In, values: ["0.1", "0.2"]}
```

```
template:
  metadata:
    name: nginx
     labels:
       project: chapter3
       service: web
       version: "0.1"
  spec:
    containers:
      - name: nginx
        image: nginx
        ports:
        - containerPort: 80
```

Deployments

Deployment is the best primitive to manage and deploy our software in Kubernetes after version 1.2. It supports gracefully deploying, rolling updating, and rolling back pods and ReplicaSets. We define our desired update of the software by deployment declaratively, and then deployment will do it for us progressively.

Before deployment, ReplicationController and kubectl rolling-update were the major way to implement rolling-update for the software, which is more imperative and slower. Deployment now becomes the major high-level object to manage our application.

Let's have a glimpse of how it works. In this section, we'll get a taste of how deployment is created, how to perform rolling-update and rollback. Chapter 7, *Continuous Delivery* has more information with practical examples about how we integrate with deployments into our continuous delivery pipeline.

First, we could use the kubectl run command to create a deployment for us:

```
// using kubectl run to launch the Pods
# kubectl run nginx --image=nginx:1.12.0 --replicas=2 --port=80
deployment "nginx" created
// check the deployment status
# kubectl get deployments
NAME     DESIRED     CURRENT     UP-TO-DATE     AVAILABLE     AGE
nginx    2           2           2              2             4h
```

Before Kubernetes 1.2, the kubectl run command would create pods instead.

There are two pods that are deployed by deployment:

```
// check if pods match our desired count
# kubectl get pods
NAME                      READY    STATUS     RESTARTS    AGE
nginx-2371676037-2brn5    1/1      Running    0           4h
nginx-2371676037-gjfhp    1/1      Running    0           4h
```

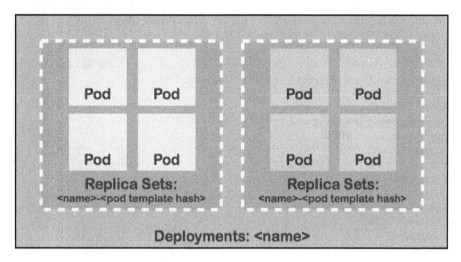

The relationship in deployments, ReplicaSets, and pods

If we delete one of the pods, the replaced pod will be scheduled and launched immediately. That's because deployments creates a ReplicaSet behind the scenes, which will ensure the number of replicas is matched with our desired count. In general, deployments manage ReplicaSets, ReplicaSets manage pods. Note that we shouldn't manually manipulate ReplicaSets that deployments managed, just like there is no sense to change pods directly if they're managed by ReplicaSets:

```
// list replica sets
# kubectl get rs
NAME               DESIRED    CURRENT    READY    AGE
nginx-2371676037   2          2          2        4h
```

We could also expose the port for deployment by the `kubectl` command:

```
// expose port 80 to service port 80
# kubectl expose deployment nginx --port=80 --target-port=80
service "nginx" exposed
// list services
# kubectl get services
NAME            CLUSTER-IP    EXTERNAL-IP    PORT(S)    AGE
kubernetes      10.0.0.1      <none>         443/TCP    3d
nginx           10.0.0.94     <none>         80/TCP     5s
```

Deployments can be created by spec as well. The previous deployments and service launched by kubectl can be converted to the following spec:

```
// create deployments by spec
# cat 3-2-3_deployments.yaml
apiVersion: apps/v1beta1
kind: Deployment
metadata:
  name: nginx
spec:
  replicas: 2
  template:
   metadata:
    labels:
     run: nginx
   spec:
    containers:
    - name: nginx
      image: nginx:1.12.0
      ports:
      - containerPort: 80
---
kind: Service
apiVersion: v1
metadata:
  name: nginx
  labels:
   run: nginx
spec:
  selector:
   run: nginx
  ports:
    - protocol: TCP
      port: 80
      targetPort: 80
      name: http
// create deployments and service
```

```
# kubectl create -f 3-2-3_deployments.yaml
deployment "nginx" created
service "nginx" created
```

For performing rolling update, we'll have to add rolling update strategy. There are three parameters used to control the process:

Parameters	Description	Default value
minReadySeconds	Warm-up time. How long a newly created pod is considered to be available. By default, Kubernetes assumes the application will be available once it is successfully launched.	0
maxSurge	How many pods can be surged when doing rolling update process.	25%
maxUnavailable	How many pods can be unavailable when doing rolling update process.	25%

The `minReadySecond` is an important setting. If our application is not available immediately when the pod is up, pods are rolling too fast without proper waiting. Although all the new pods are up, the application might be still warming up; there are chances a service outage might occur. In the following example, we'll add the configuration into the `Deployment.spec` section:

```
// add to Deployments.spec, save as 3-2-3_deployments_rollingupdate.yaml
minReadySeconds: 3
strategy:
  type: RollingUpdate
  rollingUpdate:
   maxSurge: 1
   maxUnavailable: 1
```

It indicates that we allow one of the pods to be unavailable at a time and one more pod could be launched when rolling the pods. The warm-up time before proceeding to the next operation will be three seconds. We can use either `kubectl edit deployments nginx` (edit directly) or `kubectl replace -f 3-2-3_deployments_rollingupdate.yaml` to update the strategy.

Let's say we want to simulate new software rollout, from nginx 1.12.0 to 1.13.1. We still could use the preceding two commands to change image version, or use `kubectl set image deployment nginx nginx=nginx:1.13.1` to trigger the update. If we use `kubectl describe` to check what's going on, we will see deployments have triggered rolling updates on ReplicaSets by deleting/creating pods:

```
// check detailed rs information
# kubectl describe rs nginx-2371676037
Name:      nginx-2371676037
Namespace: default
Selector:  pod-template-hash=2371676037    ,run=nginx
Labels:    pod-template-hash=2371676037
           run=nginx
Annotations:  deployment.kubernetes.io/desired-replicas=2
              deployment.kubernetes.io/max-replicas=3
              deployment.kubernetes.io/revision=4
              deployment.kubernetes.io/revision-history=2
Replicas:  2 current / 2 desired
Pods Status:  2 Running / 0 Waiting / 0 Succeeded / 0 Failed
Pod Template:
  Labels:  pod-template-hash=2371676037
           run=nginx
Containers:
nginx:
Image:     nginx:1.13.1
Port:      80/TCP
...
Events:
FirstSeen  LastSeen  Count  From         SubObjectPath  Type      Reason
Message
---------  --------  -----  ----         -------------  --------  ------
-------
3m    3m    1   replicaset-controller      Normal    SuccessfulCreate
Created pod: nginx-2371676037-f2ndj
3m    3m    1   replicaset-controller      Normal    SuccessfulCreate
Created pod: nginx-2371676037-91c8j
3m    3m    1   replicaset-controller      Normal    SuccessfulDelete
Deleted pod: nginx-2371676037-f2ndj
3m    3m    1   replicaset-controller      Normal    SuccessfulDelete
Deleted pod: nginx-2371676037-91c8j
```

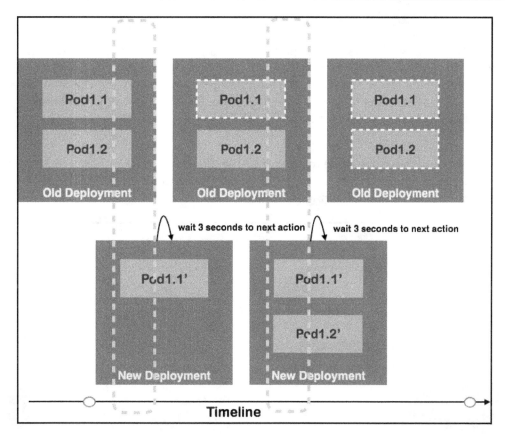

Illustration of deployments

The preceding figure shows the illustration of the deployment. At a certain point of time, we have two (desired count) and one (`maxSurge`) pods. After launching each new pod, Kubernetes will wait three (`minReadySeconds`) seconds and then performs the next action.

If we use the command `kubectl set image deployment nginx nginx=nginx:1.12.0` to previous version 1.12.0, deployments will do the rollback for us.

Services

Service in Kubernetes is an abstraction layer for routing traffic to a logical set of pods. With service, we don't need to trace the IP address of each pod. Service usually uses label selector to select the pods that it needs to route to (in some cases service is created without selector in purpose). The service abstraction is powerful. It enables the decoupling and makes communication between micro-services possible. Currently Kubernetes service supports TCP and UDP.

Service doesn't care how we create the pod. Just like ReplicationController, it only cares that the pods match its label selectors, so the pods could belong to different ReplicationControllers. The following is an illustration:

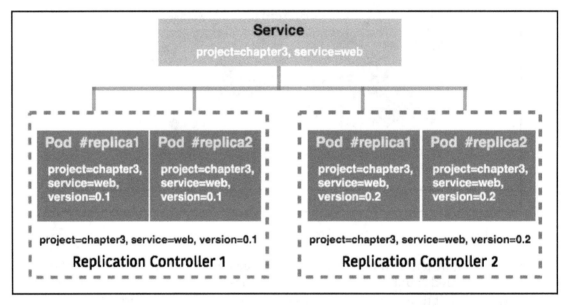

Service maps pods via label selector

In the graph, all the pods match the service selector, so service will be responsible to distribute the traffic into all the pods without explicit assignment.

Service types

There are four types of services: ClusterIP, NodePort, LoadBalancer, and ExternalName.

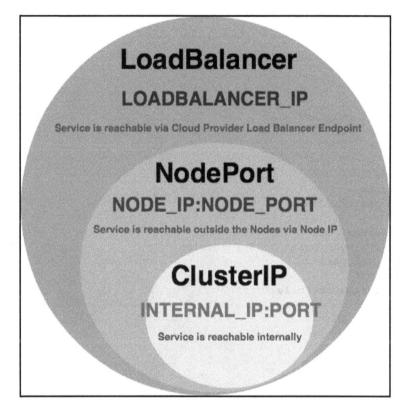

LoadBalancer includes the features of NodePort and ClusterIP

ClusterIP

ClusterIP is the default service type. It exposes the service on a cluster-internal IP. Pods in the cluster could reach the service via the IP address, environment variables, or DNS. In the following example, we'll learn how to use both native service environment variables and DNS to access the pods behind services in the cluster.

Before starting a service, we'd like to create two sets of RC shown in the figure:

```
// create RC 1 with nginx 1.12.0 version
# cat 3-2-3_rc1.yaml
apiVersion: v1
kind: ReplicationController
metadata:
```

```
    name: nginx-1.12
spec:
  replicas: 2
  selector:
   project: chapter3
   service: web
   version: "0.1"
template:
  metadata:
   name: nginx
   labels:
     project: chapter3
     service: web
     version: "0.1"
  spec:
  containers:
 - name: nginx
   image: nginx:1.12.0
   ports:
 - containerPort: 80
// create RC 2 with nginx 1.13.1 version
# cat 3-2-3_rc2.yaml
apiVersion: v1
kind: ReplicationController
metadata:
  name: nginx-1.13
spec:
  replicas: 2
  selector:
    project: chapter3
    service: web
    version: "0.2"
 template:
  metadata:
  name: nginx
  labels:
   project: chapter3
   service: web
   version: "0.2"
spec:
  containers:
- name: nginx
  image: nginx:1.13.1
  ports:
 - containerPort: 80
```

Then we could make our pod selector, targeting project and service labels:

```
// simple nginx service
# cat 3-2-3_service.yaml
kind: Service
apiVersion: v1
metadata:
  name: nginx-service
spec:
  selector:
   project: chapter3
   service: web
  ports:
  - protocol: TCP
    port: 80
    targetPort: 80
    name: http
// create the RCs
# kubectl create -f 3-2-3_rc1.yaml
replicationcontroller "nginx-1.12" created
# kubectl create -f 3-2-3_rc2.yaml
replicationcontroller "nginx-1.13" created
// create the service
# kubectl create -f 3-2-3_service.yaml
service "nginx-service" created
```

 Since `service` object might create a DNS label, service name must follow the combination of characters a-z, 0-9, or - (hyphen). A hyphen at the beginning or end of a label is not allowed.

Then we could use `kubectl describe service <service_name>` to check the service information:

```
// check nginx-service information
# kubectl describe service nginx-service
Name:       nginx-service
Namespace:    default
Labels:       <none>
Annotations:    <none>
Selector:    project=chapter3,service=web
Type:       ClusterIP
IP:       10.0.0.188
Port:       http  80/TCP
Endpoints:    172.17.0.5:80,172.17.0.6:80,172.17.0.7:80 + 1 more...
Session Affinity:  None
Events:       <none>
```

One service could expose multiple ports. Just extend `.spec.ports` list in the service spec.

We can see it's a ClusterIP type service, assigned internal IP is 10.0.0.188. Endpoints show we have four IPs behind the service. Pod IP could be found by the `kubectl describe pods <pod_name>` command. Kubernetes creates an `endpoints` object along with a `service` object for routing the traffic to matching pods.

When the service is created with selectors, Kubernetes will create corresponding endpoints entries and keep updating, which will tell the destination that service routes into:

```
// list current endpoints. Nginx-service endpoints are created and pointing
to the ip of our 4 nginx pods.
# kubectl get endpoints
NAME            ENDPOINTS                                        AGE
kubernetes      10.0.2.15:8443                                   2d
nginx-service   172.17.0.5:80,172.17.0.6:80,172.17.0.7:80 + 1 more...   10s
```

ClusterIP could be defined within your cluster, though most of the time we don't explicitly use IP address to access clusters. Using `.spec.clusterIP` could do the work.

By default, Kubernetes will expose seven environment variables for each service. In most cases, the first two will be used for using `kube-dns` addon to do service discovery for us:

- `${SVCNAME}_SERVICE_HOST`
- `${SVCNAME}_SERVICE_PORT`
- `${SVCNAME}_PORT`
- `${SVCNAME}_PORT_${PORT}_${PROTOCAL}`
- `${SVCNAME}_PORT_${PORT}_${PROTOCAL}_PROTO`
- `${SVCNAME}_PORT_${PORT}_${PROTOCAL}_PORT`
- `${SVCNAME}_PORT_${PORT}_${PROTOCAL}_ADDR`

In the following example, we'll use `${SVCNAME}_SERVICE_HOST` in another pod to check if we could access our nginx pods:

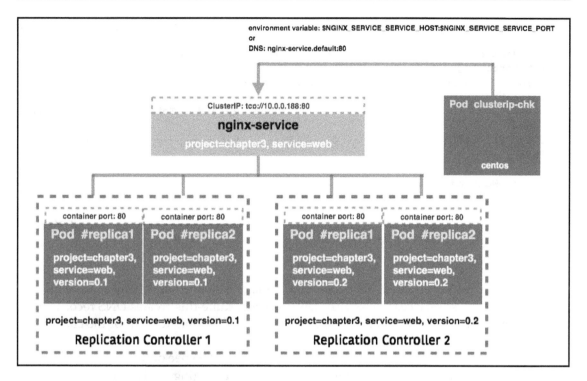

The illustration of accessing ClusterIP via environment variables and DNS names

We'll then create a pod called `clusterip-chk` to access nginx containers via `nginx-service`:

```
// access nginx service via ${NGINX_SERVICE_SERVICE_HOST}
# cat 3-2-3_clusterip_chk.yaml
apiVersion: v1
kind: Pod
metadata:
  name: clusterip-chk
spec:
  containers:
  - name: centos
    image: centos
    command: ["/bin/sh", "-c", "while : ;do curl
http://${NGINX_SERVICE_SERVICE_HOST}:80/; sleep 10; done"]
```

We could check the `stdout` of `cluserip-chk` pod via the `kubectl logs` command:

```
// check stdout, see if we can access nginx pod successfully
# kubectl logs -f clusterip-chk
% Total    % Received % Xferd  Average Speed   Time    Time     Time
Current
                                Dload  Upload   Total   Spent    Left
Speed
100   612  100   612    0     0   156k      0 --:--:-- --:--:-- --:--:--
199k
  ...
<title>Welcome to nginx!</title>
    ...
```

This abstraction level decouples the communication between pods. Pods are mortal. With RC and service, we can build robust services without caring whether one pod might influence all micro-services.

With `kube-dns` addon enabled, the pods in the same cluster and same namespace with services could access services via services DNS records. Kube-dns creates DNS records for newly created services by watching the Kubernetes API. The DNS format for the cluster IP is `$servicename.$namespace`, and the port is `_$portname_$protocal.$servicename.$namespace`. The spec of the `clusterip_chk` pod will be similar with environment variables one. Just changing the URL to `http://nginx-service.default:_http_tcp.nginx-service.default/` in our previous example, and they should work exactly the same!

NodePort

If the service is set as NodePort, Kubernetes will allocate a port within a certain range on each node. Any traffic going to nodes on that port will be routed to the service port. Port number could be user-specified. If not specified, Kubernetes will randomly choose a port from range 30000 to 32767 without collision. On the other hand, if specified, the user should be responsible to manage the collision by themselves. NodePort includes the feature of ClusterIP. Kubernetes assigns an internal IP to the service. In the following example, we'll see how we create a NodePort service and leverage it:

```
// write a nodeport type service
# cat 3-2-3_nodeport.yaml
kind: Service
apiVersion: v1
metadata:
  name: nginx-nodeport
spec:
  type: NodePort
```

```
    selector:
      project: chapter3
      service: web
    ports:
      - protocol: TCP
        port: 80
        targetPort: 80
// create a nodeport service
# kubectl create -f 3-2-3_nodeport.yaml
service "nginx-nodeport" created
```

Then you should be able to access the service via `http://${NODE_IP}:80`. Node could be any node. The `kube-proxy` watches any update of service and endpoints, and updates iptables rules accordingly (if using default iptables proxy-mode).

 If you're using minikube, you could access the service via the `minikube service [-n NAMESPACE] [--url] NAME` command. In this example, it's `minikube service nginx-nodeport`.

LoadBalancer

This type is only usable with cloud provider support, such as Google Cloud Platform (Chapter 10, *Kubernetes on GCP*) and Amazon Web Service (Chapter 9, *Kubernetes on AWS*). By creating LoadBalancer service, Kubernetes will provision a load balancer by the Cloud provider to the service.

ExternalName (kube-dns version >= 1.7)

Sometimes we leverage different services in the cloud. Kubernetes is flexible enough to be hybrid. ExternalName is one of the bridges to create a **CNAME** for external endpoints into the cluster.

Service without selectors

Service uses selectors to match the pods to direct the traffic. However, sometimes you need to implement a proxy to be the bridge between Kubernetes cluster and another namespace, another cluster, or external resources. In the following example, we'll demonstrate how to implement a proxy for http://www.google.com in your cluster. It's just an example while the source of the proxy might be the endpoint of your databases or other resources in the cloud:

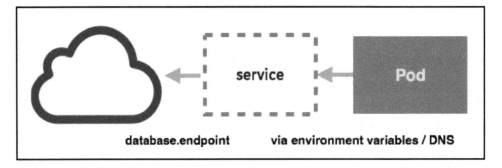

Illustration of how service without selector works

The configuration file is similar to the previous one, just without the selector section:

```
// create a service without selectors
# cat 3-2-3_service_wo_selector_srv.yaml
kind: Service
apiVersion: v1
metadata:
  name: google-proxy
spec:
  ports:
    - protocol: TCP
      port: 80
      targetPort: 80
// create service without selectors
# kubectl create -f 3-2-3_service_wo_selector_srv.yaml
service "google-proxy" created
```

No Kubernetes endpoint will be created since there is no selector. Kubernetes doesn't know where to route the traffic since no selector could match the pods. We'll have to create that on our own.

In the `Endpoints` object, the source addresses can't be DNS name, so we'll use `nslookup` to find the current Google IP from the domain, and add them into `Endpoints.subsets.addresses.ip`:

```
// get an IP from google.com
# nslookup www.google.com
Server:      192.168.1.1
Address:     192.168.1.1#53
Non-authoritative answer:
Name:  google.com
Address: 172.217.0.238
// create endpoints for the ip from google.com
# cat 3-2-3_service_wo_selector_endpoints.yaml
kind: Endpoints
apiVersion: v1
metadata:
  name: google-proxy
subsets:
  - addresses:
      - ip: 172.217.0.238
    ports:
      - port: 80
// create Endpoints
# kubectl create -f 3-2-3_service_wo_selector_endpoints.yaml
endpoints "google-proxy" created
```

Let's create another pod in the cluster to access our Google proxy:

```
// pod for accessing google proxy
# cat 3-2-3_proxy-chk.yaml
apiVersion: v1
kind: Pod
metadata:
  name: proxy-chk
spec:
  containers:
  - name: centos
    image: centos
    command: ["/bin/sh", "-c", "while : ;do curl -L
http://${GOOGLE_PROXY_SERVICE_HOST}:80/; sleep 10; done"]
// create the pod
# kubectl create -f 3-2-3_proxy-chk.yaml
pod "proxy-chk" created
```

Let's check the `stdout` from the pod:

```
// get logs from proxy-chk
# kubectl logs proxy-chk
% Total    % Received % Xferd  Average Speed   Time    Time     Time
Current
                                 Dload  Upload   Total   Spent    Left
Speed
100   219  100   219    0     0   2596      0 --:--:-- --:--:-- --:--:--
2607
100   258  100   258    0     0   1931      0 --:--:-- --:--:-- --:--:--
1931
<!doctype html><html itemscope="" itemtype="http://schema.org/WebPage"
lang="en-CA">
 . . .
```

Hurray! We can now confirm the proxy works. The traffic to the service will be routed to the endpoints we specified. If it doesn't work, make sure you add the proper inbound rules to the network of your external resources.

Endpoints don't support DNS as source. Alternatively, we could use ExternalName, which doesn't have selectors either. It requires kube-dns version >= 1.7.

 In some use cases, users need neither load balancing nor proxy functionalities for the service. In that case, we can set `CluterIP = "None"` as so-called headless services. For more information, please refer to
`https://kubernetes.io/docs/concepts/services-networking/service/#headless-services`.

Volumes

A container is ephemeral, so is its disk. We either use the `docker commit [CONTAINER]` command or mount data volumes into a container (`Chapter 2`, *DevOps with Container*). In Kubernetes' world, volume management becomes critical, since pods might run on any node. Also, ensuring that containers in the same pod could share the same files becomes extremely hard. This is a large topic in Kubernetes. `Chapter 4`, *Working with Storage and Resources* introduces volume management.

Secrets

Secret, just like its name, is an object that stores the secrets in key-value format for providing sensitive information to pods, which could be a password, access key, or token. Secret is not landed to the disk; instead, it's stored in a per-node `tmpfs` filesystem. Kubelet on the mode will create a `tmpfs` filesystem to store secret. Secret is not designed to store large amounts of data due to storage management consideration. The current size limit of one secret is 1MB.

We can create a secret based on a file, directory, or specified literal value by launching kubectl to create a secret command or by spec. There are three types of secret format: generic (or opaque, if encoded), docker registry, and TLS.

Generic/opaque is the text that we'll use in our application. Docker registry is used to store the credential of a private docker registry. TLS secret is used to store the CA certificate bundle for cluster administration.

The docker-registry type of secret is also called **imagePullSecrets**, which is used to pass the password of a private docker registry via kubelet when pulling the image. This comes in handy so that we don't need to do `docker login` for each provisioned node. The command is `kubectl create secret docker-registry <registry_name> --docker-server=<docker_server> --docker-username=<docker_username> --docker-password=<docker_password> --docker-email=<docker_email>`

We'll start with a generic-type of example to show how it works:

```
// create a secret by command line
# kubectl create secret generic mypassword --from-file=./mypassword.txt
secret "mypassword" created
```

The options for creating secrets based on directory and literal value are pretty similar with the file ones. If specifying a directory after `--from-file`, the files in the directory will be iterated, the file name will be the secret key if its a legal secret name, and other non-regular files will be ignored subdirectories, symlinks, devices, pipes. On the other hand, `--from-literal=<key>=<value>` is the option if you want to specify plain text directly from the command, for example, `--from-literal=username=root`.

Here, we create a secret name `mypassword` from the file `mypassword.txt`. By default, the key of the secret is the file name, which is equivalent to the `--from-file=mypassword=./mypassword.txt` option. We could append multiple `--from-file` as well. Using the `kubectl get secret <secret_name> -o yaml` command could check out the detailed information of the secret:

```
// get the detailed info of the secret
# kubectl get secret mypassword -o yaml
apiVersion: v1
data:
  mypassword: bXlwYXNzd29yZA==
kind: Secret
metadata:
  creationTimestamp: 2017-06-13T08:09:35Z
  name: mypassword
  namespace: default
  resourceVersion: "256749"
  selfLink: /api/v1/namespaces/default/secrets/mypassword
  uid: a33576b0-500f-11e7-9c45-080027cafd37
type: Opaque
```

We can see the type of the secret becomes `Opaque` since the text has been encrypted by kubectl. It's base64 encoded. We could use a simple bash command to decode it:

```
# echo "bXlwYXNzd29yZA==" | base64 --decode
mypassword
```

There are two ways for a pod to retrieve the secret. The first one is by file, and the second one is by environment variable. The first method is implemented by volume. The syntax is adding `containers.volumeMounts` in container specs, and adding a volumes section with secret configuration.

Retrieving secret via files

Let's see how to read secrets from files inside a pod first:

```
// example for how a Pod retrieve secret
# cat 3-2-3_pod_vol_secret.yaml
apiVersion: v1
kind: Pod
metadata:
  name: secret-access
spec:
  containers:
  - name: centos
    image: centos
    command: ["/bin/sh", "-c", "cat /secret/password-example; done"]
```

```
      volumeMounts:
        - name: secret-vol
          mountPath: /secret
          readOnly: true
    volumes:
      - name: secret-vol
        secret:
          secretName: mypassword
          # items are optional
          items:
          - key: mypassword
            path: password-example
```

```
// create the pod
# kubectl create -f 3-2-3_pod_vol_secret.yaml
pod "secret-access" created
```

The secret file will be mounted in /<mount_point>/<secret_name> without specifying itemskey and path, or /<mount_point>/<path> in the pod. In this case, it's under /secret/password-example. If we describe the pod, we can find there are two mount points in this pod. First is the read-only volume storing our secret, the second one stores the credentials to communicate with API servers, which is created and managed by Kubernetes. We'll learn more in Chapter 5, *Network and Security*:

```
# kubectl describe pod secret-access
...
Mounts:
      /secret from secret-vol (ro)
      /var/run/secrets/kubernetes.io/serviceaccount from default-token-
jd1dq (ro)
...
```

We can delete a secret by using the kubectl delete secret <secret_name> command.

After describing the pod, we can find a FailedMount event, since the volume no longer exists:

```
# kubectl describe pod secret-access
...
FailedMount  MountVolume.SetUp failed for volume
"kubernetes.io/secret/28889b1d-5015-11e7-9c45-080027cafd37-secret-vol"
(spec.Name: "secret-vol") pod "28889b1d-5015-11e7-9c45-080027cafd37" (UID:
"28889b1d-5015-11e7-9c45-080027cafd37") with: secrets "mypassword" not
found
...
```

Same idea, if the pod is generated before a secret is created, the pod will encounter failure as well.

We will now learn how to create a secret by command line. Next we'll briefly introduce its spec format:

```
// secret example
# cat 3-2-3_secret.yaml
apiVersion: v1
kind: Secret
metadata:
  name: mypassword
type: Opaque
data:
  mypassword: bXlwYXNzd29yZA==
```

Since the spec is plain text, we need to encode the secret by our own `echo -n <password> | base64`. Please note that the type here becomes `Opaque`. Following along it should work the same as the one we create via command line.

Retrieving secret via environment variables

Alternatively, we could use environment variables to retrieve secret, which is more flexible to use for short credentials, such as a password. This way, applications are able to use environment variables to retrieve database passwords without tackling files and volumes:

Secret should always be created before the pods that need it. Otherwise the pods won't get launched successfully.

```
// example to use environment variable to retrieve the secret
# cat 3-2-3_pod_ev_secret.yaml
apiVersion: v1
kind: Pod
metadata:
  name: secret-access-ev
spec:
  containers:
  - name: centos
    image: centos
    command: ["/bin/sh", "-c", "while : ;do echo $MY_PASSWORD; sleep 10;
done"]
    env:
        - name: MY_PASSWORD
          valueFrom:
           secretKeyRef:
```

```
            name: mypassword
            key: mypassword
// create the pod
# kubectl create -f 3-2-3_pod_ev_secret.yaml
pod "secret-access-ev" created
```

The declaration is under `spec.containers[].env[]`. We'll need the secret name and the key name. Both are `mypassword` in this case. The example should work the same with the one retrieving via files.

ConfigMap

ConfigMap is a mean that is able to leave your configuration outside of a Docker image. It injects the configuration data as key-values pairs into pods. Its properties are similar to secret, more specifically, secret is used to store sensitive data, such as password, and ConfigMap is used to store insensitive configuration data.

Same as secret, ConfigMap could be based on a file, directory, or specified literal value. With similar syntax/command with secrets, ConfigMap uses `kubectl create configmap` instead:

```
// create configmap
# kubectl create configmap example --from-file=config/app.properties --
from-file=config/database.properties
configmap "example" created
```

Since two `config` files are located in the same folder name `config`, we could pass a `config` folder instead of specifying the files one by one. The equivalent command to create is `kubectl create configmap example --from-file=config` in this case.

If we describe the ConfigMap, it will show current information:

```
// check out detailed information for configmap
# kubectl describe configmap example
Name:       example
Namespace:  default
Labels:     <none>
Annotations:  <none>
Data
====
app.properties:
----
name=DevOps-with-Kubernetes
port=4420
database.properties:
----
```

```
endpoint=k8s.us-east-1.rds.amazonaws.com
port=1521
```

We could use `kubectl edit configmap <configmap_name>` to update the configuration after creation.

 We also could use `literal` as the input. The equivalent commands for the preceding example will be `kubectl create configmap example --from-literal=app.properties.name=name=DevOps-with-Kubernetes` which is not always so practical when we have many configurations in an app.

Let's see how to leverage it inside a pod. There are two ways to use ConfigMap inside a pod too: by volume or environment variables.

Using ConfigMap via volume

Similar to previous examples in the secret section, we mount a volume with syntax `configmap`, and add `volumeMounts` inside a container template. The command in `centos` will loop to `cat ${MOUNTPOINT}/$CONFIG_FILENAME`:

```
cat 3-2-3_pod_vol_configmap.yaml
apiVersion: v1
kind: Pod
metadata:
  name: configmap-vol
spec:
  containers:
    - name: configmap
      image: centos
      command: ["/bin/sh", "-c", "while : ;do cat
/src/app/config/database.properties; sleep 10; done"]
      volumeMounts:
        - name: config-volume
          mountPath: /src/app/config
  volumes:
    - name: config-volume
      configMap:
        name: example
// create configmap
# kubectl create -f 3-2-3_pod_vol_configmap.yaml
pod "configmap-vol" created
// check out the logs
# kubectl logs -f configmap-vol
endpoint=k8s.us-east-1.rds.amazonaws.com
port=1521
```

We then could use this method to inject our non-sensitive configuration into the pod.

Using ConfigMap via environment variables

For using ConfigMap inside a pod, you'll have to use `configMapKeyRef` as the value source in the `env` section. It will populate whole ConfigMap pairs to environment variables:

```
# cat 3-2-3_pod_ev_configmap.yaml
apiVersion: v1
kind: Pod
metadata:
  name: config-ev
spec:
  containers:
  - name: centos
    image: centos
    command: ["/bin/sh", "-c", "while : ;do echo $DATABASE_ENDPOINT; sleep
10;
    done"]
 env:
          - name: MY_PASSWORD
            valueFrom:
             secretKeyRef:
              name: mypassword
              key: mypassword
// create configmap
# kubectl create -f 3-2-3_pod_ev_configmap.yaml
pod "configmap-ev" created
// check out the logs
# kubectl logs configmap-ev
endpoint=k8s.us-east-1.rds.amazonaws.com port=1521
```

The Kubernetes system itself also leverages ConfigMap for doing some authentication. For example, kube-dns uses it to put client CA files. You could check the system ConfigMap by adding `--namespace=kube-system` when describing ConfigMaps.

Multi-containers orchestration

In this section, we'll revisit our ticketing service: a kiosk web service as frontend, providing interface for get/put tickets. There is a Redis acting as cache, to manage how many tickets we have. Redis also acts as a publisher/subscriber channel. Once a ticket is sold, kiosk will publish an event into it. Subscriber is called recorder, which will write a timestamp and record it to the MySQL database. Please refer to the last section in `Chapter 2`, *DevOps with Container* for the detailed Dockerfile and Docker compose implementation. We'll use `Deployment`, `Service`, `Secret`, `Volume`, and `ConfigMap` objects to implement this example in Kubernetes. Source code can be found at `https://github.com/DevOps-with-Kubernetes/examples/tree/master/chapter3/3-3_kio sk`.

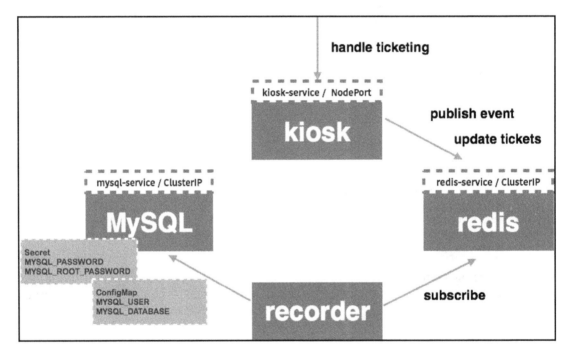

An example of kiosk in Kubernetes world

We'll need four kinds of pods. Deployment is the best choice to manage/deploy the pods. It will reduce the pain when we do the deployment in the future by its deployment strategy feature. Since kiosk, Redis, and MySQL will be accessed by other components, we'll associate services to their pods. MySQL acts as a datastore, for the simplicity, we'll mount a local volume to it. Please note that Kubernetes offers a bunch of choices. Please check out the details and examples in `Chapter 4`, *Working with Storage and Resources*. Sensitive information such as our MySQL root and user password, we'll want them to be stored in secrets. The other insensitive configuration, such as DB name or DB username, we'll leave to ConfigMap.

We'll launch MySQL first, as recorder depends on it. Before creating MySQL, we'll have to create corresponding `secret` and `ConfigMap` first. To create `secret`, we need to generate base64 encrypted data:

```
// generate base64 secret for MYSQL_PASSWORD and MYSQL_ROOT_PASSWORD
# echo -n "pass" | base64
cGFzcw==
# echo -n "mysqlpass" | base64
bXlzcWxwYXNz
```

Then we're able to create the secret:

```
# cat secret.yaml
apiVersion: v1
kind: Secret
metadata:
  name: mysql-user
type: Opaque
data:
  password: cGFzcw==
---
# MYSQL_ROOT_PASSWORD
apiVersion: v1
kind: Secret
metadata:
  name: mysql-root
type: Opaque
data:
  password: bXlzcWxwYXNz
// create mysql secret
# kubectl create -f secret.yaml --record
secret "mysql-user" created
secret "mysql-root" created
```

Then we come to our ConfigMap. Here, we put database user and database name as an example:

```
# cat config.yaml
kind: ConfigMap
apiVersion: v1
metadata:
  name: mysql-config
data:
  user: user
  database: db
// create ConfigMap
# kubectl create -f config.yaml --record
configmap "mysql-config" created
```

Then it's time to launch MySQL and its service:

```
// MySQL Deployment
# cat mysql.yaml
apiVersion: apps/v1beta1
kind: Deployment
metadata:
  name: lmysql
spec:
  replicas: 1
  template:
   metadata:
    labels:
      tier: database
      version: "5.7"
    spec:
      containers:
      - name: lmysql
        image: mysql:5.7
        volumeMounts:
         - mountPath: /var/lib/mysql
           name: mysql-vol
        ports:
         - containerPort: 3306
        env:
         - name: MYSQL_ROOT_PASSWORD
           valueFrom:
            secretKeyRef:
             name: mysql-root
             key: password
         - name: MYSQL_DATABASE
           valueFrom:
             configMapKeyRef:
```

```
                  name: mysql-config
                  key: database
                - name: MYSQL_USER
                  valueFrom:
                   configMapKeyRef:
                    name: mysql-config
                    key: user
                - name: MYSQL_PASSWORD
                  valueFrom:
                   secretKeyRef:
                   name: mysql-user
                   key: password
       volumes:
      - name: mysql-vol
       hostPath:
        path: /mysql/data
---
kind: Service
apiVersion: v1
metadata:
  name: lmysql-service
spec:
  selector:
   tier: database
 ports:
  - protocol: TCP
    port: 3306
    targetPort: 3306
    name: tcp3306
```

We can put more than one spec into a file by adding three dashes as separation. Here we mount `hostPath` `/mysql/data` into pods with the path `/var/lib/mysql`. In the environment section, we leverage the syntax of secret and ConfigMap by `secretKeyRef` and `configMapKeyRef`.

After creating MySQL, Redis would be the next good candidate, since it is others' dependency, but it needs no prerequisite:

```
// create Redis deployment
# cat redis.yaml
apiVersion: apps/v1beta1
kind: Deployment
metadata:
  name: lcredis
spec:
  replicas: 1
  template:
```

```
    metadata:
     labels:
      tier: cache
      version: "3.0"
    spec:
      containers:
      - name: lcredis
        image: redis:3.0
        ports:
        - containerPort: 6379
minReadySeconds: 1
strategy:
  type: RollingUpdate
  rollingUpdate:
  maxSurge: 1
  maxUnavailable: 1
---
kind: Service
apiVersion: v1
metadata:
  name: lcredis-service
spec:
  selector:
   tier: cache
  ports:
  - protocol: TCP
    port: 6379
    targetPort: 6379
    name: tcp6379
// create redis deployements and service
# kubectl create -f redis.yaml
deployment "lcredis" created
service "lcredis-service" created
```

Then it would be a good time to start kiosk:

```
# cat kiosk-example.yaml
apiVersion: apps/v1beta1
kind: Deployment
metadata:
  name: kiosk-example
spec:
  replicas: 5
  template:
   metadata:
    labels:
      tier: frontend
      version: "3"
```

```
    annotations:
      maintainer: cywu
  spec:
   containers:
   - name: kiosk-example
     image: devopswithkubernetes/kiosk-example
     ports:
     - containerPort: 5000
     env:
     - name: REDIS_HOST
       value: lcredis-service.default
 minReadySeconds: 5
 strategy:
  type: RollingUpdate
  rollingUpdate:
    maxSurge: 1
    maxUnavailable: 1
---
kind: Service
apiVersion: v1
metadata:
  name: kiosk-service
spec:
  type: NodePort
  selector:
   tier: frontend
 ports:
    - protocol: TCP
      port: 80
      targetPort: 5000
      name: tcp5000
// launch the spec
# kubectl create -f kiosk-example.yaml
deployment "kiosk-example" created
service "kiosk-service" created
```

Here, we expose `lcredis-service.default` to environment variables to kiosk pods, which is the DNS name that kube-dns creates for `Service` object (referred to as service in this chapter). Thus, kiosk could access Redis host via environment variables.

In the end, we'll create recorder. Recorder doesn't expose any interface to others, so it doesn't need a `Service` object:

```
# cat recorder-example.yaml
apiVersion: apps/v1beta1
kind: Deployment
metadata:
  name: recorder-example
spec:
  replicas: 3
  template:
   metadata:
    labels:
     tier: backend
     version: "3"
    annotations:
     maintainer: cywu
   spec:
    containers:
    - name: recorder-example
      image: devopswithkubernetes/recorder-example
      env:
     - name: REDIS_HOST
       value: lcredis-service.default
     - name: MYSQL_HOST
       value: lmysql-service.default
     - name: MYSQL_USER
       value: root
     - name: MYSQL_ROOT_PASSWORD
       valueFrom:
        secretKeyRef:
          name: mysql-root
          key: password
minReadySeconds: 3
strategy:
  type: RollingUpdate
  rollingUpdate:
   maxSurge: 1
   maxUnavailable: 1
// create recorder deployment
# kubectl create -f recorder-example.yaml
deployment "recorder-example" created
```

Recorder needs to access both Redis and MySQL. It uses root credential that is injected via secret. Both endpoints for Redis and MySQL are accessed via service DNS name `<service_name>.<namespace>`.

We then could check `deployment` objects:

```
// check deployment details
# kubectl get deployments
NAME              DESIRED  CURRENT  UP-TO-DATE  AVAILABLE  AGE
kiosk-example     5        5        5           5          1h
lcredis           1        1        1           1          1h
lmysql            1        1        1           1          1h
recorder-example  3        3        3           3          1h
```

As expected, we have four `deployment` objects with different desired count for pods.

As we expose kiosk as NodePort, we should be able to access its service endpoint and see if it works properly. Assume we have a node, IP is `192.168.99.100`, and the NodePort that Kubernetes allocates is 30520.

> If you're using minikube, `minikube service [-n NAMESPACE] [--url] NAME` could help you access service NodePort via your default browser:
> ```
> // open kiosk console
>
> # minikube service kiosk-service
>
> Opening kubernetes service default/kiosk-service in
> default browser...
> ```

Then we could know the IP and the port.

We could then create and a get ticket by `POST` and `GET` `/tickets`:

```
// post ticket
# curl -XPOST -F 'value=100' http://192.168.99.100:30520/tickets
SUCCESS
// get ticket
# curl -XGET http://192.168.99.100:30520/tickets
100
```

Summary

In this chapter, we learned the basic concept of Kubernetes. We learned Kubernetes master has kube-apiserver to handle the requests, and controller managers are the control center of Kubernetes, for example, it ensures our desired container amount is fulfilled, controls the endpoint to associate pods and services, and controls API access token. We also have Kubernetes nodes, which are the workers to host the containers, receive the information from master, and route the traffic based on the configuration.

We then used minikube to demonstrate basic Kubernetes objects, including pod, ReplicaSets, ReplicationControllers, deployments, services, secrets, and ConfigMap. In the end, we demonstrated how to combine all the concepts we've learned into kiosk application deployment.

As we mentioned previously, the data inside containers will be gone when a container is gone. Therefore, volume is extremely important to persist the data in container world. In the next chapter, we'll be learning how volume works and its options, how to use persistent volume, and so on.

4
Working with Storage and Resources

In `Chapter 3`, *Getting Started with Kubernetes* we introduced the basic function of Kubernetes. Once you start to deploy some containers by Kubernetes, you need to consider the application's data lifecycle and CPU/memory resource management.

In this chapter, we will discuss the following topics:

- How a container behaves with volume
- Introduce Kubernetes volume functionalities
- Best practice and pitfalls of Kubernetes Persistent Volume
- Kubernetes resource management

Kubernetes volume management

Kubernetes and Docker use a local host disk by default. The Docker application may store and load any data onto the disk, for example, log data, temporary files, and application data. As long as the host has enough space and the application has necessary permission, data will exist as long as a container exists. In other words, when a container is closed the application exits, crashes, and reassigns a container to another host, and the data will be lost.

Container volume lifecycle

In order to understand Kubernetes volume management, you need to understand the Docker volume lifecycle. The following example is how Docker behaves with a volume when a container restarts:

```
//run CentOS Container
$ docker run -it centos
# ls
anaconda-post.log  dev  home  lib64       media  opt   root  sbin  sys  usr
bin                etc  lib   lost+found  mnt    proc  run   srv   tmp  var

//create one file (/I_WAS_HERE) at root directory
# touch /I_WAS_HERE
# ls /
I_WAS_HERE         bin  etc   lib    lost+found  mnt  proc  run   srv  tmp
var
anaconda-post.log  dev  home  lib64  media            opt   root  sbin sys  usr

//Exit container
# exit
exit

//re-run CentOS Container
# docker run -it centos

//previous file (/I_WAS_HERE) was disappeared
# ls /
anaconda-post.log  dev  home  lib64       media  opt   root  sbin  sys  usr
bin                etc  lib   lost+found  mnt    proc  run   srv   tmp  var
```

On Kubernetes, it also needs to care pod restart. In the case of a resource shortage, Kubernetes may stop a container and then restart a container on the same or another Kubernetes node.

The following example shows how Kubernetes behaves when there is a resource shortage. One pod is killed and restarted when an out of memory error is received:

```
//there are 2 pod on the same Node
$ kubectl get pods
NAME                       READY     STATUS     RESTARTS     AGE
Besteffort                 1/1       Running    0            1h
guaranteed                 1/1       Running    0            1h

//when application consumes a lot of memory, one Pod has been killed
$ kubectl get pods
NAME                       READY     STATUS     RESTARTS     AGE
```

```
Besteffort                    0/1        Error        0         1h
guaranteed                    1/1        Running      0         1h

//clashed Pod is restarting
$ kubectl get pods
NAME                          READY      STATUS                  RESTARTS   AGE
Besteffort                    0/1        CrashLoopBackOff        0          1h
guaranteed                    1/1        Running                 0          1h

//few moment later, Pod has been restarted
$ kubectl get pods
NAME                          READY      STATUS      RESTARTS   AGE
Besteffort                    1/1        Running     1          1h
guaranteed                    1/1        Running     0          1h
```

Sharing volume between containers within a pod

Chapter 3, *Getting Started with Kubernetes* described that multiple containers within the same Kubernetes pod can share the same pod IP address, network port, and IPC, therefore, applications can communicate with each other through a localhost network; however, the filesystem is segregated.

The following diagram shows that **Tomcat** and **nginx** are in the same pod. Those applications can communicate with each other via localhost. However, they can't access each other's `config` file:

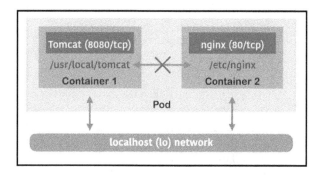

Some applications won't affect these scenarios and behavior, but some applications may have some use cases that require them to use a shared directory or file. Therefore, developers and Kubernetes administrators need to be aware of the different types of stateless and stateful applications.

Stateless and stateful applications

In terms of stateless applications, in this case use ephemeral volume. The application on the container doesn't need to preserve the data. Although stateless applications may write the data onto the filesystem while a container exists, but it is not important in terms of the application's lifecycle.

For example, the `tomcat` container runs some web applications. It also writes an application log under `/usr/local/tomcat/logs/`, but it won't be affected if it loses a `log` file.

However, what if you start to analyze an application log? Need to preserve due to auditing purpose? In this scenario, Tomcat can still be stateless, but share the `/usr/local/tomcat/logs` volume to another container such as Logstash (`https://www.elastic.co/products/logstash`). Then Logstash will send a log to the chosen analytic store, such as Elasticsearch (`https://www.elastic.co/products/elasticsearch`).

In this case, the `tomcat` container and `logstash` container *must be in the same Kubernetes pod* and share the `/usr/local/tomcat/logs` volume as follows:

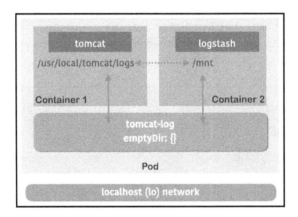

The preceding figure shows how Tomcat and Logstash can share the `log` file using the Kubernetes `emptyDir` volume (`https://kubernetes.io/docs/concepts/storage/volumes/#emptydir`).

Tomcat and Logstash didn't use network via localhost, but share the filesystem between
`/usr/local/tomcat/logs` from the Tomcat container and `/mnt` from the Logstash
container through Kubernetes `emptyDir` volume:

```
$ cat tomcat-logstash.yaml
apiVersion: apps/v1beta1
kind: Deployment
metadata:
  name: tomcat
spec:
  replicas: 1
  template:
    metadata:
      labels:
        run: tomcat
    spec:
      containers:
        - image: tomcat
          name: tomcat
          ports:
            - containerPort: 8080
          env:
            - name: UMASK
              value: "0022"
          volumeMounts:
            - mountPath: /usr/local/tomcat/logs
              name: tomcat-log
        - image: logstash
          name: logstash
          args: ["-e input { file { path => \"/mnt/localhost_access_log.*\" } } output { stdout { codec => ru
bydebug } elasticsearch { hosts => [\"http://elasticsearch-svc.default.svc.cluster.local:9200\"] } }"]
          volumeMounts:
            - mountPath: /mnt
              name: tomcat-log
      volumes:
        - name: tomcat-log
          emptyDir: {}
```

Let's create `tomcat` and `logstash` pod, and then see whether Logstash can see the Tomcat application log under `/mnt`:

```
chapter4 — kubectl exec -it tomcat-1439976938-h7kbf -c logstash /bin/bash — 108×12
                    kubectl exec -it tomcat-1439976938-h7kbf -c logstash /bin/bash
$ kubectl create -f tomcat-logstash.yaml
deployment "tomcat" created
$
$ kubectl get pods
NAME                       READY      STATUS      RESTARTS    AGE
tomcat-1439976938-h7kbf    2/2        Running     0           11s
$
$ kubectl exec -it tomcat-1439976938-h7kbf -c logstash /bin/bash
root@tomcat-1439976938-h7kbf:/# ls /mnt
catalina.2017-06-16.log        localhost.2017-06-16.log              manager.2017-06-16.log
host-manager.2017-06-16.log  localhost_access_log.2017-06-16.txt
root@tomcat-1439976938-h7kbf:/#
```

In this scenario, in the final destination Elasticsearch must be stateful. In terms of stateful means use Persistent Volume. The Elasticsearch container must preserve the data even if the container is restarted. In addition, you do not need to configure the Elasticsearch container within the same pod as Tomcat/Logstash. Because Elasticsearch should be a centralized log datastore, it can be separate from the Tomcat/Logstash pod and scaled independently.

Once you determine that your application needs a Persistent Volume, there are some different types of volume and different ways to manage Persistent Volumes.

Kubernetes Persistent Volume and dynamic provisioning

Kubernetes supports a variety of Persistent Volume. For example, public cloud storage such as AWS EBS and Google Persistent Disk. It also supports network (distributed) filesystems such as NFS, GlusterFS, and Ceph. In addition, it can also support a block device such as iSCSI and Fibre Channel. Based on environment and infrastructure, a Kubernetes administrator can choose the best match types of Persistent Volume.

The following example is using GCP Persistent Disk as Persistent Volume. The first step is creating a GCP Persistent Disk and naming it `gce-pd-1`.

If you use AWS EBS or Google Persistent Disk, the Kubernetes node must be in the AWS or Google Cloud Platform.

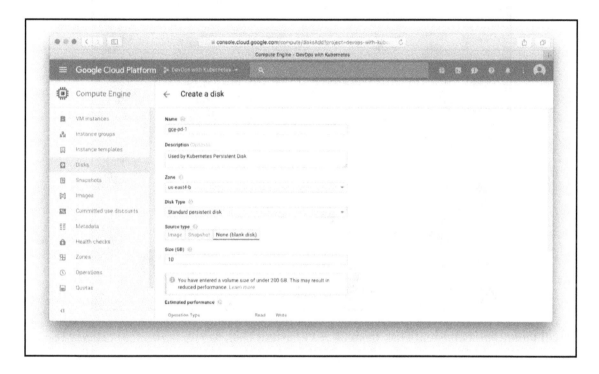

Then specify the name `gce-pd-1` in the `Deployment` definition:

```
● ● ●                     chapter4 — -bash — 80×25
                              -bash                                    +
$ cat tomcat-pv.yml
apiVersion: apps/v1beta1
kind: Deployment
metadata:
  name: tomcat
spec:
  replicas: 1
  template:
    metadata:
      labels:
        run: tomcat
    spec:
      containers:
        - image: tomcat
          name: tomcat
          ports:
          - containerPort: 8080
          volumeMounts:
          - mountPath: /usr/local/tomcat/logs
            name: tomcat-log
      volumes:
      - name: tomcat-log
        gcePersistentDisk:
          pdName: gce-pd-1
          fsType: ext4
```

It will mount the Persistent Disk from GCE Persistent Disk to `/usr/local/tomcat/logs`, which can persist Tomcat application logs.

Persistent Volume claiming the abstraction layer

Specifying a Persistent Volume into a configuration file directly, which makes a tight couple with a particular infrastructure. In previous example, this was Google Cloud Platform and also the disk name (`gce-pd-1`). From a container management point of view, pod definition shouldn't be locked-in to the specific environment because the infrastructure could be different based on the environment. The ideal pod definition should be flexible or abstract the actual infrastructure that specifies only volume name and mount point.

Therefore, Kubernetes provides an abstraction layer that associates between the pod and the Persistent Volume, which is called the **Persistent Volume Claim** (**PVC**). It allows us to decouple from the infrastructure. The Kubernetes administrator just needs to pre-allocate a necessary size of the Persistent Volume in advance. Then Kubernetes will bind between the Persistent Volume and PVC:

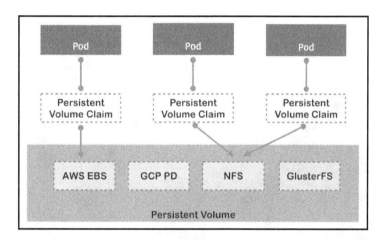

The following example is a definition of pod that uses PVC; let's reuse the previous example (gce-pd-1) to register with Kubernetes first:

```
$ cat pv-gce-pd-1.yml
apiVersion: "v1"
kind: "PersistentVolume"
metadata:
  name: pv-1
spec:
  capacity:
    storage: "10Gi"
  accessModes:
    - "ReadWriteOnce"
  gcePersistentDisk:
    fsType: "ext4"
    pdName: "gce-pd-1"
$
$ kubectl create -f pv-gce-pd-1.yml
persistentvolume "pv-1" created
$
$ kubectl get pv
NAME   CAPACITY   ACCESSMODES   RECLAIMPOLICY   STATUS      CLAIM   STORAGECLASS   REASON   AGE
pv-1   10Gi       RWO           Retain          Available                                  1m
```

Then, create a PVC that associates with Persistent Volume (pv-1).

Note that setting it as storageClassName: "" means, that it should explicitly use static provisioning. Some of the Kubernetes environments such as **Google Container Engine** (**GKE**), are already set up with Dynamic Provisioning. If we don't specify storageClassName: "", Kubernetes will ignore the existing PersistentVolume and allocates a new PersistentVolume when creating the PersistentVolumeClaim.

```
$ cat pvc-1.yml
apiVersion: v1
kind: PersistentVolumeClaim
metadata:
    name: pvc-1
spec:
  storageClassName: ""
  accessModes:
    - ReadWriteOnce
  resources:
    requests:
      storage: 10Gi
$
$ kubectl create -f pvc-1.yml
persistentvolumeclaim "pvc-1" created
$
$ kubectl get pvc
NAME        STATUS     VOLUME      CAPACITY    ACCESSMODES    STORAGECLASS    AGE
pvc-1       Bound      pv-1        10Gi        RWO                            23s
$
$ kubectl get pv
NAME       CAPACITY    ACCESSMODES    RECLAIMPOLICY    STATUS     CLAIM            STORAGECLASS    REASON    AGE
pv-1       10Gi        RWO            Retain           Bound      default/pvc-1                              5m
```

Now, `tomcat` setting has been decoupled from the specific volume to "`pvc-1`":

```
$ cat tomcat-pvc.yml
apiVersion: apps/v1beta1
kind: Deployment
metadata:
  name: tomcat
spec:
  replicas: 1
  template:
    metadata:
      labels:
        run: tomcat
    spec:
      containers:
        - image: tomcat
          name: tomcat
          ports:
          - containerPort: 8080
          volumeMounts:
          - mountPath: /usr/local/tomcat/logs
            name: tomcat-log
      volumes:
      - name: tomcat-log
        persistentVolumeClaim:
          claimName: "pvc-1"
```

Dynamic Provisioning and StorageClass

PVC gives a degree of flexibility for Persistent Volume management. However, pre-allocating some Persistent Volumes pools might not be cost efficient, especially in a public cloud.

Kubernetes also helps this kind of situation by supporting Dynamic Provision for Persistent Volume. Kubernetes administrator defines the *provisioner* of the Persistent Volume, which is called `StorageClass`. Then, the Persistent Volume Claim asks `StorageClass` to dynamically allocate a Persistent Volume and then associates it with the PVC:

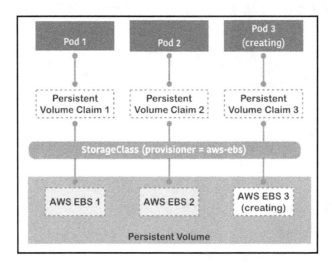

In the following example, AWS EBS is used as the `StorageClass`, and then, when creating the PVC, `StorageClass` dynamically create EBS registers it with Kubernetes Persistent Volume, and then attaches to PVC:

```
$ cat storageclass-aws.yml
kind: StorageClass
apiVersion: storage.k8s.io/v1
metadata:
  name: aws-sc
provisioner: kubernetes.io/aws-ebs
parameters:
  type: gp2
$
$ kubectl create -f storageclass-aws.yml
storageclass "aws-sc" created
$
$ kubectl get storageclass
NAME      TYPE
aws-sc    kubernetes.io/aws-ebs
```

Once `StorageClass` has been successfully created, create a PVC without PV, but specify the `StorageClass` name. In this example, this would be `"aws-sc"`, as shown in the following screenshot:

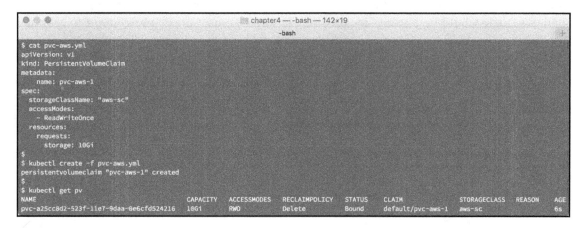

Then, PVC asks `StorageClass` to create a Persistent Volume automatically on AWS as follows:

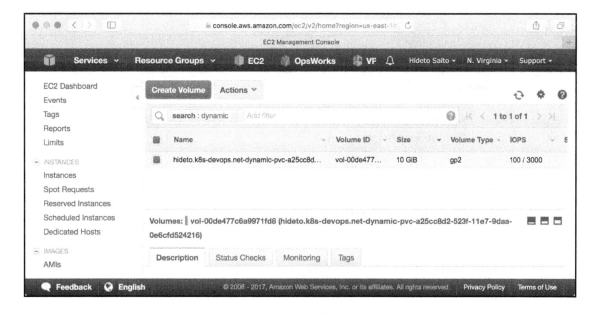

Note that a Kubernetes provisioning tool such as kops
(`https://github.com/kubernetes/kops`) and also Google Container Engine
(`https://cloud.google.com/container-engine/`) create a `StorageClass` by default. For
example, kops sets up a default `StorageClass` as AWS EBS on an AWS environment. As
well as Google Cloud Persistent disk on GKE. For more information, please refer to `Chapter`
`9`, *Kubernetes on AWS* and `Chapter 10`, *Kubernetes on GCP*:

```
//default Storage Class on AWS
$ kubectl get sc
NAME            TYPE
default         kubernetes.io/aws-ebs
gp2 (default)   kubernetes.io/aws-ebs

//default Storage Class on GKE
$ kubectl get sc
NAME               TYPE
standard (default) kubernetes.io/gce-pd
```

A problem case of ephemeral and persistent setting

You may determine your application as stateless, because `datastore` function is handled
by another pod or system. However, there are some pitfalls that sometimes applications
actually store important files that you aren't aware of. For example, Grafana
(`https://grafana.com/grafana`), it connects time series datasources such as Graphite
(`https://graphiteapp.org`) and InfluxDB
(`https://www.influxdata.com/time-series-database/`), so that people may determine
whether Grafana is a stateless application.

However, Grafana itself also uses databases to store the user, organization, and dashboard
metadata. By default, Grafana uses SQLite3 components and stores the database as
`/var/lib/grafana/grafana.db`. Therefore, when a container is restarted, the Grafana
setting will be all reset.

The following example demonstrates how Grafana behaves with ephemeral volume:

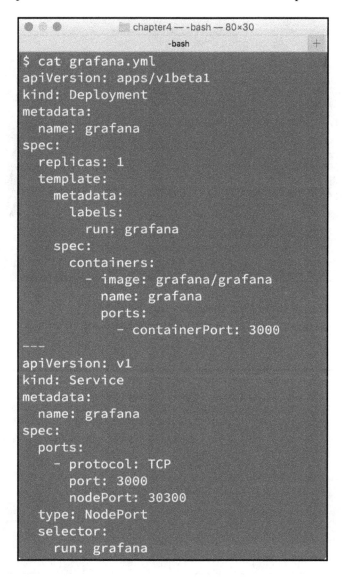

```
$ cat grafana.yml
apiVersion: apps/v1beta1
kind: Deployment
metadata:
  name: grafana
spec:
  replicas: 1
  template:
    metadata:
      labels:
        run: grafana
    spec:
      containers:
        - image: grafana/grafana
          name: grafana
          ports:
            - containerPort: 3000
---
apiVersion: v1
kind: Service
metadata:
  name: grafana
spec:
  ports:
    - protocol: TCP
      port: 3000
      nodePort: 30300
  type: NodePort
  selector:
    run: grafana
```

Let's create a Grafana `organizations` named `kubernetes org` as follows:

Then, look at the `Grafana` directory, there is a database file (`/var/lib/grafana/grafana.db`) timestamp that has been updated after creating a Grafana `organization`:

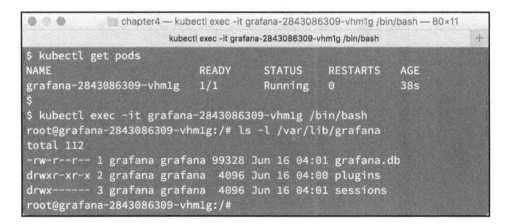

When the pod is deleted, ReplicaSet will start a new pod and check whether a Grafana `organization` exists or not:

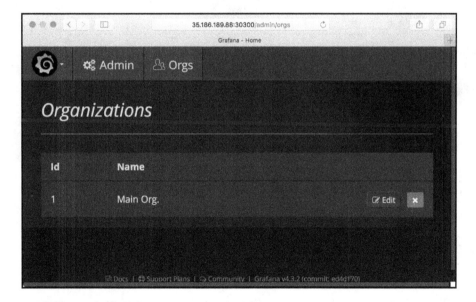

```
chapter4 — kubectl exec -it grafana-2843086309-qp2rh /bin/bash — 80×12
kubectl exec -it grafana-2843086309-qp2rh /bin/bash

$ kubectl delete pod grafana-2843086309-vhm1g; kubectl get pods
pod "grafana-2843086309-vhm1g" deleted
NAME                        READY    STATUS             RESTARTS    AGE
grafana-2843086309-qp2rh    0/1      ContainerCreating  0           0s
grafana-2843086309-vhm1g    1/1      Terminating        0           2m
$
$ kubectl exec -it grafana-2843086309-qp2rh /bin/bash
root@grafana-2843086309-qp2rh:/# ls -l /var/lib/grafana
total 108
-rw-r--r-- 1 grafana grafana 99328 Jun 16 04:03 grafana.db
drwxr-xr-x 2 grafana grafana  4096 Jun 16 04:03 plugins
root@grafana-2843086309-qp2rh:/#
```

It looks like the `sessions` directory has disappeared and `grafana.db` is also recreated by the Docker image again. Then if you access Web Console, the Grafana `organization` will also disappear:

How about just using Persistent Volume for Grafana? But using ReplicaSet with Persistent Volume, it doesn't replicate (scale) properly. Because all of the pods attempt to mount the same Persistent Volume. In most cases, only the first pod can mount the Persistent Volume, then another pod will try to mount, and if it can't, it will give up. This happens if the Persistent Volume is capable of only RWO (read write once, only one pod can write).

In the following example, Grafana uses Persistent Volume to mount `/var/lib/grafana`; however, it can't scale because Google Persistent Disk is RWO:

```
chapter4 — -bash — 80×34
                                  -bash                                    +
$ cat grafana-pv.yml
apiVersion: apps/v1beta1
kind: Deployment
metadata:
  name: grafana
spec:
  replicas: 1
  template:
    metadata:
      labels:
        run: grafana
    spec:
      containers:
        - image: grafana/grafana
          name: grafana
          ports:
            - containerPort: 3000
          volumeMounts:
            - mountPath: /var/lib/grafana
              name: grafana-data
      volumes:
        - name: grafana-data
          gcePersistentDisk:
            pdName: gce-pd-1
            fsType: ext4
$
$ kubectl create -f grafana-pv.yml
deployment "grafana" created
$
$ kubectl scale deploy grafana --replicas=3
error: Scaling the resource failed with: Deployment.apps "grafana" is invalid: s
pec.template.spec.volumes[0].gcePersistentDisk.readOnly: Invalid value: false: m
ust be true for replicated pods > 1; GCE PD can only be mounted on multiple mach
ines if it is read-only; Current resource version 1374730
```

Even if the Persistent Volume has a capability of RWX (read write many, many pods can mount to read and write simultaneously), such as NFS, it won't complain if multiple pods try to bind the same volume. However, we still need to consider whether multiple application instances can use the same folder/file or not. For example, if it replicates Grafana to two or more pods, it will be conflicted with multiple Grafana instances that try to write to the same `/var/lib/grafana/grafana.db`, and then data could be corrupted, as shown in the following screenshot:

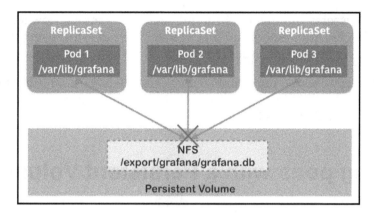

In this scenario, Grafana must use backend databases such as MySQL or PostgreSQL instead of SQLite3 as follows. It allows multiple Grafana instances to read/write Grafana metadata properly:

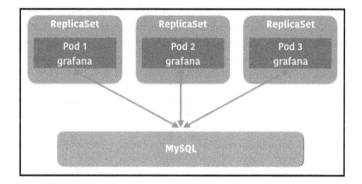

Because RDBMS basically supports to connecting with multiple application instances via network, therefore, this scenario is perfectly suited being used by multiple pods. Note that Grafana supports using RDBMS as a backend metadata store; however, not all applications support RDBMS.

For the Grafana configuration that uses MySQL/PostgreSQL, please visit the online documentation via:

`http://docs.grafana.org/installation/configuration/#database`.

Therefore, the Kubernetes administrator carefully needs to monitor how an application behaves with volumes. And understand that in some use cases, just using Persistent Volume may not help because of issues that might arise when scaling pods.

If multiple pods need to access the centralized volume, then consider using the database as previously shown, if applicable. On the other hand, if multiple pods need an individual volume, consider using StatefulSet.

Replicating pods with a Persistent Volume using StatefulSet

StatefulSet was introduced in Kubernetes 1.5; it consists of a bond between the pod and the Persistent Volume. When scaling a pod that increases or decreases, pod and Persistent Volume are created or deleted together.

In addition, pod creation process is serial. For example, when requesting Kubernetes to scale two additional StatefulSet, Kubernetes creates **Persistent Volume Claim 1** and **Pod 1** first, and then creates **Persistent Volume Claim 2** and **Pod 2**, but not simultaneously. It helps the administrator if an application registers to a registry during the application bootstrap:

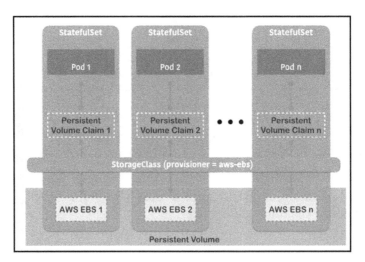

Even if one pod is dead, StatefulSet preserves the position of the pod (pod name, IP address, and related Kubernetes metadata) and also the Persistent Volume. Then, it attempts to recreate a container that reassigns to the same pod and mounts the same Persistent Volume.

It helps to keep the number of pods/Persistent Volumes and the application remains online using the Kubernetes scheduler:

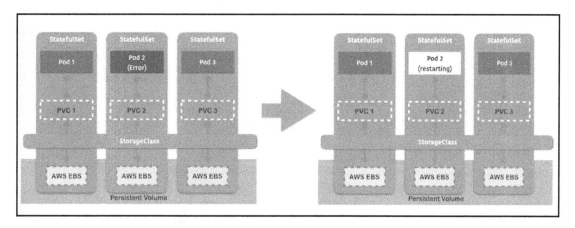

StatefulSet with Persistent Volume requires Dynamic Provisioning and `StorageClass` because StatefulSet can be scalable. Kubernetes needs to know how to provision the Persistent Volume when adding more pods.

Persistent Volume example

In this chapter, there are some Persistent Volume examples that have been introduced. Based on the environment and scenario, the Kubernetes administrator needs to configure Kubernetes properly.

The following are some examples that build Elasticsearch clusters using different role nodes to configure different types of Persistent Volume. They will help you to decide how to configure and manage the Persistent Volume.

Elasticsearch cluster scenario

Elasticsearch is capable of setting up a cluster by using multiple nodes. As of Elasticsearch version 2.4, there are several different types, such as master, data, and coordinate nodes (`https://www.elastic.co/guide/en/elasticsearch/reference/2.4/modules-node.html`). Each node has a different role and responsibility in the cluster, therefore the corresponding Kubernetes configuration and Persistent Volume should align with the proper settings.

The following diagram shows the components and roles of Elasticsearch nodes. The master node is the only node in the cluster that manages all Elasticsearch node registration and configuration. It can also have a backup node (master-eligible node) that can serve as the master node at any time:

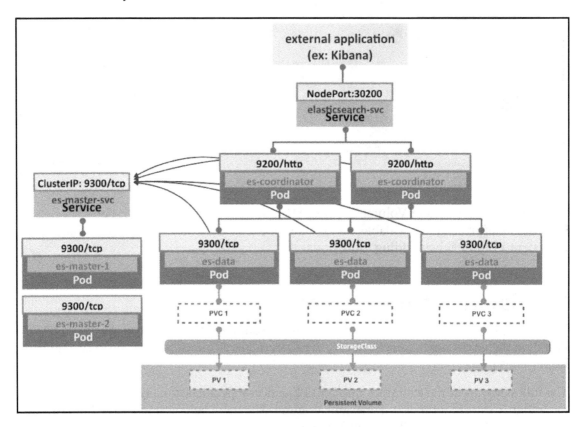

Data nodes hold and operate datastores in Elasticsearch. And the coordinating node handles HTTP requests from other applications, and then load balances/dispatches to the data nodes.

Elasticsearch master node

The master node is the only node in the cluster. In addition, other nodes need to point to the master node because of registration. Therefore, the master node should use Kubernetes StatefulSet to assign a stable DNS name, such as `es-master-1`. Therefore, we have to use the Kubernetes service to assign DNS with a headless mode that assigns the DNS name to the pod IP address directly.

On the other hand, if the Persistent Volume is not required, because the master node does not need to persist an application's data.

Elasticsearch master-eligible node

The master-eligible node is a standby for the master node, and therefore there's no need to create another `Kubernetes` object. This means that scaling the master StatefulSet that assigns `es-master-2`, `es-master-3`, and `es-master-N` is enough. When the master node does not respond, there is a master node election within the master-eligible nodes to choose and elevate one node as the master node.

Elasticsearch data node

The Elasticsearch data node is responsible for storing the data. In addition, we need to scale out if greater data capacity and/or more query requests are needed. Therefore, we can use StatefulSet with Persistent Volume to stabilize the pod and Persistent Volume. On the other hand, there's no need to have the DNS name, therefore no need to setup Kubernetes service for Elasticsearch data node.

Elasticsearch coordinating node

The coordinating node is a load balancer role in the Elasticsearch. Therefore, we need to scale out to handle HTTP traffic from external sources and persisting the data is not required. Therefore, we can use Kubernetes ReplicaSet with the Kubernetes service to expose the HTTP to the external service.

The following example shows the commands used when we create all of the preceding Elasticsearch nodes by Kubernetes:

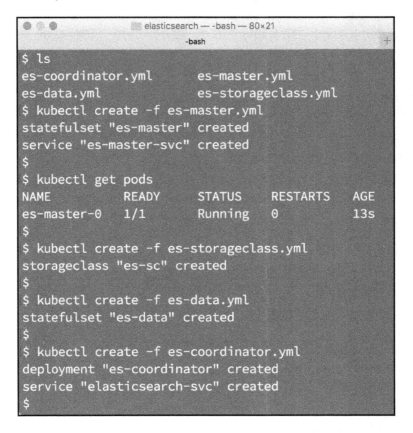

In addition, the following screenshot is the result we obtain after creating the preceding instances:

```
●  ●  ●                    elasticsearch — -bash — 80×22
                                    -bash                                          +
$ kubectl get pods
NAME                            READY     STATUS      RESTARTS     AGE
es-coordinator-3248971439-s9xmd  1/1      Running     0            6m
es-data-0                        1/1      Running     0            9m
es-data-1                        1/1      Running     0            8m
es-data-2                        1/1      Running     0            8m
es-master-0                      1/1      Running     0            10m
$
$ kubectl get deploy
NAME             DESIRED    CURRENT    UP-TO-DATE    AVAILABLE    AGE
es-coordinator   1          1          1             1            6m
$
$ kubectl get statefulset
NAME          DESIRED    CURRENT    AGE
es-data       3          3          9m
es-master     1          1          10m
$
$ kubectl get service
NAME               CLUSTER-IP       EXTERNAL-IP    PORT(S)            AGE
elasticsearch-svc  10.15.243.217    <nodes>        9200:30200/TCP     7m
es-master-svc      None             <none>         9300/TCP           10m
kubernetes         10.15.240.1      <none>         443/TCP            9d
```

```
●  ●  ●                              elasticsearch — -bash — 151×16
                                             -bash                                                                    +
$ kubectl get storageclass
NAME                 TYPE
es-sc                kubernetes.io/gce-pd
standard (default)   kubernetes.io/gce-pd
$
$ kubectl get pvc
NAME                STATUS   VOLUME                                          CAPACITY   ACCESSMODES   STORAGECLASS   AGE
es-data-es-data-0   Bound    pvc-799495f7-524b-11e7-9ac8-42010a960006        1Gi        RWO           es-sc          7m
es-data-es-data-1   Bound    pvc-952038a4-524b-11e7-9ac8-42010a960006        1Gi        RWO           es-sc          7m
es-data-es-data-2   Bound    pvc-9fc111a8-524b-11e7-9ac8-42010a960006        1Gi        RWO           es-sc          6m
$
$ kubectl get pv
NAME                                         CAPACITY   ACCESSMODES   RECLAIMPOLICY   STATUS   CLAIM                       STORAGECLASS   REASON   AGE
pvc-799495f7-524b-11e7-9ac8-42010a960006     1Gi        RWO           Delete          Bound    default/es-data-es-data-0   es-sc                   7m
pvc-952038a4-524b-11e7-9ac8-42010a960006     1Gi        RWO           Delete          Bound    default/es-data-es-data-1   es-sc                   7m
pvc-9fc111a8-524b-11e7-9ac8-42010a960006     1Gi        RWO           Delete          Bound    default/es-data-es-data-2   es-sc                   6m
```

In this case, external service (Kubernetes node:`30020`) is an entry point for external applications. For testing purposes, let's install `elasticsearch-head` (`https://github.com/mobz/elasticsearch-head`) to visualize the cluster information.

Connect Elasticsearch coordination node to install the `elasticsearch-head` plugin:

```
elasticsearch — kubectl exec -it es-coordinator-3248971439-s9xmd /bin/bash — 80×20
                 kubectl exec -it es-coordinator-3248971439-s9xmd /bin/bash                +

$ kubectl exec -it es-coordinator-3248971439-s9xmd /bin/bash
< bin/plugin install mobz/elasticsearch-head

-> Installing mobz/elasticsearch-head...
Trying https://github.com/mobz/elasticsearch-head/archive/master.zip ...
Downloading .............................................................
.............................................................................
.............................................................................
.............................................................................
.............................................................................
.............................................................................
.............................................................................
.............................................................................
............................................DONE
Verifying https://github.com/mobz/elasticsearch-head/archive/master.zip checksum
s if available ...
NOTE: Unable to verify checksum for downloaded plugin (unable to find .sha1 or .
md5 file to verify)
Installed head into /usr/share/elasticsearch/plugins/head
root@es-coordinator-3248971439-s9xmd:/usr/share/elasticsearch#
```

Then, access any Kubernetes node, URL as
`http://<kubernetes-node>:30200/_plugin/head`. The following UI contains the
cluster node information:

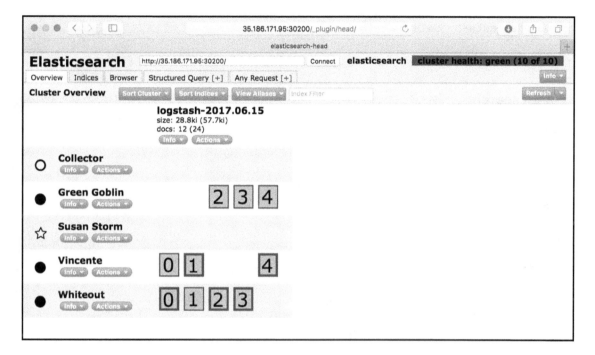

The star icon indicates the Elasticsearch master node, the three black bullets are data nodes
and the white circle bullet is the coordinator node.

In this configuration, if one data node is down, no service impact will occur, as shown in the following snippet:

```
//simulate to occur one data node down
$ kubectl delete pod es-data-0
pod "es-data-0" deleted
```

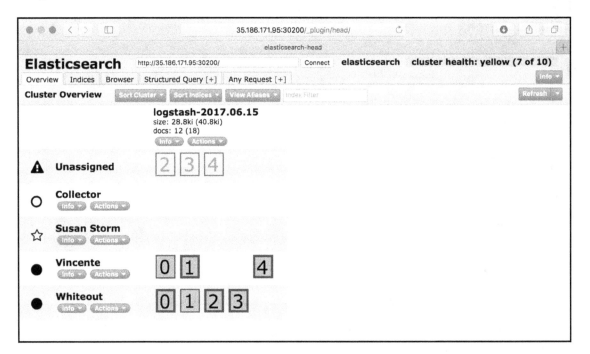

A few moments later, the new pod mounts the same PVC, which preserved `es-data-0` data. And then the Elasticsearch data node registers to master node again, after which the cluster health is back to green (normal), as shown in the following screenshot:

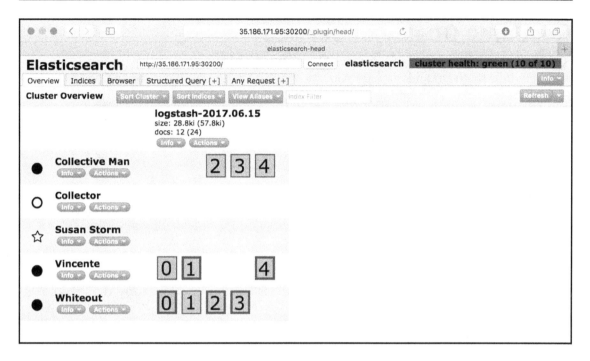

Due to StatefulSet and Persistent Volume, the application data is not lost on `es-data-0`. If you need more disk space, increase the number of data nodes. If you need to support more traffic, increase the number of coordinator nodes. If a backup of the master node is required, increase the number of master nodes to make some master-eligible nodes.

Overall, the Persistent Volume combination of StatefulSet is very powerful, and can make the application flexible and scalable.

Kubernetes resource management

`Chapter 3`, *Getting Started with Kubernetes* mentioned that Kubernetes has a scheduler that manages Kubernetes node and then determines where to deploy a pod. When node has enough resources such as CPU and memory, Kubernetes administrator can feel free to deploy an application. However, once it reaches its resource limit, the Kubernetes scheduler behaves different based on its configuration. Therefore, the Kubernetes administrator has to understand how to configure and utilize machine resources.

Resource Quality of Service

Kubernetes has the concept of **Resource QoS** (**Quality of Service**), which helps an administrator to assign and manage pods by different priorities. Based on the pod's setting, Kubernetes classifies each pod as:

- Guaranteed pod
- Burstable pod
- BestEffort pod

The priority would be Guaranteed > Burstable > BestEffort, which means if the BestEffort pod and the Guaranteed pod exist in the same node, then when one of the pods consumes memory and to causes a node resource shortage, one of the BestEffort pods will be terminated to save the Guaranteed pod.

In order to configure Resource QoS, you have to set the resource request and/or resource limit in the pod definition. The following example is a definition of resource request and resource limit for nginx:

```
$ cat burstable.yml
apiVersion: v1
kind: Pod
metadata:
  name: burstable-pod
spec:
  containers:
  - name: nginx
    image: nginx
    resources:
      requests:
        cpu: 0.1
        memory: 10Mi
      limits:
        cpu: 0.5
        memory: 300Mi
```

This example indicates the following:

Type of resource definition	Resource name	Value	Mean
requests	cpu	0.1	At least 10% of 1 CPU core
	memory	10Mi	At least 10 Mbytes of memory
limits	cpu	0.5	Maximum 50 % of 1 CPU core
	memory	300Mi	Maximum 300 Mbyte of memory

For the CPU resource, acceptable value expressions for either cores (0.1, 0.2 ... 1.0, 2.0) or millicpu (100m, 200m ... 1000m, 2000m). 1000 m is equivalent to 1 core. For example, if Kubernetes node has 2 cores CPU (or 1 core with hyperthreading), there are total of 2.0 cores or 2000 millicpu, as follows:

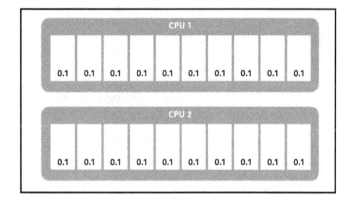

If you run the nginx example (`requests.cpu: 0.1`), it occupies at least 0.1 core, as shown in the following figure:

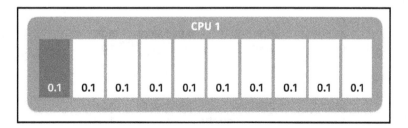

As long as the CPU has enough spaces, it may occupy up to 0.5 cores (`limits.cpu: 0.5`), as shown in the following figure:

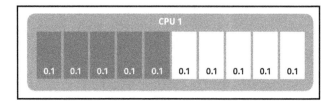

You can also see the configuration by using the `kubectl describe nodes` command as follows:

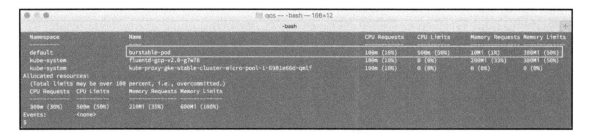

Note that it shows a percentage that depends on the Kubernetes node's spec in the preceding example; as you can see the node has 1 core and 600 MB memory.

On the other hand, if it exceeds the memory limit, the Kubernetes scheduler determines that this pod is out of memory, and then it will kill a pod (`OOMKilled`):

```
//Pod is reaching to the memory limit
$ kubectl get pods
NAME            READY      STATUS      RESTARTS     AGE
burstable-pod   1/1        Running     0            10m

//got OOMKilled
$ kubectl get pods
NAME            READY      STATUS      RESTARTS     AGE
burstable-pod   0/1        OOMKilled   0            10m

//restarting Pod
$ kubectl get pods
NAME            READY      STATUS            RESTARTS   AGE
burstable-pod   0/1        CrashLoopBackOff  0          11m

//restarted
$ kubectl get pods
```

```
NAME            READY    STATUS      RESTARTS    AGE
burstable-pod   1/1      Running     1           12m
```

Configuring the BestEffort pod

The BestEffort pod has the lowest priority in the Resource QoS configuration. Therefore, in case of a resource shortage, this pod will be the first one to be terminated. The use case of using BestEffort would be a stateless and recoverable application such as:

- Worker process
- Proxy or cache node

In the case of a resource shortage, this pod should yield CPU and memory resource to other higher priority pods. In order to configure a pod as the BestEffort pod, you need to set resource limit as 0, or not specify resource limit. For example:

```
//no resource setting
$ cat besteffort-implicit.yml
apiVersion: v1
kind: Pod
metadata:
  name: besteffort
spec:
  containers:
  - name: nginx
    image: nginx

//resource limit setting as 0
$ cat besteffort-explicit.yml
apiVersion: v1
kind: Pod
metadata:
  name: besteffort
spec:
  containers:
  - name: nginx
    image: nginx
    resources:
     limits:
      cpu: 0
      memory: 0
```

Note that the resource setting is inherited by the `namespace default` setting. Therefore, if you intend to configure the pod as the BestEffort pod using the implicit setting, it might not configure as BestEffort if the namespace has a default resource setting as follows:

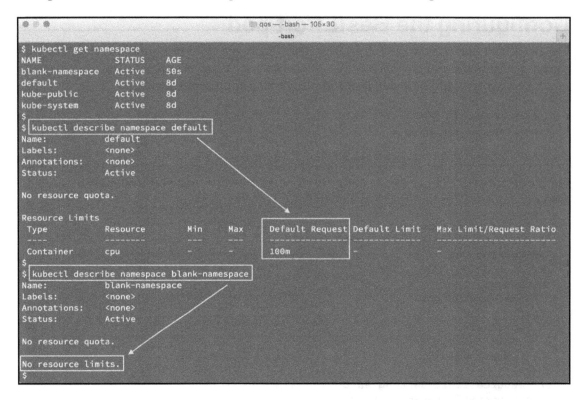

In this case, if you deploy to the default namespace using implicit setting, it applies a default CPU request as `request.cpu: 0.1` and then it becomes Burstable. On the other hand, if you deploy to `blank-namespace`, apply `request.cpu: 0`, and then it will become BestEffort.

Configuring as the Guaranteed pod

Guaranteed is the highest priority in Resource QoS. In the case of a resource shortage, the Kubernetes scheduler will try to retain the Guaranteed pod to the last.

Therefore, the usage of a Guaranteed pod would be a mission critical node such as:

- Backend database with Persistent Volume
- Master node (such as Elasticsearch master node and HDFS name node)

In order to configure as the Guaranteed pod, explicitly set the resource limit and resource request as the same value, or only set the resource limit. However, again, if the namespace has default resource setting, it might cause different results:

```
$ cat guaranteed.yml
apiVersion: v1
kind: Pod
metadata:
  name: guaranteed-pod
spec:
  containers:
    - name: nginx
      image: nginx
      resources:
       limits:
         cpu: 0.3
         memory: 350Mi
       requests:
         cpu: 0.3
         memory: 350Mi

$ kubectl get pods
NAME              READY       STATUS     RESTARTS    AGE
guaranteed-pod    1/1         Running    0           52s

$ kubectl describe pod guaranteed-pod | grep -i qos
QoS Class:   Guaranteed
```

Because Guaranteed pod has to set resource limit, if you are not 100% sure about the necessary CPU/memory resource of your application, especially maximum memory usage; you should use Burstable setting to monitor the application behavior for a while. Otherwise Kubernetes scheduler might terminate a pod (OOMKilled) even if the node has enough memory.

Configuring as Burstable pod

The Burstable pod has a higher priority than BestEffort, but lower than Guaranteed. Unlike Guaranteed pod, resource limit setting is not mandatory; therefore pod can consume CPU and memory as much as possible while node resource is available. Therefore, it is good to be used by any type of application.

If you already know the minimal memory size of an application, you should specify request resource, which helps Kubernetes scheduler to assign to the right node. For example, there are two nodes that have 1 GB memory each. Node 1 already assigns 600 MB memory and node 2 assigns 200 MB memory to other pods.

If we create one more pod that has a resource request memory as 500 MB, then Kubernetes scheduler assigns this pod to node 2. However, if the pod doesn't have a resource request, the result will vary either node 1 or node 2. Because Kubernetes doesn't know how much memory this pod will consume:

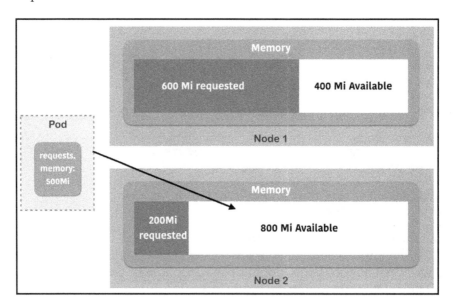

There is still important behavior of Resource QoS to discuss. The granularity of Resource QoS unit is pod level, not a container level. This means, if you configure a pod that has two containers, you intend to set container A as Guaranteed (request/limit are same value), and container B is Burstable (set only request). Unfortunately, Kubernetes configures this pod as Burstable because Kubernetes doesn't know what the limit of container B is.

The following example demonstrate that failed to configure as Guaranteed pod, it eventually configured as Burstable:

```
// supposed nginx is Guaranteed, tomcat as Burstable...
$ cat guaranteed-fail.yml
apiVersion: v1
kind: Pod
metadata:
  name: burstable-pod
spec:
  containers:
  - name: nginx
    image: nginx
    resources:
     limits:
        cpu: 0.3
        memory: 350Mi
     requests:
        cpu: 0.3
        memory: 350Mi
  - name: tomcat
    image: tomcat
    resources:
      requests:
        cpu: 0.2
        memory: 100Mi


$ kubectl create -f guaranteed-fail.yml
pod "guaranteed-fail" created

//at the result, Pod is configured as Burstable
$ kubectl describe pod guaranteed-fail | grep -i qos
QoS Class:  Burstable
```

Even though, change to configure resource limit only, but if container A has CPU limit only, then container B has memory limit only, then result will also be Burstable again because Kubernetes knows only either limit:

```
//nginx set only cpu limit, tomcat set only memory limit
$ cat guaranteed-fail2.yml
apiVersion: v1
kind: Pod
metadata:
  name: guaranteed-fail2
spec:
  containers:
  - name: nginx
    image: nginx
    resources:
      limits:
        cpu: 0.3
  - name: tomcat
    image: tomcat
    resources:
      requests:
        memory: 100Mi


$ kubectl create -f guaranteed-fail2.yml
pod "guaranteed-fail2" created

//result is Burstable again
$ kubectl describe pod |grep -i qos
QoS Class:  Burstable
```

Therefore, if you intend to configure pod as Guaranteed, you must set all containers as Guaranteed.

Monitoring resource usage

When you start to configure to set a resource request and/or limit, your pod may not be scheduled to deploy by Kubernetes scheduler due to insufficient resources. In order to understand allocatable resources and available resources, use the `kubectl describe nodes` command to see the status.

The following example shows one node that has 600 MB memory and one core CPU. So allocatable resources are as follows:

```
●  ●  ●            qos — saito@gke-stable-cluster-micro-pool-1-6981e66d-47c7:~ — -bash — 112×19
                      saito@gke-stable-cluster-micro-pool-1-6981e66d-47c7:~ — -bash                    +
Addresses:              10.150.0.7,35.186.189.88,gke-stable-cluster-micro-pool-1-6981e66d-47c7
Capacity:
 cpu:           1
 memory:        608356Ki
 pods:          110
Allocatable:
 cpu:           1
 memory:        608356Ki
 pods:          110
System Info:
 Machine ID:            264835d12e1e9386a67c9d2c1969c714
 System UUID:           264835D1-2E1E-9386-A67C-9D2C1969C714
 Boot ID:               cd7782b3-0d2f-47ef-9f95-4ff0d3902be7
 Kernel Version:        4.4.35+
 OS Image:              Container-Optimized OS from Google
 Operating System:      linux
 Architecture:          amd64
 Container Runtime Version:  docker://1.11.2
 Kubelet Version:       v1.6.4
```

However, this node already runs some Burstable pod (use resource request) already as follows:

```
●  ●  ●            qos — saito@gke-stable-cluster-micro-pool-1-6981e66d-47c7:~ — -bash — 112×19
                      saito@gke-stable-cluster-micro-pool-1-6981e66d-47c7:~ — -bash                    +
 ----   ----------        ---------------- --------------
   kube-system                    fluentd-gcp-v2.0-s9wh4                                      100m (10
%)      0 (0%)      200Mi (33%)    300Mi (50%)
   kube-system                    heapster-v1.3.0-2541477364-vzcvc                           138m (13
%)      138m (13%)   302456Ki (49%)  302456Ki (49%)
   kube-system                    kube-dns-autoscaler-2528518105-8p57v                       20m (2%0
 (0%)        10Mi (1%)    0 (0%)
   kube-system                    kube-proxy-gke-stable-cluster-micro-pool-1-6981e66d-47c7   100m (10
%)      0 (0%)      0 (0%)         0 (0%)
   kube-system                    kubernetes-dashboard-2917854236-6981d                      100m (10
%)      100m (10%)   50Mi (8%)      50Mi (8%)
   kube-system                    l7-default-backend-1044750973-g20g7                        10m (1%1
0m (1%) 20Mi (3%)     20Mi (3%)
Allocated resources:
  (Total limits may be over 100 percent, i.e., overcommitted.)
  CPU Requests  CPU Limits   Memory Requests Memory Limits
  ------------  ----------   --------------- -------------
  468m (46%)    248m (24%)   589176Ki (96%)  681336Ki (111%)
$ ▊
```

The available memory is limited as approximately 20 MB. Therefore, if you submit Burstable pod that request more than 20 MB, it is never scheduled, as shown in the following screenshot:

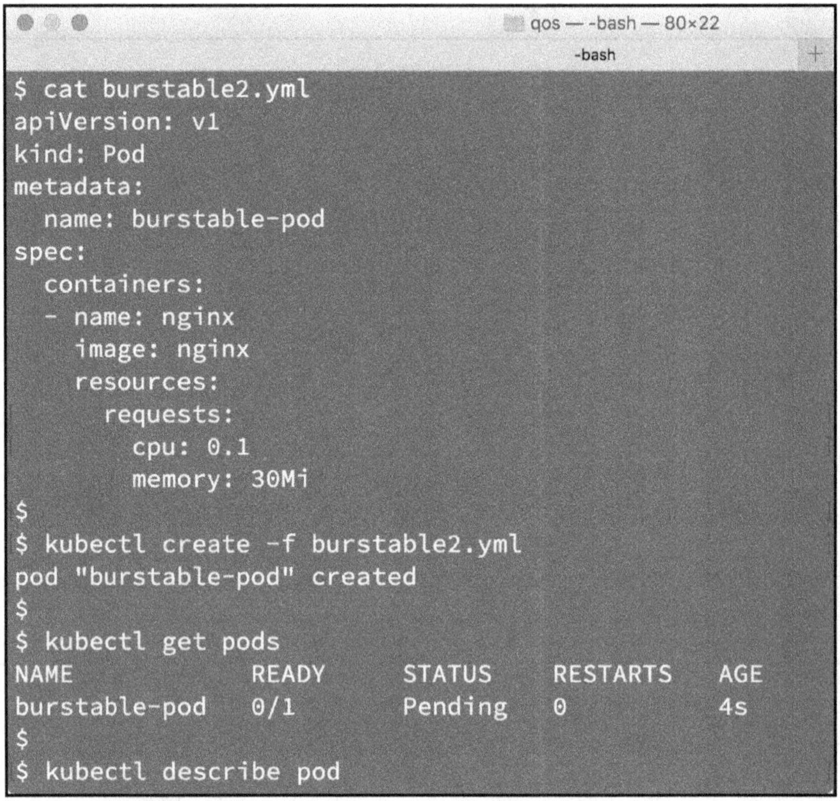

```
$ cat burstable2.yml
apiVersion: v1
kind: Pod
metadata:
  name: burstable-pod
spec:
  containers:
  - name: nginx
    image: nginx
    resources:
      requests:
        cpu: 0.1
        memory: 30Mi
$
$ kubectl create -f burstable2.yml
pod "burstable-pod" created
$
$ kubectl get pods
NAME             READY    STATUS    RESTARTS    AGE
burstable-pod    0/1      Pending   0           4s
$
$ kubectl describe pod
```

The error event can be captured by the `kubectl describe pod` command:

```
● ● ●                       qos — -bash — 80×22
                                   -bash                                        +
)
Conditions:
  Type            Status
  PodScheduled    False
Volumes:
  default-token-xj95q:
    Type:         Secret (a volume populated by a Secret)
    SecretName:   default-token-xj95q
    Optional:     false
QoS Class:        Burstable
Node-Selectors:   <none>
Tolerations:      node.alpha.kubernetes.io/notReady=:Exists:NoExecute for 300s
                  node.alpha.kubernetes.io/unreachable=:Exists:NoExecute for 300s
Events:
  FirstSeen       LastSeen      Count     From                  SubObjectPath   T
ype               Reason                  Message
  ---------       --------      -----     ----                  -------------   -
-------- ------                 --------
    25s           12s           3         default-scheduler                     W
arning            FailedScheduling        No nodes are available that match all of
  the following predicates:: Insufficient memory (1).
$
```

In this case, you need to add more Kubernetes nodes to support more resources.

Summary

In this chapter, we have covered Stateless and Stateful applications that use ephemeral volume or Persistent Volume. Both have pitfalls when an application restarts or a pod scales. In addition, Persistent Volume management on Kubernetes has been kept enhanced to make it easier, as you can see from such tools as StatefulSet and Dynamic Provisioning.

Also, Resource QoS helps Kubernetes scheduler to assign a pod to the right node based on request and limit based on priorities.

The next chapter will introduce Kubernetes network and security, which configures pod and services more easier, and makes them scalable and secure.

5
Network and Security

We've learned how to deploy containers with different resources in Kubernetes in Chapter 3, *Getting Started with Kubernetes*, and know how to use volume to persist the data, dynamic provisioning, and different storage classes. Next, we'll learn how Kubernetes routes the traffic to make all of this possible. Networking always plays an important role in the software world. We'll describe the networking from containers on a single host, multiple hosts and finally to Kubernetes.

- Docker networking
- Kubernetes networking
- Ingress
- Network policy

Kubernetes networking

There are plenty of choices you can use to implement networking in Kubernetes. Kubernetes itself doesn't care how you implement it, but you must meet its three fundamental requirements:

- All containers should be accessible to each other without NAT, regardless of which nodes they are on
- All nodes should communicate with all containers
- The IP container should see itself the same way as the others see it

Before getting into anything further, we'll first review how does the default container networking works. That's the pillar of the network to make all of this possible.

Docker networking

Let's review how Docker networking works before getting into Kubernetes networking. In Chapter 2, *DevOps with Container*, we learned three modes of container networking, bridge, none, and host.

Bridge is the default networking model. Docker creates and attaches virtual Ethernet device (also known as veth) and assigns network namespace to each container.

 The **network namespace** is a feature in Linux, which is logically another copy of a network stack. It has its own routing tables, arp tables, and network devices. It's a fundamental concept of container networking.

Veth always comes in a pair, one is in network namespace and the other is in the bridge. When the traffic comes into the host network, it will be routed into the bridge. The packet will be dispatched to its veth, and will go into the namespace inside the container, as shown in the following figure:

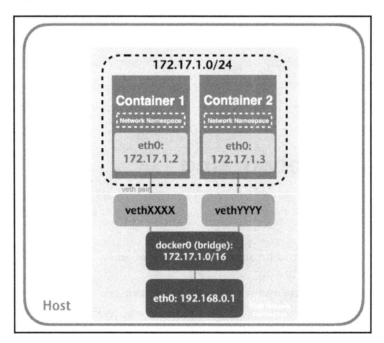

Let's take a closer look. In the following example, we'll use a minikube node as the docker host. Firstly, we'll have to use `minikube ssh` to ssh into the node because we're not using Kubernetes yet. After we get into the minikube node, let's launch a container to interact with us:

```
// launch a busybox container with `top` command, also, expose container
port 8080 to host port 8000.
# docker run -d -p 8000:8080 --name=busybox busybox top
737e4d87ba86633f39b4e541f15cd077d688a1c8bfb83156d38566fc5c81f469
```

Let's see the implementation of outbound traffic within a container. `docker exec <container_name or container_id>` can run a command in a running container. Lets use `ip link list` to list down all the interfaces:

```
// show all the network interfaces in busybox container
// docker exec <container_name> <command>
# docker exec busybox ip link list
1: lo: <LOOPBACK,UP,LOWER_UP> mtu 65536 qdisc noqueue qlen 1
   link/loopback 00:00:00:00:00:00 brd 00:00:00:00:00:00
2: sit0@NONE: <NOARP> mtu 1480 qdisc noop qlen 1
   link/sit 0.0.0.0 brd 0.0.0.0
53: eth0@if54: <BROADCAST,MULTICAST,UP,LOWER_UP,M-DOWN>
   mtu 1500 qdisc noqueue
   link/ether 02:42:ac:11:00:07 brd ff:ff:ff:ff:ff:ff
```

We can see that we have three interfaces inside the `busybox` container. One is with ID `53` with the name `eth0@if54`. The number after `if` is the other interface ID in the pair. In this case, the pair ID is `54`. If we run the same command on the host, we could see the veth in the host is pointing to the `eth0` inside the container:

```
// show all the network interfaces from the host
# ip link list
1: lo: <LOOPBACK,UP,LOWER_UP> mtu 65536 qdisc noqueue
   state UNKNOWN mode DEFAULT group default qlen 1
   link/loopback 00:00:00:00:00:00 brd 00:00:00:00:00:00
2: eth0: <BROADCAST,MULTICAST,UP,LOWER_UP> mtu 1500 qdisc
   pfifo_fast state UP mode DEFAULT group default qlen
   1000
   link/ether 08:00:27:ca:fd:37 brd ff:ff:ff:ff:ff:ff
...
54: vethfeec36a@if53: <BROADCAST,MULTICAST,UP,LOWER_UP>
   mtu 1500 qdisc noqueue master docker0 state UP mode
   DEFAULT group default
   link/ether ce:25:25:9e:6c:07 brd ff:ff:ff:ff:ff:ff link-netnsid 5
```

We have a veth on the host named `vethfeec36a@if53`. It pairs with `eth0@if54` in the container network namespace. The veth 54 is attached to the `docker0` bridge, and eventually accesses the internet via eth0. If we take a look at the iptables rules, we can find a masquerading rule (also known as SNAT) on the host that Docker creates for outbound traffic, which will make internet access available for containers:

```
// list iptables nat rules. Showing only POSTROUTING rules which allows
packets to be altered before they leave the host.
# sudo iptables -t nat -nL POSTROUTING
Chain POSTROUTING (policy ACCEPT)
target        prot opt source                destination
...
MASQUERADE    all  --  172.17.0.0/16         0.0.0.0/0
...
```

On the other hand, for the inbound traffic, Docker creates a custom filter chain on prerouting and creates forwarding rules in the `DOCKER` filter chain dynamically. If we expose a container port `8080` and map it to a host port `8000`, we can see we're listening to port `8000` on any IP address (`0.0.0.0/0`), which will then be routed to container port `8080`:

```
// list iptables nat rules
# sudo iptables -t nat -nL
Chain PREROUTING (policy ACCEPT)
target        prot opt source                destination
...
DOCKER        all  --  0.0.0.0/0             0.0.0.0/0          ADDRTYPE
match dst-type LOCAL
...
Chain OUTPUT (policy ACCEPT)
target        prot opt source                destination
DOCKER        all  --  0.0.0.0/0             !127.0.0.0/8       ADDRTYPE
match dst-type LOCAL
...
Chain DOCKER (2 references)
target        prot opt source                destination
RETURN        all  --  0.0.0.0/0             0.0.0.0/0
...
DNAT          tcp  --  0.0.0.0/0             0.0.0.0/0          tcp dpt:8000
to:172.17.0.7:8080
...
```

Now we know how packet goes in/out of containers. Let's have a look at how containers in a pod communicates with each other.

Container-to-container communications

Pods in Kubernetes have their own real IP addresses. Containers within a pod share network namespace, so they see each other as *localhost*. This is implemented by the **network container** by default, which acts as a bridge to dispatch the traffic for every container in a pod. Let's see how this works in the following example. Let's use the first example from Chapter 3, *Getting Started with Kubernetes*, which includes two containers, nginx and centos inside one pod:

```
#cat 5-1-1_pod.yaml
apiVersion: v1
kind: Pod
metadata:
  name: example
spec:
  containers:
    - name: web
      image: nginx
    - name: centos
      image: centos
      command: ["/bin/sh", "-c", "while : ;do curl http://localhost:80/;
sleep 10; done"]
// create the Pod
#kubectl create -f 5-1-1_pod.yaml
pod "example" created
```

Then, we will describe the pod and see its container ID:

```
# kubectl describe pods example
Name:        example
Node:        minikube/192.168.99.100
. . .
Containers:
  web:
    Container ID: docker://
d9bd923572ab186870284535044e7f3132d5cac11ecb18576078b9c7bae86c73
    Image:        nginx
. . .
centos:
    Container ID: docker:
//f4c019d289d4b958cd17ecbe9fe22a5ce5952cb380c8ca4f9299e10bf5e94a0f
    Image:        centos
. . .
```

In this example, `web` is with container ID `d9bd923572ab` and `centos` is with container ID `f4c019d289d4`. If we go into the node `minikube/192.168.99.100` using `docker ps`, we can check how many containers Kubernetes actually launches since we're in minikube, which launches lots of other cluster containers. Check out the latest launch time by `CREATED` column, where we will find that there are three containers that have just been launched:

```
# docker ps
CONTAINER ID          IMAGE                                              COMMAND
CREATED               STATUS              PORTS
NAMES
f4c019d289d4          36540f359ca3                                       "/bin/sh -c
'while : "   2 minutes ago         Up 2 minutes
k8s_centos_example_default_9843fc27-677b-11e7-9a8c-080027cafd37_1
d9bd923572ab          e4e6d42c70b3                                       "nginx -g
'daemon off"   2 minutes ago         Up 2 minutes
k8s_web_example_default_9843fc27-677b-11e7-9a8c-080027cafd37_1
4ddd3221cc47          gcr.io/google_containers/pause-amd64:3.0   "/pause"
2 minutes ago         Up 2 minutes
```

There is an additional container `4ddd3221cc47` that was launched. Before digging into which container it is, let's check the network mode of our `web` container. We will find that the containers in our example pod are running in containers with mapped container mode:

```
# docker inspect d9bd923572ab | grep NetworkMode
"NetworkMode":
"container:4ddd3221cc4792207ce0a2b3bac5d758a5c7ae321634436fa3e6dd627a31ca76
",
```

`4ddd3221cc47` container is the so-called network container in this case, which holds network namespace to let `web` and `centos` containers join. Containers in the same network namespace share the same IP address and same network configuration. This is the default implementation in Kubernetes to achieve container-to-container communications, which is mapped to the first requirement.

Pod-to-pod communications

Pod IP addresses are accessible from other pods no matter which nodes they're on. This fits the second requirement. We'll describe the pods' communication within the same node and across nodes in the upcoming section.

Pod communication within the same node

Pod-to-pod communication within the same node goes through the bridge by default. Let's say we have two pods, which have their own network namespaces. When pod1 wants to talk to pod2, the packet passes through pod1's namespace to the corresponding veth pair **vethXXXX** and eventually goes to the bridge. The bridge then broadcasts the destination IP to help the packet find its way, **vethYYYY** responses. The packet then arrives at pod2:

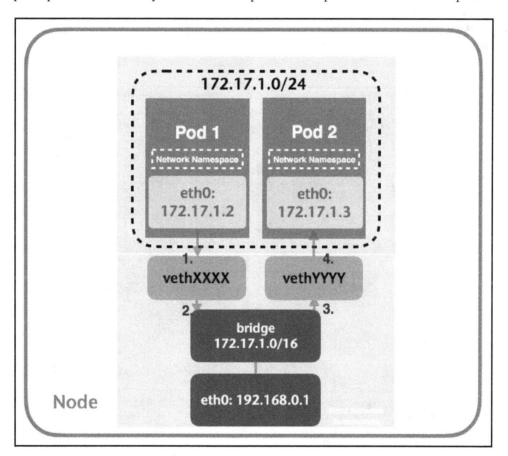

However, Kubernetes is all about clusters. How does traffic get routed when the pods are in different nodes?

Pod communication across nodes

According to the second requirement, all nodes must communicate with all containers. Kubernetes delegates the implementation to the **container network interface** (**CNI**). Users could choose different implementations, by L2, L3, or overlay. Overlay networking is one of the common solutions, known as **packet encapsulation**. It wraps a message before leaving the source, gets delivered, and unwraps the message at the destination. This leads to a situation where overlay increases the network latency and complexity. As long as all the containers can access each other across nodes, you're free to use any technology, such as L2 adjacency or L3 gateway. For more information about CNI, refer to its spec (`https://github.com/containernetworking/cni/blob/master/SPEC.md`):

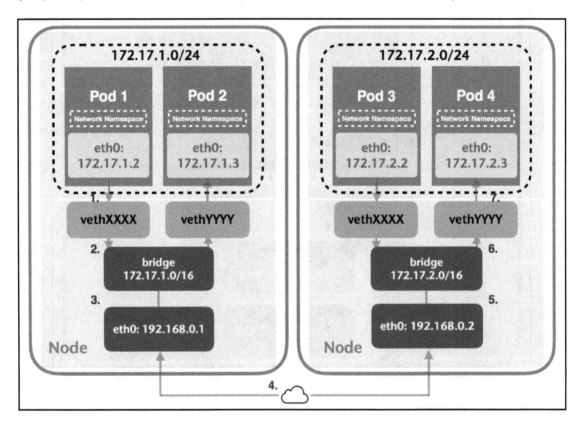

Let's say we have a packet from pod1 to pod4. The packet leaves from container interface and reaches to the veth pair, then passes through the bridge and node's network interface. Network implementation comes into play in step 4. As long as the packet could be routed to the target node, you are free to use any options. In the following example, we'll launch minikube with the `--network-plugin=cni` option. With CNI enabled, the parameters will be passed through kubelet in the node. Kubelet has a default network plugin, but you could probe any supported plugin when it starts up. Before starting minikube, you could use `minikube stop` first if it's been started or `minikube delete` to delete the whole cluster thoroughly before doing anything further. Although minikube is a single node environment, which might not completely represent the production scenario we'll encounter, this just gives you a basic idea of how all of this works. We will learn the deployment of networking options in the real world in `Chapter 9`, *Kubernetes on AWS* and `Chapter 10`, *Kubernetes on GCP*.

```
// start minikube with cni option
# minikube start --network-plugin=cni
...
Kubectl is now configured to use the cluster.
```

When we specify the `network-plugin` option, it will use the directory specified in `--network-plugin-dir` for plugins on startup. In the CNI plugin, the default plugin directory is `/opt/cni/net.d`. After the cluster comes up, let's log in to the node and see the setting inside via `minikube ssh`:

```
# minikube ssh
$ ifconfig
...
mybridge  Link encap:Ethernet  HWaddr 0A:58:0A:01:00:01
          inet addr:10.1.0.1  Bcast:0.0.0.0
          Mask:255.255.0.0
...
```

We will find that there is one new bridge in the node, and if we create the example pod again by `5-1-1_pod.yml`, we will find that the IP address of the pod becomes `10.1.0.x`, which is attaching to `mybridge` instead of `docker0`.

```
# kubectl create -f 5-1-1_pod.yaml
pod "example" created
# kubectl describe po example
Name:         example
Namespace:    default
Node:         minikube/192.168.99.100
Start Time:   Sun, 23 Jul 2017 14:24:24 -0400
Labels:           <none>
Annotations:      <none>
```

```
Status:              Running
IP:          10.1.0.4
```

Why is that? That's because we specify that we'll use CNI as the network plugin, and `docker0` will not be used (also known as **container network model** or **libnetwork**). CNI creates a virtual interface, attaches it to the underlay network, and sets the IP address and routes and maps it to the pods' namespace eventually. Let's take a look at the configuration located at `/etc/cni/net.d/`:

```
# cat /etc/cni/net.d/k8s.conf
{
  "name": "rkt.kubernetes.io",
  "type": "bridge",
  "bridge": "mybridge",
  "mtu": 1460,
  "addIf": "true",
  "isGateway": true,
  "ipMasq": true,
  "ipam": {
    "type": "host-local",
    "subnet": "10.1.0.0/16",
    "gateway": "10.1.0.1",
    "routes": [
      {
        "dst": "0.0.0.0/0"
      }
    ]
  }
}
```

In this example, we use the bridge CNI plugin to reuse the L2 bridge for pod containers. If the packet is from `10.1.0.0/16`, and its destination is to anywhere, it'll go through this gateway. Just like the diagram we saw earlier, we could have another node with CNI enabled with `10.1.2.0/16` subnet, so that ARP packets could go out to the physical interface on the node that the target pod is located at. It then achieves pod-to-pod communication across nodes.

Let's check the rules in iptables:

```
// check the rules in iptables
# sudo iptables -t nat -nL
...
Chain POSTROUTING (policy ACCEPT)
target       prot opt source                  destination
KUBE-POSTROUTING  all  --  0.0.0.0/0           0.0.0.0/0           /*
kubernetes postrouting rules */
MASQUERADE  all  --  172.17.0.0/16         0.0.0.0/0
CNI-25df152800e33f7b16fc085a  all  --  10.1.0.0/16         0.0.0.0/0
/* name: "rkt.kubernetes.io" id:
"328287949eb4d4483a3a8035d65cc326417ae7384270844e59c2f4e963d87e18" */
CNI-f1931fed74271104c4d10006  all  --  10.1.0.0/16         0.0.0.0/0
/* name: "rkt.kubernetes.io" id:
"08c562ff4d67496fdae1c08facb2766ca30533552b8bd0682630f203b18f8c0a" */
```

All the related rules have been switched to `10.1.0.0/16` CIDR.

Pod-to-service communications

Kubernetes is dynamic. Pods are created and deleted all the time. The Kubernetes service is an abstraction to define a set of pods by label selectors. We normally use the service to access pods instead of specifying a pod explicitly. When we create a service, an `endpoint` object will be created, which describes a set of pod IPs that the label selector in that service has selected.

> In some cases, `endpoint` object will not be created with service creation. For example, services without selectors will not create a corresponding `endpoint` object. For more information, refer to the service without selectors section in `Chapter 3`, *Getting Started with Kubernetes*.

Then, how does traffic get from pod to the pod behind service? By default, Kubernetes uses iptables to perform the magic by `kube-proxy`. This is explained in the following figure.

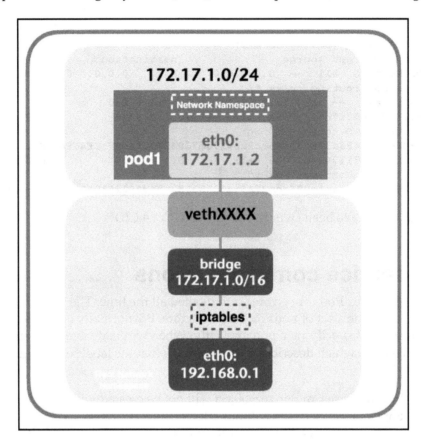

Let's reuse the `3-2-3_rc1.yaml` and `3-2-3_nodeport.yaml` examples from Chapter 3, *Getting Started with Kubernetes,* to observe the default behavior:

```
// create two pods with nginx and one service to observe default
networking. Users are free to use any other kind of solution.
# kubectl create -f 3-2-3_rc1.yaml
replicationcontroller "nginx-1.12" created
# kubectl create -f 3-2-3_nodeport.yaml
service "nginx-nodeport" created
```

Let's observe iptable rules and see how this works. As shown next, our service IP is `10.0.0.167`, two pods IP addresses underneath are `10.1.0.4` and `10.1.0.5`.

```
// kubectl describe svc nginx-nodeport
Name:              nginx-nodeport
Namespace:         default
Selector:          project=chapter3,service=web
Type:              NodePort
IP:                10.0.0.167
Port:              <unset>        80/TCP
NodePort:          <unset>        32261/TCP
Endpoints:         10.1.0.4:80,10.1.0.5:80
...
```

Let's get into minikube node by `minikube ssh` and check its iptable rules:

```
# sudo iptables -t nat -nL
...
Chain KUBE-SERVICES (2 references)
target      prot opt source                 destination
KUBE-SVC-37ROJ3MK6RKFMQ2B  tcp  --  0.0.0.0/0            10.0.0.167
/* default/nginx-nodeport: cluster IP */ tcp dpt:80
KUBE-NODEPORTS  all  --  0.0.0.0/0            0.0.0.0/0            /*
kubernetes service nodeports; NOTE: this must be the last rule in this
chain */ ADDRTYPE match dst-type LOCAL
Chain KUBE-SVC-37ROJ3MK6RKFMQ2B (2 references)
target      prot opt source                 destination
KUBE-SEP-SVVBOHTYP7PAP3J5  all  --  0.0.0.0/0            0.0.0.0/0
/* default/nginx-nodeport: */ statistic mode random probability
0.50000000000
KUBE-SEP-AYS7I6ZPYFC6YNNF  all  --  0.0.0.0/0            0.0.0.0/0
/* default/nginx-nodeport: */
Chain KUBE-SEP-SVVBOHTYP7PAP3J5 (1 references)
target      prot opt source                 destination
KUBE-MARK-MASQ  all  --  10.1.0.4            0.0.0.0/0            /*
default/nginx-nodeport: */
DNAT        tcp  --  0.0.0.0/0            0.0.0.0/0            /*
default/nginx-nodeport: */ tcp to:10.1.0.4:80
Chain KUBE-SEP-AYS7I6ZPYFC6YNNF (1 references)
target      prot opt source                 destination
KUBE-MARK-MASQ  all  --  10.1.0.5            0.0.0.0/0            /*
default/nginx-nodeport: */
DNAT        tcp  --  0.0.0.0/0            0.0.0.0/0            /*
default/nginx-nodeport: */ tcp to:10.1.0.5:80
...
```

The key point here is that the service exposes the cluster IP to outside traffic from the target KUBE-SVC-37ROJ3MK6RKFMQ2B, which links to two custom chains KUBE-SEP-SVVBOHTYP7PAP3J5 and KUBE-SEP-AYS7I6ZPYFC6YNNF with statistic mode random probability 0.5. This means, iptables will generate a random number and tune it based on the probability distribution 0.5 to the destination. These two custom chains have the DNAT target set to the corresponding pod IP. The DNAT target is responsible for changing the packets' destination IP address. By default, conntrack is enabled to track the destination and source of connection when the traffic comes in. All of this results in a routing behavior. When the traffic comes to service, iptables will randomly pick one of the pods to route, and modify the destination IP from service IP to real pod IP, and un-DNAT to go all the way back.

External-to-service communications

The ability to serve external traffic to Kubernetes is critical. Kubernetes provides two API objects to achieve this:

- **Service**: External network LoadBalancer or NodePort (L4)
- **Ingress:** HTTP(S) LoadBalancer (L7)

For ingress, we'll learn more in the next section. We'll focus on L4 first. Based on what we've learned about pod-to-pod communication across nodes, how the packet goes in and out between service and pod. The following figure shows how it works. Let's say we have two services, one service A has three pods (pod a, pod b, and pod c) and another service B gets only one pod (pod d). When the traffic comes in from LoadBalancer, the packet will be dispatched to one of the nodes. Most of the cloud LoadBalancer itself is not aware of pods or containers. It only knows about the node. If the node passes the health check, then it will be the candidate for the destination. Assume that we want to access service B, it currently only has one pod running on one node. However, LoadBalancer sends the packet to another node that doesn't have any of our desired pods running. The traffic route will look like this:

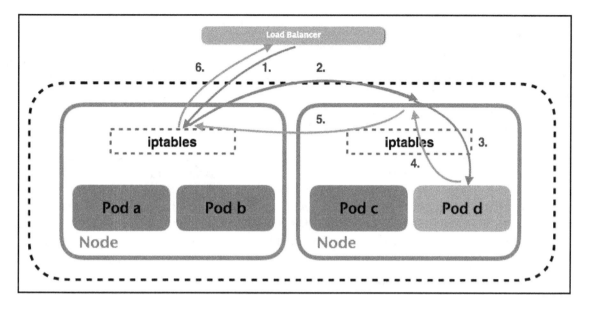

The packet routing journey will be:

1. LoadBalancer will choose one of the nodes to forward the packet. In GCE, it selects the instance based on a hash of the source IP and port, destination IP and port, and protocol. In AWS, it's based on a round-robin algorithm.
2. Here, the routing destination will be changed to pod d (DNAT) and forward it to the other node similar to pod-to-pod communication across nodes.
3. Then, comes service-to-pod communication. The packet arrives at pod d with the response accordingly.
4. Pod-to-service communication is manipulated by iptables as well.
5. The packet will be forwarded to the original node.
6. The source and destination will be un-DNAT to LoadBalancer and client, and sent all the way back.

 In Kubernetes 1.7, there is a new attribute in service called **externalTrafficPolicy**. You can set its value to local, then after the traffic goes into a node, Kubernetes will route the pods on that node, if any.

Ingress

Pods and services in Kubernetes have their own IP; however, it is normally not the interface you'd provide to the external internet. Though there is service with node IP configured, the port in the node IP can't be duplicated among the services. It is cumbersome to decide which port to manage with which service. Furthermore, the node comes and goes, it wouldn't be clever to provide a static node IP to external service.

Ingress defines a set of rules that allows the inbound connection to access Kubernetes cluster services. It brings the traffic into the cluster at L7, allocates and forwards a port on each VM to the service port. This is shown in the following figure. We define a set of rules and post them as source type ingress to the API server. When the traffic comes in, the ingress controller will then fulfill and route the ingress by the ingress rules. As shown in the following figure, ingress is used to route external traffic to the kubernetes endpoints by different URLs:

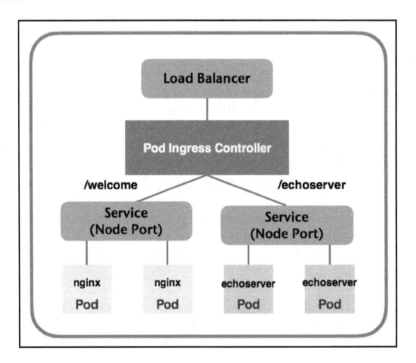

Now, we will go through an example and see how this works. In this example, we'll create two services named `nginx` and `echoserver` with ingress path `/welcome` and `/echoserver` configured. We can run this in minikube. The old version of minikube doesn't enable ingress by default; we'll have to enable it first:

```
// start over our minikube local
# minikube delete && minikube start
// enable ingress in minikube
# minikube addons enable ingress
ingress was successfully enabled
// check current setting for addons in minikube
# minikube addons list
- registry: disabled
- registry-creds: disabled
- addon-manager: enabled
- dashboard: enabled
- default-storageclass: enabled
- kube-dns: enabled
- heapster: disabled
- ingress: enabled
```

Enabling ingress in minikube will create an nginx ingress controller and a `ConfigMap` to store nginx configuration (refer to https://github.com/kubernetes/ingress/blob/master/controllers/nginx/README.md), and a RC and service as default HTTP backend for handling unmapped requests. We could observe them by adding `--namespace=kube-system` in the `kubectl` command. Next, let's create our backend resources. Here is our nginx `Deployment` and `Service`:

```
# cat 5-2-1_nginx.yaml
apiVersion: apps/v1beta1
kind: Deployment
metadata:
  name: nginx
spec:
  replicas: 2
  template:
    metadata:
    labels:
      project: chapter5
      service: nginx
    spec:
      containers:
        - name: nginx
          image: nginx
          ports:
          - containerPort: 80
---
```

```
kind: Service
apiVersion: v1
metadata:
  name: nginx
spec:
  type: NodePort
  selector:
    project: chapter5
    service: nginx
  ports:
    - protocol: TCP
      port: 80
      targetPort: 80
// create nginx RS and service
# kubectl create -f 5-2-1_nginx.yaml
deployment "nginx" created
service "nginx" created
```

We'll then create another service with RS:

```
// another backend named echoserver
# cat 5-2-1_echoserver.yaml
apiVersion: apps/v1beta1
kind: Deployment
metadata:
  name: echoserver
spec:
  replicas: 1
  template:
    metadata:
      name: echoserver
      labels:
       project: chapter5
       service: echoserver
    spec:
      containers:
      - name: echoserver
        image: gcr.io/google_containers/echoserver:1.4
        ports:
      - containerPort: 8080
---
kind: Service
apiVersion: v1
metadata:
  name: echoserver
spec:
  type: NodePort
  selector:
```

```
      project: chapter5
      service: echoserver
    ports:
      - protocol: TCP
        port: 8080
        targetPort: 8080
// create RS and SVC by above configuration file
# kubectl create -f 5-2-1_echoserver.yaml
deployment "echoserver" created
service "echoserver" created
```

Next, we'll create the ingress resource. There is an annotation named
`ingress.kubernetes.io/rewrite-target`. This is required if the service requests are
coming from the root URL. Without a rewrite annotation, we'll get **404** as response. Refer to
`https://github.com/kubernetes/ingress/blob/master/controllers/nginx/configurati`
`on.md#annotations` for more supported annotation in nginx ingress controller:

```
# cat 5-2-1_ingress.yaml
apiVersion: extensions/v1beta1
kind: Ingress
metadata:
  name: ingress-example
  annotations:
    ingress.kubernetes.io/rewrite-target: /
spec:
  rules:
  - host: devops.k8s
    http:
     paths:
    - path: /welcome
      backend:
        serviceName: nginx
        servicePort: 80
    - path: /echoserver
      backend:
        serviceName: echoserver
        servicePort: 8080
// create ingress
# kubectl create -f 5-2-1_ingress.yaml
ingress "ingress-example" created
```

In some cloud providers, service LoadBalancer controller is supported. It could be integrated with ingress via the `status.loadBalancer.ingress` syntax in the configuration file. For more information, refer to https://github.com/kubernetes/contrib/tree/master/service-loadbalancer.

Since our host is set to `devops.k8s`, it will only return if we access it from that hostname. You could either configure the DNS record in the DNS server, or modify the hosts file in local. For simplicity, we'll just add a line with the `ip hostname` format in the host file:

```
// normally host file located in /etc/hosts in linux
# sudo sh -c "echo `minikube ip` devops.k8s >> /etc/hosts"
```

Then we should be able to access our service by the URL directly:

```
# curl http://devops.k8s/welcome
...
<title>Welcome to nginx!</title>
...
// check echoserver
# curl http://devops.k8s/echoserver
CLIENT VALUES:
client_address=172.17.0.4
command=GET
real path=/
query=nil
request_version=1.1
request_uri=http://devops.k8s:8080/
```

The pod ingress controller dispatches the traffic based on the URL path. The routing path is similar to external-to-service communication. The packet hops between nodes and pods. Kubernetes is pluggable. Lots of third-party implementation is going on. We only scratch the surface here while iptables is just a default and common implementation. Networking evolves a lot in every single release. At the time of this writing, Kubernetes had just released version 1.7.

Network policy

Network policy works as a software firewall to the pods. By default, every pod could communicate with each other without any boundaries. Network policy is one of the isolations you could apply to the pods. It defines who can access which pods in which port by namespace selector and pod selector. Network policy in a namespace is additive, and once a pod has policy on, it denies any other ingress (also known as default deny all).

Currently, there are multiple network providers that support network policy, such as Calico (`https://www.projectcalico.org/calico-network-policy-comes-to-kubernetes/`), Romana (`https://github.com/romana/romana`), Weave Net (`https://www.weave.works/docs/net/latest/kube-addon/#npc`), Contiv (`http://contiv.github.io/documents/networking/policies.html`) and Trireme (`https://github.com/aporeto-inc/trireme-kubernetes`). Users are free to choose any options. For simplicity, we're going to use Calico with minikube. To do that, we'll have to launch minikube with the `--network-plugin=cni` option. Network policy is still pretty new in Kubernetes at this point. We're running Kubernetes version v.1.7.0 with v.1.0.7 minikube ISO to deploy Calico by self-hosted solution (`http://docs.projectcalico.org/v1.5/getting-started/kubernetes/installation/hosted/`). First, we'll have to download a `calico.yaml` (`https://github.com/projectcalico/calico/blob/master/v2.4/getting-started/kubernetes/installation/hosted/calico.yaml`) file to create Calico nodes and policy controller. `etcd_endpoints` needs to be configured. To find out the IP of etcd, we need to access localkube resources.

```
// find out etcd ip
# minikube ssh -- "sudo /usr/local/bin/localkube --host-ip"
2017-07-27 04:10:58.941493 I | proto: duplicate proto type registered:
google.protobuf.Any
2017-07-27 04:10:58.941822 I | proto: duplicate proto type registered:
google.protobuf.Duration
2017-07-27 04:10:58.942028 I | proto: duplicate proto type registered:
google.protobuf.Timestamp
localkube host ip:  10.0.2.15
```

The default port of etcd is `2379`. In this case, we modify `etcd_endpoint` in `calico.yaml` from `http://127.0.0.1:2379` to `http://10.0.2.15:2379`:

```
// launch calico
# kubectl apply -f calico.yaml
configmap "calico-config" created
secret "calico-etcd-secrets" created
daemonset "calico-node" created
deployment "calico-policy-controller" created
job "configure-calico" created
```

```
// list the pods in kube-system
# kubectl get pods --namespace=kube-system
NAME                                         READY    STATUS     RESTARTS
AGE
calico-node-ss243                            2/2      Running    0
1m
calico-policy-controller-2249040168-r2270    1/1      Running    0
1m
```

Let's reuse `5-2-1_nginx.yaml` as the example:

```
# kubectl create -f 5-2-1_nginx.yaml
replicaset "nginx" created
service "nginx" created
// list the services
# kubectl get svc
NAME         CLUSTER-IP    EXTERNAL-IP    PORT(S)        AGE
kubernetes   10.0.0.1      <none>         443/TCP        47m
nginx        10.0.0.42     <nodes>        80:31071/TCP   5m
```

We will find that our nginx service has IP `10.0.0.42`. Let's launch a simple bash and use `wget` to see if we can access our nginx:

```
# kubectl run busybox -i -t --image=busybox /bin/sh
If you don't see a command prompt, try pressing enter.
/ # wget --spider 10.0.0.42
Connecting to 10.0.0.42 (10.0.0.42:80)
```

The `--spider` parameter is used to check whether the URL exists. In this case, busybox can access nginx successfully. Next, let's apply a `NetworkPolicy` to our nginx pods:

```
// declare a network policy
# cat 5-3-1_networkpolicy.yaml
kind: NetworkPolicy
apiVersion: networking.k8s.io/v1
metadata:
  name: nginx-networkpolicy
spec:
  podSelector:
  matchLabels:
    service: nginx
  ingress:
  - from:
    - podSelector:
        matchLabels:
          project: chapter5
```

We can see some important syntax here. The `podSelector` is used to select pods, which should match the labels of the target pod. Another one is `ingress[].from[].podSelector`, which is used to define who can access these pods. In this case, all the pods with `project=chapter5` labels are eligible to access the pods with `server=nginx` labels. If we go back to our busybox pod, we're unable to contact nginx anymore because right now, the nginx pod has NetworkPolicy on. By default, it is deny all, so busybox won't be able to talk to nginx:

```
// in busybox pod, or you could use `kubectl attach <pod_name> -c busybox -
i -t` to re-attach to the pod
# wget --spider --timeout=1 10.0.0.42
Connecting to 10.0.0.42 (10.0.0.42:80)
wget: download timed out
```

We could use `kubectl edit deployment busybox` to add the label `project=chaper5` into busybox pods.

> Refer to the labels and selectors section in `Chapter 3`, *Getting Started with Kubernetes* if you forget how to do so.

After that, we can contact nginx pod again:

```
// inside busybox pod
/ # wget --spider 10.0.0.42
Connecting to 10.0.0.42 (10.0.0.42:80)
```

With the help of the preceding example, we have an idea how to apply network policy. We could also apply some default polices to deny all or allow all by tweaking the selector to select nobody or everybody. For example, deny all behavior could be achieved as follows:

```
# cat 5-3-1_np_denyall.yaml
apiVersion: networking.k8s.io/v1
kind: NetworkPolicy
metadata:
  name: default-deny
spec:
  podSelector:
```

This way, all pods that don't match labels will deny all other traffic. Alternatively, we could create a `NetworkPolicy` whose ingress is listed from everywhere. Then the pods running in this namespace could be accessed by anyone else.

```
# cat 5-3-1_np_allowall.yaml
apiVersion: networking.k8s.io/v1
kind: NetworkPolicy
metadata:
  name: allow-all
spec:
  podSelector:
  ingress:
  - {}
```

Summary

In this chapter, we have learned how containers communicate with each other as it is essential, and we introduced how pod-to-pod communication works. Service is an abstraction to route the traffic to any of the pods underneath, if label selectors match. We learned how service works with pod by iptables magic. We got to know how packet routes from external to a pod and the DNAT, un-DAT tricks. We also learned new API objects such as *ingress*, which allow us to use the URL path to route to different services in the backend. In the end, another object `NetworkPolicy` was introduced. It provides a second layer of security, acting as a software firewall rule. With network policy, we can make certain pods communicate only with certain pods. For example, only data retrieval service can talk to the database container. All of these things make Kubernetes more flexible, secure, and powerful.

Until now, we've learned the basic concepts of Kubernetes. Next, we'll get a clearer understanding of what is happening inside your cluster by monitoring cluster metrics and analyzing applications and system logs for Kubernetes. Monitoring and logging tools are essential for every DevOps, which also play an extremely important role in dynamic clusters such as Kubernetes. So we'll get an insight into the activities of the cluster, such as scheduling, deployment, scaling, and service discovery. The next chapter will help you better understand the act of operating Kubernetes in the real world.

6
Monitoring and Logging

Monitoring and logging are a crucial part of a site's reliability. We've learned how to leverage various controllers to take care of our application, and about utilizing service together with Ingress to serve our web applications. Next, in this chapter, we'll learn how to keep track of our application by means of the following topics:

- Getting status snapshot of a container
- Monitoring in Kubernetes
- Converging metrics from Kubernetes by Prometheus
- Concepts of logging in Kubernetes
- Logging with Fluentd and Elasticsearch

Inspecting a container

Whenever our application behaves abnormally, we will definitely want to know what happened, using all means, such as checking logs, resource usage, processes watchdog, or even getting into the running host directly to dig problems out. In Kubernetes, we have `kubectl get` and `kubectl describe` that can query deployment states, which will help us determine if an application has crashed or works as desired.

Further, if we want to know what is going on from the outputs of an application, we also have `kubectl logs` that redirects a container's `stdout` to our Terminal. For CPU and memory usage stats, there's also a top-like command we can employ, `kubectl top`. `kubectl top node`, which gives an overview of the resource usages of nodes, and `kubectl top pod <POD_NAME>` which displays per-pod usage:

```
# kubectl top node
NAME           CPU(cores)    CPU%        MEMORY(bytes)    MEMORY%
node-1         42m           4%          273Mi            12%
node-2         152m          15%         1283Mi           75%
# kubectl top pod mypod-name-2587489005-xq72v
NAME                                  CPU(cores)    MEMORY(bytes)
mypod-name-2587489005-xq72v    0m                0Mi
```

 To use `kubectl top`, you'll need Heapster deployed in your cluster. We'll discuss this later in the chapter.

What if we leave something such as logs inside a container and they are not sent out anywhere? We know there's a `docker exec` execute command inside a running container, but it's unlikely that we have access to nodes every time. Fortunately, `kubectl` allows us to do the same thing with the `kubectl exec` command. Its usage is similar to the Docker one. For example, we can run a shell inside the container in a pod like this:

```
$ kubectl exec -it mypod-name-2587489005-xq72v /bin/sh
/ #
/ # hostname
mypod-name-2587489005-xq72v
```

It's pretty much the same as logging onto a host by SSH, and it enables us to troubleshoot with tools we are familiar with, as we've done in non-container worlds.

Kubernetes dashboard

In addition to the command-line utility, there is a dashboard that aggregates almost every information we have just discussed on a decent web-UI:

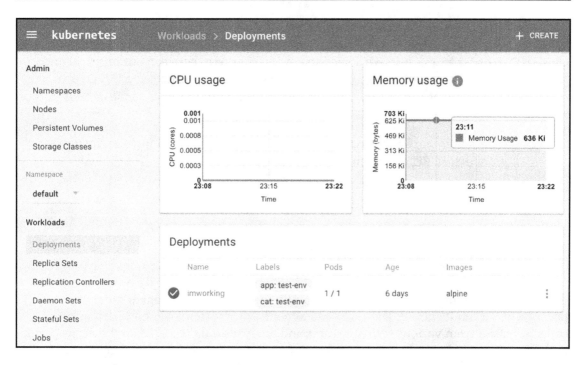

It's in fact a general purpose graphical user interface of a Kubernetes cluster, as it also allows us to create, edit, and delete resources. Deploying it is quite easy; all we need to do is apply a template:

```
$ kubectl create -f \
https://raw.githubusercontent.com/kubernetes/dashboard/v1.6.3/src/deploy/
kubernetes-dashboard.yaml
```

This template is for the Kubernetes cluster with **RBAC (role-based access control)** enabled. Check the dashboard's project repository (`https://github.com/kubernetes/dashboard`) if you need other deployment options. Regarding RBAC, we'll talk about this in `Chapter 8`, *Cluster Administration*. Many managed Kubernetes services, such as Google Container Engine, pre-deployed the dashboard in the cluster so that we don't need to install it on our own. To determine whether the dashboard exists in our cluster or not, use `kubectl cluster-info`.

We'll see **kubernetes-dashboard is running at ...** if it's installed. The service for the dashboard deployed with the default template or provisioned by cloud providers is usually ClusterIP. In order to access it, we'll need to establish a proxy between our terminal and Kubernetes' API server with `kubectl proxy`. Once the proxy is up, we are then able to access the dashboard at `http://localhost:8001/ui`. The port `8001` is the default port of `kubectl proxy`.

 As with `kubectl top`, you'll need Heapster deployed in your cluster to see the CPU and memory stats.

Monitoring in Kubernetes

Since we now know how to examine our applications in Kubernetes, it's quite natural that we should have a mechanism to do so constantly to detect any incident at the first occurrence. To put it another way, we need a monitoring system. A monitoring system collects metrics from various sources, stores and analyzes data received, and then responds to exceptions. In a classical setup of application monitoring, we would gather metrics from, at the very least, three different layers of our infrastructure to ensure our service's availability as well as quality.

Application

The data we're concerned with at this level involves the internal states of an application, which can help us determine what's going on inside our service. For example, the following screenshot is from Elasticsearch Marvel (`https://www.elastic.co/guide/en/marvel/current/introduction.html`), called **Monitoring** from version 5 onward), which is a monitoring solution for an Elasticsearch cluster. It brings together the information about our cluster, particularly Elasticsearch specific metrics:

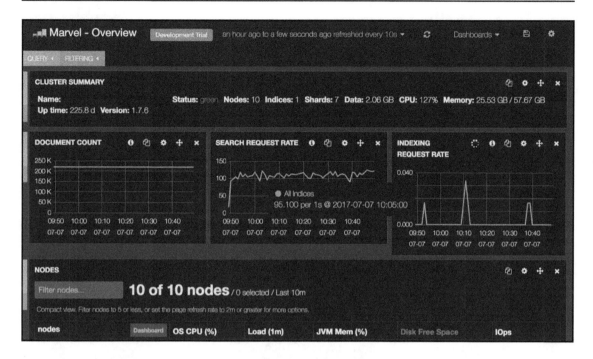

In addition, we would leverage profiling tools in conjunction with tracing tools to instrument our program, which augments dimensions that enables us to inspect our service in a finer granularity. Especially nowadays, an application might be composed of dozens of services in a distributed way. Without utilizing tracing tools, such as OpenTracing (http://opentracing.io) implementations, identifying performance culprits can be extremely difficult.

Host

Collecting tasks at the host level is usually performed by agents provided by the monitoring framework. The agent extracts and sends out comprehensive metrics about a host such as loads, disks, connections, or stats of processes that assist in determining a host's health.

External resources

Aside from the aforementioned two components, we also need to check dependent components' statuses. For instance, say we have an application that consumes a queue and executes corresponding tasks; we should also take care about the metrics, such as the queue length and the consuming rate. If the consuming rate is low and the queue length keeps growing, our application is supposedly hitting trouble.

These principles also apply to containers on Kubernetes, as running a container on a host is almost identical to running a process. Nonetheless, due to the fact that there is a subtle distinction between the way containers on Kubernetes and on traditional hosts utilize resources, we still need to take the differences into consideration when employing a monitoring strategy. For instance, containers of an application on Kubernetes would spread across multiple hosts, and also would not always be on the same hosts. It would be grueling to produce a consistent recording of one application if we are still adopting the host-centric monitoring approach. Therefore, rather than observing resource usages at the host level only, we should pile a container layer to our monitoring stack. Moreover, since Kubernetes is, in reality, the infrastructure to our applications, we absolutely should take it into account as well.

Container

As mentioned, metrics collected at the container level and what we get at the host level are pretty much the same thing, particularly the usage of system resources. Notwithstanding the seeming redundancy, it's the very key which facilitates us to resolve difficulties on monitoring moving containers. The idea is quite simple: what we need to do is attach logical information to metrics, such as pod labels or their controller name. In this way, metrics coming out from containers across distinct hosts could be meaningfully grouped. Consider the following diagram; say we want to know how many bytes transmitted (**tx**) on **App 2**, we could sum up **tx** metrics over the **App 2** label and it yields **20 MB:**

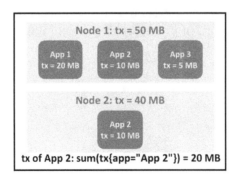

Another difference is that metrics on CPU throttling are reported at container level only. If performance issues are encountered at a certain application but the CPU resource on the host is spare, we can check if it's throttled with the associated metrics.

Kubernetes

Kubernetes is responsible for managing, scheduling, and orchestrating our applications. Accordingly, once an application has crashed, Kubernetes is certainly one of the first places we would want to look. In particular, when the crash happens after rolling out a new deployment, the state of associated objects would be reflected instantly on Kubernetes.

To sum up, components that should be monitored are illustrated in the following diagram:

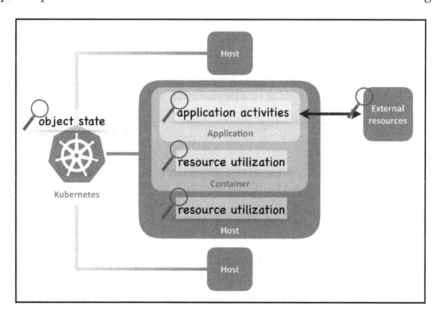

Getting monitoring essentials for Kubernetes

For every layer of the monitoring stack, we can always find a counterpart collector. For instance, at the application level, we can dump metrics manually; at the host level, we would install a metrics collector on every box; as for Kubernetes, there are APIs for exporting the metrics that we are interested in, and, at the very least, we have `kubectl` at hand.

When it comes to the container level collector, what options do we have? Perhaps installing the host metrics collector inside the image of our application does the job, but we'll soon realize that it could make our container way too clumsy in terms of size as well as resource utilizations. Fortunately, there's already a solution for such needs, namely cAdvisor (https://github.com/google/cadvisor), the answer to the container level metrics collector. Briefly speaking, cAdvisor aggregates the resource usages and performance statistics of every running container on a machine. Notice that the deployment of cAdvisor is one per host instead of one per container, which is more reasonable for containerized applications. In Kubernetes, we don't even care about deploying cAdvisor, as it has already been embedded into kubelet.

cAdvisor is accessible via port 4194 on every node. Prior to Kubernetes 1.7, the data gathered by cAdvisor was able to be collected via the kubelet port (10250/10255) as well. To access cAdvisor, we can access the instance port 4194 or through kubectl proxy at http://localhost:8001/api/v1/nodes/<nodename>:4194/proxy/ or access http://<node-ip>:4194/ directly.

The following screenshot is from the cAdvisor Web UI. You will see a similar page once connected. For viewing the metrics that cAdvisor grabbed, visit the endpoint, /metrics.

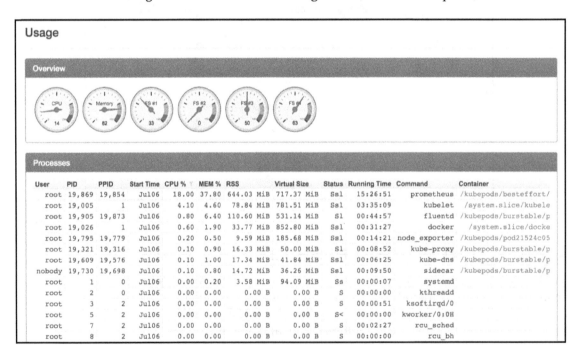

Another important component in the monitoring pipeline is Heapster
(`https://github.com/kubernetes/heapster`). It retrieves monitoring statistics from every
node, specifically kubelet on nodes processing, and writes to external sinks afterward. It
also exposes aggregated metrics via the REST API. The function of Heapster sounds rather
redundant with cAdvisor, but they play different roles in the monitoring pipeline in
practice. Heapster gathers cluster-wide statistics; cAdvisor is a host-wide component. That
is to say, Heapster empowers a Kubernetes cluster with the basic monitoring ability. The
following diagram illustrates how it interacts with other components in a cluster:

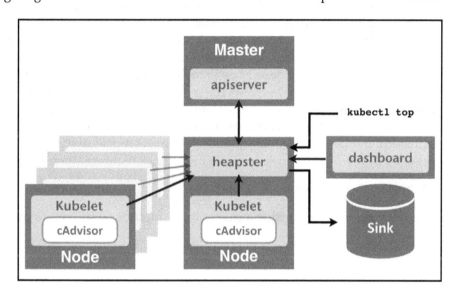

As a matter of fact, it's unnecessary to install Heapster if your monitoring framework offers
a similar tool that also scrapes metrics from kubelet. However, since it's a default
monitoring component in Kubernetes' ecosystem, many tools rely on it, such as `kubectl`
`top` and the Kubernetes dashboard mentioned earlier.

Before deploying Heapster, check if the monitoring tool you're using is supported as a
Heapster sink in this document:
`https://github.com/kubernetes/heapster/blob/master/docs/sink-configuration.md`.

If not, we can just have a standalone setup and make the dashboard and `kubectl top`
work by applying this template:

```
$ kubectl create -f \
https://raw.githubusercontent.com/kubernetes/heapster/master/deploy/kube-co
nfig/standalone/heapster-controller.yaml
```

Remember to apply this template if RBAC is enabled:

```
$ kubectl create -f \
https://raw.githubusercontent.com/kubernetes/heapster/master/deploy/kube-co
nfig/rbac/heapster-rbac.yaml
```

After Heapster is installed, the `kubectl top` command and the Kubernetes dashboard should display resource usages properly.

While cAdvisor and Heapster focus on physical metrics, we also want the logical states of objects being displayed on our monitoring dashboard. kube-state-metrics (`https://github.com/kubernetes/kube-state-metrics`) is the very piece that completes our monitoring stack. It watches Kubernetes masters and transforms the object statues we see from `kubectl get` or `kubectl describe` to metrics in Prometheus format (`https://prometheus.io/docs/instrumenting/exposition_formats/`). As long as the monitoring system supports this format, we can scrape the states into the metrics storage and be alerted on events such as unexplainable restart counts. To install kube-state-metrics, first download the templates inside the `kubernetes` folder under the project repository(`https://github.com/kubernetes/kube-state-metrics/tree/master/kubernetes`), and then apply them:

```
$ kubectl apply -f kubernetes
```

Afterwards, we can view the states inside a cluster in the metrics on its service endpoint:

```
http://kube-state-metrics.kube-system:8080/metrics
```

Hands-on monitoring

So far, we've learned lots of principles to fabricate an impervious monitoring system in Kubernetes toward a robust service, and it's time to implement a pragmatic one. Because the vast majority of Kubernetes components expose their instrumented metrics on a conventional path in Prometheus format, we are free to use any monitoring tool with which we are acquainted as long as the tool understands the format. In this section, we'll set up an example with an open-source project, Prometheus (`https://prometheus.io`), which is a platform-independent monitoring tool. Its popularity in Kubernetes' ecosystem is for not only its powerfulness but also for its being backed by the **Cloud Native Computing Foundation** (`https://www.cncf.io/`), who also sponsors the Kubernetes project.

Meeting Prometheus

The Prometheus framework comprises several components, as illustrated in the following diagram:

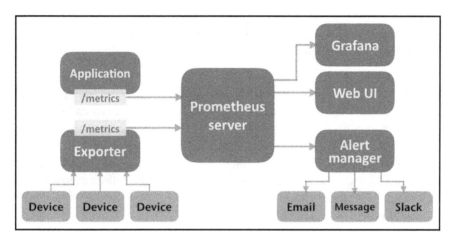

As with all other monitoring frameworks, Prometheus relies on agents scraping out statistics from the components of our system, and those agents are the exporters at the left of the diagram. Besides this, Prometheus adopts the pull model on metrics collecting, which is to say that it's not receiving metrics passively, but actively pulls data back from the metrics' endpoints on exporters. If an application exposes a metric's endpoint, Prometheus is able to scrape that data as well. The default storage backend is an embedded LevelDB, and can be switched to other remote storages such as InfluxDB or Graphite. Prometheus is also responsible for sending alerts according to pre-configured rules to **Alert manager**. **Alert manager** handles alarm sending tasks. It groups alarms received and dispatches them to tools that actually send messages, such as email, Slack, PagerDuty, and so on. In addition to alerts, we would also like to visualize collected metrics for getting a quick overview of our system, and Grafana is what comes in handy here.

Deploying Prometheus

The templates we've prepared for this chapter can be found here:
`https://github.com/DevOps-with-Kubernetes/examples/tree/master/chapter6`

Under **6-1_prometheus** are manifests for this section, including a Prometheus deployment, exporters, and related resources. They'll be settled at a dedicated namespace, `monitoring`, except components required to work in `kube-system` namespaces. Please review them carefully, and now let's create resources in the following order:

```
$ kubectl apply -f monitoring-ns.yml
$ kubectl apply -f prometheus/config/prom-config-default.yml
$ kubectl apply -f prometheus
```

Usages of resources are confined to a relatively low level at provided setups. If you'd like to use them in a more formal way, adjusting parameters according to actual requirements is recommended. After the Prometheus server is up, we can connect to its Web-UI at port `9090` by `kubectl port-forward`. We can use NodePort or Ingress to connect to the UI if modifying its service (`prometheus/prom-svc.yml`) accordingly. The first page we will see when entering the UI is Prometheus' expression browser, where we build queries and visualize metrics. Under the default settings, Prometheus will collect metrics from itself. All valid scraping targets can be found at path `/targets`. To speak to Prometheus, we have to gain some understanding of its language: **PromQL**.

Working with PromQL

PromQL has three data types: instant vector, range vector, and scalar. An instant vector is a time series of data sampled; a range vector is a set of time series containing data within a certain time range; a scalar is a numeric floating value. Metrics stored inside Prometheus are identified with a metric name and labels, and we can find the name of any collected metric with the drop-down list next to the **Execute** button on the expression browser. If we query Prometheus with metric names, say `http_requests_total`, we'll get lots of results as instant vectors match the name but with different labels. Likewise, we can also query a particular set of labels only with `{}` syntax. For example, the query `{code="400",method="get"}` means that we want any metric that has the label `code`, `method` equals to `400`, and `get` respectively. Combining names and labels in a query is also valid, such as `http_requests_total{code="400",method="get"}`. PromQL grants us the detective ability to inspect our applications or systems from all kinds of clues so long as related metrics are collected.

In addition to the basic queries just mentioned, there's so much more to PromQL, such as querying labels with regex and logical operators, joining and aggregating metrics with functions, and even performing operations between different metrics. For instance, the following expression gives us the total memory consumed by a `kube-dns` deployment in the `kube-system` namespace:

```
sum(container_memory_usage_bytes{namespace="kube-system", pod_name=~"kube-
dns-(\\d+)-.*"} ) / 1048576
```

More detailed documents can be found at Prometheus' official site (`https://prometheus.io/docs/querying/basics/`), and it certainly should help you to unleash the power of Prometheus.

Discovering targets in Kubernetes

Since Prometheus only pulls metrics from endpoints it knows, we have to explicitly tell it where we'd like to collect data from. Under the path `/config` is the page that lists current configured targets to pull. By default, there would be one job that collects the current metrics about Prometheus itself, and it's in the conventional scraping path, `/metrics`. We would see a very long text page if connecting to the endpoint:

```
$ kubectl exec -n monitoring prometheus-1496092314-jctr6 -- \
wget -qO - localhost:9090/metrics
# HELP go_gc_duration_seconds A summary of the GC invocation durations.
# TYPE go_gc_duration_seconds summary
go_gc_duration_seconds{quantile="0"} 2.4032e-05
go_gc_duration_seconds{quantile="0.25"} 3.7359e-05
go_gc_duration_seconds{quantile="0.5"} 4.1723e-05
...
```

This is just the Prometheus metrics format we've mentioned several times. Next time when we see any page like this, we will know it's a metrics endpoint.

The default job to scrape Prometheus is configured as a static target. However, with the fact that containers in Kubernetes are created and destroyed dynamically, it's really troublesome to find out the exact address of a container, let alone set it on Prometheus. In some cases, we may utilize service DNS as a static metrics target, but this still cannot solve all cases. Fortunately, Prometheus helps us overcome the problem with its ability to discover services inside Kubernetes.

To be more specific, it's able to query Kubernetes about the information of running services, and adds or deletes them to the target configuration accordingly. Four kinds of discovery mechanisms are currently supported:

- The **node** discovery mode creates one target per node, and the target port would be kubelet's port by default.
- The **service** discovery mode creates a target for every `service` object, and all defined ports in a service would become a scraping target.
- The **pod** discovery mode works in a similar way to the service discovery role, that is, it creates targets per pod and for each pod it exposes all the defined container ports. If there is no port defined in a pod's template, it would still create a scraping target with its address only.
- The **endpoints** mode discovers `endpoint` objects created by a service. For example, if a service is backed by three pods with two ports each, then we'll have six scraping targets. In addition, for a pod, not only ports that expose to a service but also other declared container ports would be discovered.

The following diagram illustrates four discovery mechanisms: the left ones are the resources in Kubernetes, and those in the right list are targets created in Prometheus:

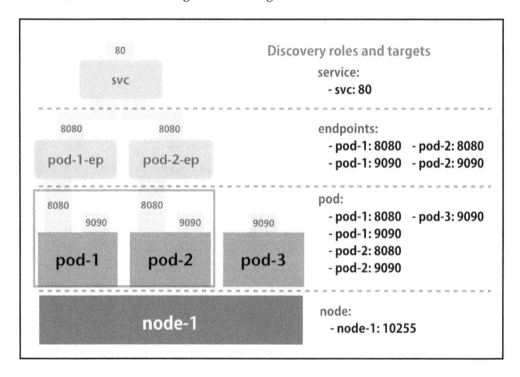

Generally speaking, not all exposed ports are served as a metrics endpoint, so we certainly don't want Prometheus to grab everything in our cluster but collect marked resources only. To achieve this, Prometheus utilizes annotations on resource manifests to distinguish which targets are to be grabbed. The annotation format is as follows:

- **On pod**: If a pod is created by a pod controller, remember to set Prometheus annotations in the pod spec rather than in the pod controller:
  - `prometheus.io/scrape`: `true` indicates that this pod should be pulled.
  - `prometheus.io/path`: Set this annotation to the path that exposes metrics; it only needs to be set if the target pod is using a path other than `/metrics`.
  - `prometheus.io/port`: If the defined port is different from the actual metrics port, override it with this annotation.

- **On service**: Since endpoints are mostly not created manually, endpoint discovery uses the annotations inherited from a service. That is to say, annotations on services effect service and endpoint discovery modes simultaneously. As such, we'd use `prometheus.io/scrape`: `'true'` to denote endpoints created by a service that are to be scraped, and use `prometheus.io/probe`: `'true'` to tag a service with metrics. Moreover, `prometheus.io/scheme` designates whether `http` or `https` is used. Other than that, the path and port annotations also work here.

The following template snippet indicates Prometheus' endpoint discovery role, but the service discovery role to create targets on pods is selected at: `9100/prom`.

```
apiVersion: v1
kind: Service
metadata:
  annotations:
    prometheus.io/scrape: 'true'
    prometheus.io/path: '/prom'
...
spec:
  ports:
 - port: 9100
```

The template `prom-config-k8s.yml` under our example repository contains the configuration to discover Kubernetes resources for Prometheus. Apply it with:

```
$ kubectl apply -f prometheus/config/prom-config-k8s.yml
```

Because it's a ConfigMap, it takes seconds to become consistent. Afterwards, reload Prometheus by sending a `SIGHUP` to the process:

```
$ kubectl exec -n monitoring ${PROM_POD_NAME} -- kill -1 1
```

The provided template is based on this example from Prometheus' official repository; you can find out more usages here:

`https://github.com/prometheus/prometheus/blob/master/documentation/examples/prometheus-kubernetes.yml`

Also, the document page describes in detail how the Prometheus configuration works:

`https://prometheus.io/docs/operating/configuration/`

Gathering data from Kubernetes

The steps for implementing the five monitoring layers discussed earlier in Prometheus are quite clear now: installing exporters, annotating them with appropriate tags, and then collecting them on auto-discovered endpoints.

The host layer monitoring in Prometheus is done by the node exporter (`https://github.com/prometheus/node_exporter`). Its Kubernetes manifest can be found under the examples for this chapter, and it contains one DaemonSet with a scrape annotation. Install it with:

```
$ kubectl apply -f exporters/prom-node-exporter.yml
```

Its corresponding configuration will be created by a pod discovery role.

The container layer collector should be cAdvisor, and it has already been installed in kubelet. Consequently, discovering it with the node mode is the only thing what we need to do.

Kubernetes monitoring is done by kube-state-metrics, which was also introduced previously. One even better thing is that it comes with Prometheus annotations, and this means that we don't need to do anything additional to configure it.

Up to this point, we've already set up a strong monitoring stack based on Prometheus. With respect to the application and external resources monitoring, there are extensive exporters in the Prometheus ecosystem to support monitoring various components inside our system. For instance, if we need statistics of our MySQL database, we could just install MySQL Server Exporter (`https://github.com/prometheus/mysqld_exporter`), which offers comprehensive and useful metrics.

In addition to those metrics already described, there are some other useful metrics from Kubernetes components that play a significant part in a variety of aspects:

- **Kubernetes API server**: The API server exposes its state at `/metrics`, and this target is enabled by default.
- **kube-controller-manager**: This component exposes metrics on port `10252`, but it's invisible on some managed Kubernetes services such as **Google Container Engine (GKE)**. If you're on a self-hosted cluster, applying `"kubernetes/self/kube-controller-manager-metrics-svc.yml"` creates endpoints for Prometheus.
- **kube-scheduler**: It uses port `10251`, and it's not visible on clusters by GKE as well. `"kubernetes/self/kube-scheduler-metrics-svc.yml"` is the template for creating a target to Prometheus.
- **kube-dns**: There are two containers in a kube-dns pod, `dnsmasq` and `sky-dns`, and their metrics ports are `10054` and `10055` respectively. The corresponding template is `kubernetes/self/ kube-dns-metrics-svc.yml`.
- **etcd**: The etcd cluster also has a Prometheus metrics endpoint on port `4001`. If your etcd cluster is self-hosted and managed by Kubernetes, you can take `"kubernetes/self/etcd-server.yml"` as a reference.
- **Nginx ingress controller**: The nginx controller publishes metrics at port `10254`. But the metrics contain only limited information. To get data such as connection counts by host or by path, you'll need to activate the `vts` module in the controller to enhance the metrics collected.

Seeing metrics with Grafana

The expression browser has a built-in graph panel that enables us to see the visualized metrics, but it's not designed to serve as a visualization dashboard for daily routines. Grafana is the best option for Prometheus. We've discussed how to set up Grafana in `Chapter 4`, *Working with Storage and Resources*, and we also provide templates in the repository for this chapter; both options do the job.

To see Prometheus metrics in Grafana, we have to add a data source first. The following configurations are required to connect to our Prometheus server:

- Type: "Prometheus"
- Url: `http://prometheus-svc.monitoring:9090`
- Access: proxy

Once it's connected, we can import a dashboard to see something in action. On Grafana's sharing page (`https://grafana.com/dashboards?dataSource=prometheus`) are rich off-the-shelf dashboards. The following screenshot is from the dashboard `#1621`:

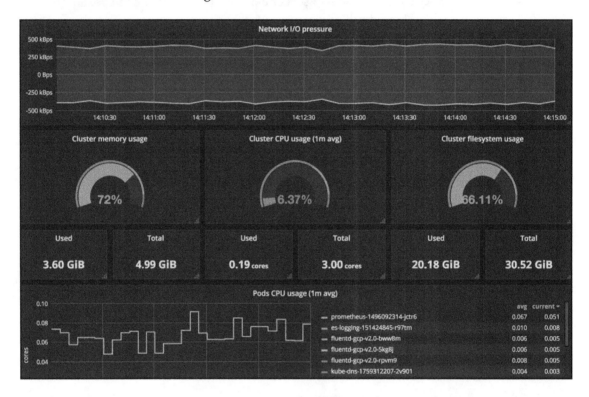

Because the graphs are drawn by data from Prometheus, we are capable of plotting any data with which we are concerned as long as we master PromQL.

Logging events

Monitoring with quantitative time series of a system status enables us to briskly dig out which components in our system failed, but it's still inadequate to diagnose with the root cause under syndromes. As a result, a logging system that gathers, persists, and searches logs is certainly helpful for uncovering the reason why something went wrong by means of correlating events with the anomalies detected.

In general, there are two main components in a logging system: the logging agent and the logging backend. The former is an abstract layer to a program. It gathers, transforms, and dispatches logs to the logging backend. A logging backend warehouses all logs received. As with monitoring, the most challenging part of building a logging system for Kubernetes is ascertaining how to gather logs from containers to a centralized logging backend. Typically, there are three ways to send out logs to a program:

- Dumping everything to `stdout/stderr`
- Writing `log` files
- Sending logs to a logging agent or logging the backend directly; programs in Kubernetes are also able to emit logs in the same manner so long as we understand how log streams flow in Kubernetes

Patterns of aggregating logs

For programs that log to a logging agent or backend directly, whether they are inside Kubernetes or not doesn't matter on the whole, as they technically don't output logs through Kubernetes. As for other cases, we'd use the following two patterns to centralize logs.

Collecting logs with a logging agent per node

We know messages we retrieved via `kubectl logs` are streams redirected from `stdout/stderr` of a container, but it's obviously not a good idea to collect logs with `kubectl logs`. Actually, `kubectl logs` gets logs from kubelet, and kubelet aggregates logs to the host path, `/var/log/containers/`, from the container engine underneath.

Therefore, setting up logging agents on every node and configuring them to tail and forward `log` files under the path are just what we need for converging standard streams of running containers, as shown in the following diagram:

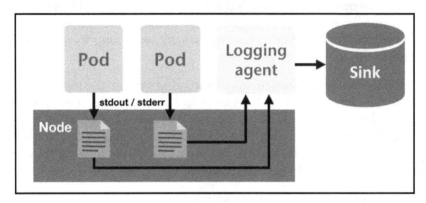

In practice, we'd also configure a logging agent to tail logs from the system and Kubernetes, components under `/var/log` on masters and nodes such as:

- `kube-proxy.log`
- `kube-apiserver.log`
- `kube-scheduler.log`
- `kube-controller-manager.log`
- `etcd.log`

Aside from `stdout/stderr`, if logs of an application are stored as files in the container and persisted via the `hostPath` volume, a node logging agent is capable of passing them to a node likewise. However, for each exported `log` file, we have to customize their corresponding configurations in the logging agent so that they can be dispatched correctly. Moreover, we also need to name `log` files properly to prevent any collision and take care of log rotation on our own, which makes it an unscalable and unmanageable logging mechanism.

Running a sidecar container to forward logs

Sometimes it's just difficult to modify our application to write logs to standard streams rather than `log` files, and we wouldn't want to face the troubles brought about by logging to `hostPath` volumes. In such a situation, we could run a Sidecar container to deal with logging within only one pod. In other words, each application pod would have two containers sharing the same `emptyDir` volume so that the Sidecar container can follow logs from the application container and send them outside their pod, as shown in the following diagram:

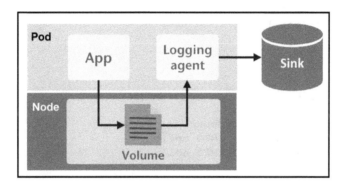

Although we don't need to worry about management of `log` files anymore, chores such as configuring logging agents for each pod and attaching metadata from Kubernetes to log entries still takes extra effort. Another choice is leveraging the Sidecar container to outputting logs to standard streams instead of running a dedicated logging agent like the following pod; the application container unremittingly writes messages to `/var/log/myapp.log`, and the Sidecar tails `myapp.log` in the shared volume.

```
---6-2_logging-sidecar.yml---
apiVersion: v1
kind: Pod
metadata:
  name: myapp
spec:
  containers:
  - image: busybox
    name: application
    args:
    - /bin/sh
    - -c
    - >
      while true; do
        echo "$(date) INFO hello" >> /var/log/myapp.log ;
        sleep 1;
```

```
        done
    volumeMounts:
    - name: log
      mountPath: /var/log
  - name: sidecar
    image: busybox
    args:
     - /bin/sh
     - -c
     - tail -fn+1 /var/log/myapp.log
    volumeMounts:
    - name: log
      mountPath: /var/log
  volumes:
  - name: log
emptyDir: {}
```

Now we can see the written log with `kubectl logs`:

```
$ kubectl logs -f myapp -c sidecar
Tue Jul 25 14:51:33 UTC 2017 INFO hello
Tue Jul 25 14:51:34 UTC 2017 INFO hello
...
```

Ingesting Kubernetes events

The event messages we saw at the output of `kubectl describe` contain valuable information and complement the metrics gathered by kube-state-metrics, which allows us to know what exactly happened to our pods or nodes. Consequently, it should be part of our logging essentials together with system and application logs. In order to achieve this, we'll need something to watch Kubernetes API servers and aggregate events into a logging sink. And there is eventer that does what we need to events.

Eventer is part of Heapster, and it currently supports Elasticsearch, InfluxDB, Riemann, and Google Cloud Logging as its sink. Eventer can also output to `stdout` directly in case the logging system we're using is not supported.

Deployment of eventer is similar to deploying Heapster, except for the container startup commands, as they are packed in the same image. The flags and options for each sink type can be found here:
(https://github.com/kubernetes/heapster/blob/master/docs/sink-configuration.md).

Example templates we provided for this chapter also include eventer, and it's configured to work with Elasticsearch. We'll describe it in the next section.

Logging with Fluentd and Elasticsearch

Thus far we've discussed various conditions on the logging we may encounter in the real world, and it's time to roll up our sleeves to fabricate a logging system with what we have learned.

The architecture of a logging system and a monitoring system are pretty much the same in some ways--collectors, storages, and the user-interface. The corresponding components we're going to set up are Fluentd/eventer, Elasticsearch, and Kibana, respectively. Templates for this section can be found under `6-3_efk`, and they'd be deployed to the namespace `monitoring` from the previous part.

Elasticsearch is a powerful text search and analysis engine, which makes it an ideal choice for persisting, processing, and analyzing logs from everything running in our cluster. The Elasticsearch template for this chapter uses a very simple setup to demonstrate the concept. If you'd like to deploy an Elasticsearch cluster for production use, leveraging the StatefulSet controller and tuning Elasticsearch with the proper configuration, as we discussed in `Chapter 4`, *Working with Storage and Resources*, is recommended. Let's deploy Elasticsearch with the following template (`https://github.com/DevOps-with-Kubernetes/examples/tree/master/chapter6/6-3_efk/`):

```
$ kubectl apply -f elasticsearch/es-config.yml
$ kubectl apply -f elasticsearch/es-logging.yml
```

Elasticsearch is ready if there's a response from `es-logging-svc:9200`.

The next step is setting up a node logging agent. As we'd run it on every node, we definitely want it as light as possible in terms of resource usages of a node, hence Fluentd (`www.fluentd.org`) is opted for. Fluentd features in lower memory footprints, which makes it a competent logging agent for our needs. Furthermore, since the logging requirement in the containerized environment is very focused, there is a sibling project, Fluent Bit (`fluentbit.io`), which aims to minimize the resource usages by trimming out functions that wouldn't be used for its target scenario. In our example, we would use the Fluentd image for Kubernetes (`https://github.com/fluent/fluentd-kubernetes-daemonset`) to conduct the first logging pattern we mentioned previously.

The image is already configured to forward container logs under `/var/log/containers` and logs of certain system components under `/var/log`. We are absolutely able to further customize its logging configuration if need be. Two templates are provided here: `fluentd-sa.yml` is the RBAC configuration for the Fluentd DaemonSet, `fluentd-ds.yml`:

```
$ kubectl apply -f fluentd/fluentd-sa.yml
$ kubectl apply -f fluentd/fluentd-ds.yml
```

Another must-have logging component is eventer. Here we prepared two templates for different conditions. If you're on a managed Kubernetes service where Heapster is already deployed, the template for a standalone eventer, `eventer-only.yml`, is used in this case. Otherwise, consider the template of running Heapster in combination with eventer in the same pod:

```
$ kubectl apply -f heapster-eventer/heapster-eventer.yml
or
$ kubectl apply -f heapster-eventer/eventer-only.yml
```

To see logs emitted to Elasticsearch, we can invoke the search API of Elasticsearch, but there's a better option, namely Kibana, a web interface that allows us to play with Elasticsearch. The template for Kibana is `elasticsearch/kibana-logging.yml` under `https://github.com/DevOps-with-Kubernetes/examples/tree/master/chapter6/6-3_efk/`.

```
$ kubectl apply -f elasticsearch/kibana-logging.yml
```

Kibana in our example is listening to port `5601`. After exposing the service out of your cluster and connecting to it with any browser, you can start to search logs from Kubernetes. The index name of the logs sent out by eventer is `heapster-*`, and it's `logstash-*` for logs forwarded by Fluentd. The following screenshot shows what a log entry looks like in Elasticsearch.

The entry is from our earlier example, myapp, and we can find that the entry is already tagged with handy metadata on Kubernetes.

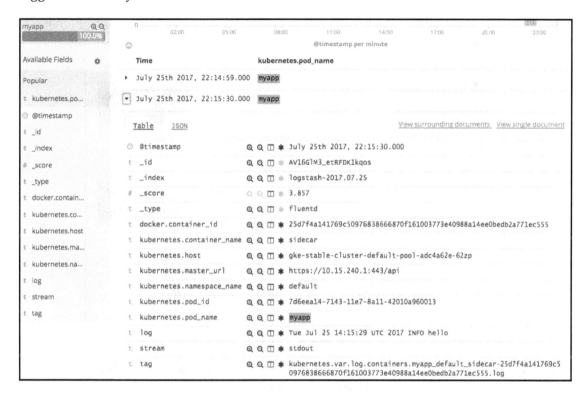

Extracting metrics from logs

The monitoring and logging system we built around our application on top of Kubernetes is shown in the following diagram:

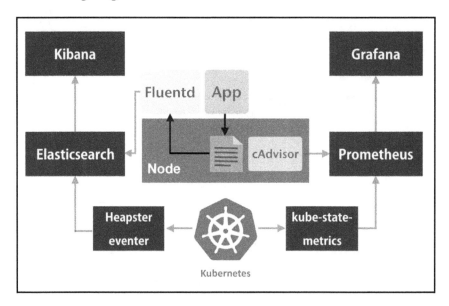

The logging part and the monitoring part look like two independent tracks, but the value of the logs is much more than a collection of short texts. They are structured data and emitted with timestamps as usual; as such, the idea to transform logs into time-series data is promising. However, although Prometheus is extremely good at processing time-series data, it cannot ingest texts without any transformation.

An access log entry from HTTPD looks like this:

```
10.1.8.10 - - [07/Jul/2017:16:47:12 0000] "GET /ping HTTP/1.1" 200 68.
```

It consists of the request IP address, time, method, handler, and so on. If we demarcate log segments by their meanings, counted sections can then be regarded as a metric sample like this: `"10.1.8.10": 1, "GET": 1, "/ping": 1, "200": 1`.

Tools such as mtail (`https://github.com/google/mtail`) and Grok Exporter (`https://github.com/fstab/grok_exporter`) count log entries and organize those numbers to metrics so that we can further process them in Prometheus.

Summary

At the start of this chapter, we described how to get the status of running containers quickly by means of built-in functions such as `kubectl`. Then we expanded the discussion to concepts and principles of monitoring, including why it is necessary to do monitoring, what to monitor, and how to monitor. Afterwards, we built a monitoring system with Prometheus as the core, and set up exporters to collecting metrics from Kubernetes. The fundamentals of Prometheus were also introduced so that we can leverage metrics to gain more understanding of our cluster as well as the applications running inside. On the logging part, we mentioned common patterns of logging and how to deal with them in Kubernetes, and deployed an EFK stack to converge logs. The system we built in this chapter facilitates the reliability of our service. Next, we are advancing to set up a pipeline to deliver our product continuously in Kubernetes.

7
Continuous Delivery

Topics we've discussed so far enable us to run our services in Kubernetes. With the monitoring system, we've gained more confidence in our service. The next thing we'd like to achieve to set our service on course is how to deliver our latest features as well as ameliorations to our service continuously in Kubernetes, and we'll learn it with the following topics in this chapter:

- Updating Kubernetes resources
- Setting up a delivery pipeline
- Techniques to improve the deployment process

Updating resources

The property of Continuous Delivery is as what we described in `Chapter 1`, *Introduction to DevOps*, a set of operations including the **Continuous Integration** (**CI**) and ensuing deployment tasks. The CI flow comprises elements like version control systems, buildings, and different levels of automated tests. Tools to implement CI functions are usually at the application layer which can be independent to underlying infrastructure, but when it comes to achieving deployment, understanding and dealing with infrastructure is inevitable since the deployment tasks are tightly bound to the platform that our application is running on. In the environment that software runs on physical or virtual machines, we'd utilize configuration management tools, orchestrators, and scripts to deploy our software. However, if we're running our service on an application platform like Heroku, or even in the Serverless pattern, designing the deployment pipeline would be a totally different story. All in all, the goal of deployment tasks is about making sure our software works properly in the right places. In Kubernetes, it's about how to rightly update resources, in particular, pods.

Triggering updates

In Chapter 3, *Getting Started with Kubernetes*, we've discussed the rolling update mechanism of pods of a Deployment. Let's recap what'd happen after the update process is triggered:

1. The Deployment creates a new ReplicaSet with 0 pod according to the updated manifest.
2. The new ReplicaSet is scaled up gradually while the previous ReplicaSet keeps shrinking.
3. The process ends after all the old pods are replaced.

Such a mechanism is done automatically by Kubernetes, and it exempts us from supervising the updating process. To trigger it, all we need to do is inform Kubernetes that the pod specification of a Deployment is updated, that is to say, modifying the manifest of one resource in Kubernetes. Suppose we have a Deployment my-app (see ex-deployment.yml under the example directory for this section), we can modify the manifest with the sub commands of kubectl as follows:

- kubectl patch: Patches a manifest of an object partially according to the input JSON parameter. If we'd like to update the image of my-app from alpine:3.5 to alpine:3.6, it'd be:

```
$ kubectl patch deployment my-app -p
'{"spec":{"template":{"spec":{"containers":[{"name":"app","image":"
alpine:3.6"}]}}}}'
```

- kubectl set: Makes changes to certain properties of an object. This is a shortcut to change some properties directly, image of a Deployment is one of the properties it supports:

```
$ kubectl set image deployment my-app app=alpine:3.6
```

- kubectl edit: Opens an editor and dumps the current manifest so that we can edit it interactively. The modified one would take effect immediately after being saved.

- `kubectl replace`: Replaces one manifest with another submitted template file. If a resource is not created yet or contains properties that can't be changed, it yields errors. For instance, there are two resources in our example template `ex-deployment.yml`, namely the Deployment `my-app` and its Service `my-app-svc`. Let's replace them with a new specification file:

```
$ kubectl replace -f ex-deployment.yml
deployment "my-app" replaced
The Service "my-app-svc" is invalid: spec.clusterIP: Invalid value:
"": field is immutable
$ echo $?
1
```

  After they are replaced, we'd see the error code would be `1` even though the result is expected, that is, updating the Deployment rather than the Service. Such behavior should be noticed especially when composing automation scripts for the CI/CD flow.

- `kubectl apply`: Applies the manifest file anyway. In other words, if a resource exists in Kubernetes, then it'd be updated, otherwise it'd be created. When `kubectl apply` is used to create resources, it's roughly equal to `kubectl create --save-config` in functionality. The applied specification file would be saved to the annotation field `kubectl.kubernetes.io/last-applied-configuration` accordingly, and we can manipulate it with sub commands `edit-last-applied`, `set-last-applied`, and `view-last-applied`. For example, we can view the template we've submitted previously, no matter what the actual content of `ex-deployment.yml` become with:

```
$ kubectl apply -f ex-deployment.yml view-last-applied
```

  The saved manifest information would exactly be the same as what we've sent, unlike the one we retrieve via `kubectl get -o yaml/json` which contains an object's live status, in addition to specifications.

Although in this section we only focus on manipulating a Deployment, but the commands here also work for updating all other Kubernetes resources like Service, Role, and so on.

Changes to `ConfigMap` and secret usually take seconds to propagate to pods.

The recommended way to interact with an Kubernetes' API server is by `kubectl`. If you're under a confined environment, there are also REST APIs for manipulating resources of Kubernetes. For example, the `kubectl patch` command we used before would become as follows:

```
$ curl -X PATCH -H 'Content-Type: application/strategic-merge-patch+json' --data
'{"spec":{"template":{"spec":{"containers":[{"name":"app","image":"alpine:3.6"}]}}}}'
'https://$KUBEAPI/apis/apps/v1beta1/namespaces/default/deployments/my-app'
```

Here the variable `$KUBEAPI` is the endpoint of the API server. See API references for more information: `https://kubernetes.io/docs/api-reference/v1.7/`.

Managing rollouts

Once the rollout process is triggered, Kubernetes would silently complete all tasks behind the backdrop. Let's try some hands-on experiments. Again, the rolling update process won't be triggered even if we've modified something with the commands mentioned earlier, unless the associated pod's specification is changed. The example we prepared is a simple script that would respond to any request with its hostname and the Alpine version it runs on. We first create the Deployment, and check its response in another Terminal constantly:

```
$ kubectl apply -f ex-deployment.yml
deployment "my-app" created
service "my-app-svc" created
$ kubectl proxy
Starting to serve on 127.0.0.1:8001
// switch to another terminal #2
$ while :; do curl
localhost:8001/api/v1/proxy/namespaces/default/services/my-app-svc:80/;
sleep 1;

done
my-app-3318684939-pwh41-v-3.5.2 is running...
my-app-3318684939-smd0t-v-3.5.2 is running...
...
```

Now we change its image to another version and see what the responses are:

```
$ kubectl set image deployment my-app app=alpine:3.6
deployment "my-app" image updated
// switch to terminal #2
my-app-99427026-7r5lr-v-3.6.2 is running...
my-app-3318684939-pwh41-v-3.5.2 is running...
...
```

Messages from version 3.5 and 3.6 are interleaved until the updating process ends. To immediately determine the status of updating processes from Kubernetes rather than polling the service endpoint, there's `kubectl rollout` for managing the rolling update process, including inspecting the progress of ongoing updates. Let's see the acting rollout with sub command `status`:

```
$ kubectl rollout status deployment my-app
Waiting for rollout to finish: 3 of 5 updated replicas are available...
Waiting for rollout to finish: 3 of 5 updated replicas are available...
Waiting for rollout to finish: 4 of 5 updated replicas are available...
Waiting for rollout to finish: 4 of 5 updated replicas are available...
deployment "my-app" successfully rolled out
```

At this moment, the output at Terminal #2 should be all from version 3.6. The sub command `history` allows us to review previous changes of the `deployment`:

```
$ kubectl rollout history deployment my-app
REVISION     CHANGE-CAUSE
1            <none>
2            <none>
```

However, the `CHANGE-CAUSE` field doesn't show any useful information that helps us to know the detail of the revision. To leverage it, add a flag `--record` after every command that leads to a change, such as what we've introduced earlier. Certainly, `kubectl create` also support the record flag.

Let's make some change to the Deployment, say, modifying the environment variable `DEMO` of pods of `my-app`. As it causes a change in the pod's specification, a rollout would start right away. This sort of behavior allows us to trigger an update without building a new image. For simplicity's sake, we use `patch` to modify the variable:

```
$ kubectl patch deployment my-app -p
'{"spec":{"template":{"spec":{"containers":[{"name":"app","env":[{"name":"D
EMO","value":"1"}]}]}}}}' --record
deployment "my-app" patched
$ kubectl rollout history deployment my-app
deployments "my-app"
```

```
REVISION        CHANGE-CAUSE
1               <none>
2               <none>
3               kubectl patch deployment my-app --
patch={"spec":{"template":{"spec":{"containers":
[{"name":"app","env":[{"name":"DEMO","value":"1"}]}]}}}} --record=true
```

The CHANGE-CAUSE of REVISION 3 notes the committed command clearly. Nonetheless, only the command would be recorded, which means any modification by edit/apply/replace wouldn't be marked down explicitly. If we'd like to get the manifest of former versions, we could retrieve the saved configuration as long as our changes are made with apply.

For all kinds of reasons, sometimes we want to roll back our application even if the rollout is successful to a certain extent. It can be achieved by the sub command undo:

```
$ kubectl rollout undo deployment my-app
deployment "my-app" rolled back
```

The whole process is basically identical to updating, that is, applying the previous manifest, and performing a rolling update. Also, we can utilize the flag --to-revision=<REVISION#> to rollback to a specific version, but only retained revisions are able to be rolled back. Kubernetes determines how many revisions it would keep according to the revisionHistoryLimit parameter in Deployment objects.

The progress of an update is controlled by kubectl rollout pause and kubectl rollout resume. As their names indicate, they should be used in pairs. The pause of a Deployment implicates not only stopping of an ongoing rollout, but also freezing any rolling updates even if the specification is modified unless it's resumed.

Updating DaemonSet and StatefulSet

Kubernetes supports various ways to orchestrate pods for different kinds of workloads. In addition to Deployments, there are DaemonSet and StatefulSet for long-running, non-batch workloads. As pods they spawned have more constraint than Deployments, we should know caveats on handling their updates

DaemonSet

DaemonSet is a controller designed for system daemons as its name suggests. Consequently, a DaemonSet launches and maintains exactly one pod per node, this is to say, the total number of pods by a DaemonSet is adhered to a number of nodes in a cluster. Due to such limitations, updating a DaemonSet is not as straightforward as updating a Deployment. For instance, Deployment has a maxSurge parameter (.spec.strategy.rollingUpdate.maxSurge) that controls how many redundant pods over desired numbers can be created during updates. But we can't employ the same strategy for the pod as a DaemonSet usually occupies host's resources like ports. It could result in errors if we have two or more system pods simultaneously on a node. As such, the update is in the form that a new pod is created after the old pod is terminated on a host.

Kubernetes implements two update strategies for DaemonSet, namely OnDelete and rollingUpdate. An example demonstrates how to write a template of DaemonSet is at 7-1_updates/ex-daemonset.yml. The update strategy is set at path .spec.updateStrategy.type, and its default is OnDelete in Kubernetes 1.7, and it becomes rollingUpdate since Kubernetes 1.8:

- OnDelete: Pods are only updated after they are deleted manually.
- rollingUpdate: It actually works like OnDelete but the deletion of pods is performed by Kubernetes automatically. There is one optional parameter .spec.updateStrategy.rollingUpdate.maxUnavailable, which is akin to the one in Deployment. Its default value is 1, which means Kubernetes replaces one pod at a time node by node.

The trigger of the rolling update process is identical to a Deployment's. Moreover, we can also utilize kubectl rollout to manage rollouts of our DaemonSet. But pause and resume are not supported.

 Rolling updates for DaemonSet are only available at Kubernetes 1.6 and onward.

StatefulSet

The updating of `StatefulSet` and `DaemonSet` are pretty much the same -- they don't create redundant pods during an update, and their update strategies also behave in a similar way. There is also a template file at `7-1_updates/ex-statefulset.yml` for practice. The option of update strategy is set at path `.spec.updateStrategy.type`:

- `OnDelete`: Pods are only updated after they are manually deleted.
- `rollingUpdate`: Like every rolling update, Kubernetes deletes and creates pods in a controlled fashion. But Kubernetes knows the order matters in `StatefulSet`, so it would replace pods in reverse ordinal. Say we have three pods in a `StatefulSet`, and they are `my-ss-0`, `my-ss-1`, `my-ss-2` respectively. The update order is then starting from `my-ss-2` to `my-ss-0`. The deletion process does not respect the pod management policy, that is to say, even if we set the pod management policies to `Parallel`, the updating would still be performed one by one.

  The only parameter for type `rollingUpdate` is partition (`.spec.updateStrategy.rollingUpdate.partition`). If it's specified, any pod with its ordinal less than the partition number would keep its current version and wouldn't be updated. For instance, if we set it to 1 in a `StatefulSet` with 3 pods, only pod-1 and pod-2 would be updated after a rollout. This parameter allows us to control the progress at certain degrees and it's particularly handy for scenarios such as waiting for data synchronization, testing the release with a canary, or maybe we just want to stage an update.

 Pod management policies and rolling updates are two features implemented in Kubernetes 1.7 and later.

Building a delivery pipeline

Implementing a continuous delivery pipeline for containerized applications is quite simple. Let's remember what we have learnt about Docker and Kubernetes so far and organize them into the CD pipeline. Suppose we've done our code, Dockerfile, and corresponding Kubernetes templates. To deploy them to our cluster, we'd go through the following steps:

1. `docker build`: Produces an executable immutable artifact.
2. `docker run`: Verifies if the build works with some simple test.

3. `docker tag`: Tags the build with meaningful versions if it's good.
4. `docker push`: Moves the build to the artifacts repository for distribution.
5. `kubectl apply`: Deploys the build to a desired environment.
6. `kubectl rollout status`: tracks the progress of deployment tasks.

That's all for a simple but viable delivery pipeline.

Choosing tools

To make the pipeline ship builds continuously, we need at least three kinds of tools, namely version control systems, build servers, and a repository for storing container artifacts. In this section, we will set a reference CD pipeline based on the SaaS tools we've introduced in previous chapters. They are *GitHub* (`https://github.com`), *Travis CI* (`https://travis-ci.org`), and *Docker Hub* (`https://hub.docker.com`), all of them are free to open source projects. There are numerous alternatives for each tool we used here, like GitLab for VCS, or hosting a Jenkins for CI. The following diagram is our CD flow based on the three services earlier:

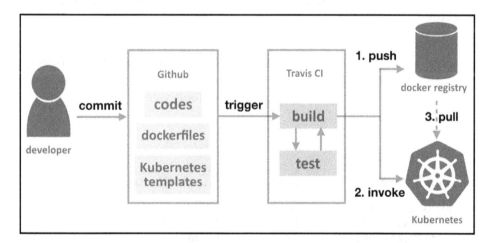

The workflow begins from committing codes into a repository on GitHub, and the commit would invoke a build job on Travis CI. Our Docker image is built at this stage. Meanwhile, we often run different levels of tests on the CI server to ensure that the quality of build is solid. Further, as running an application stack by Docker Compose or Kubernetes is easier than ever, we are capable of running tests involving many components in a build job. Afterwards, the verified image is tagged with identifiers and pushed to the public Docker Registry service, Docker Hub.

No blocks in our pipeline are dedicated to deployment tasks. Instead, we rely on Travis CI to deploy our builds. As a matter of fact, the deployment task is merely applying Kubernetes templates on certain builds after the image is pushed. Finally, the delivery is finished after the rolling update process by Kubernetes ends.

Steps explained

Our example, `my-app` is a web service that echoes `OK` constantly, and the code as well as the files for deployment are committed in our repository over in GitHub here: (`https://github.com/DevOps-with-Kubernetes/my-app`).

Before configuring our builds on Travis CI, let's create an image repository at Docker Hub first for later use. After signing in to Docker Hub, press the huge **Create Repository** at top-right, and then follow the steps on screen to create one. Image registry of `my-app` for pushing and pulling is at `devopswithkubernetes/my-app` (`https://hub.docker.com/r/devopswithkubernetes/my-app/`).

Connecting Travis CI with a GitHub repository is quite simple, all we need to do is authorize Travis CI to access our GitHub repositories, and enable Travis CI to build the repository at the profile page (`https://travis-ci.org/profile`).

The definition of a job in Travis CI is configured in a file `.travis.yml` placed under the same repository. It's a YAML format template consisting of blocks of shell scripts that tell what Travis CI should do during a build. Explanations on blocks of our `.travis.yml` (`https://github.com/DevOps-with-Kubernetes/my-app/blob/master/.travis.yml`) are the following:

env

This section defines environment variables that are visible throughout a build:

```
DOCKER_REPO=devopswithkubernetes/my-app
BUILD_IMAGE_PATH=${DOCKER_REPO}:b${TRAVIS_BUILD_NUMBER}
RELEASE_IMAGE_PATH=${DOCKER_REPO}:${TRAVIS_TAG}
RELEASE_TARGET_NAMESPACE=default
```

Here we set some variables that might be changed like the namespace and the docker registry path to where the built image is going. Besides, there're also metadata about a build passed from Travis CI in the form of environment variables, and they are documented here: `https://docs.travis-ci.com/user/environment-variables/#Default-Environment-Variables`. For example, `TRAVIS_BUILD_NUMBER` represents the number of the current build, and we use it as an identifier to distinguish our images across builds.

The other one source of environment variables is configured manually on Travis CI. Because the variables configured there would be hidden publicly, we stored some sensitive data such as credentials to Docker Hub and Kubernetes there:

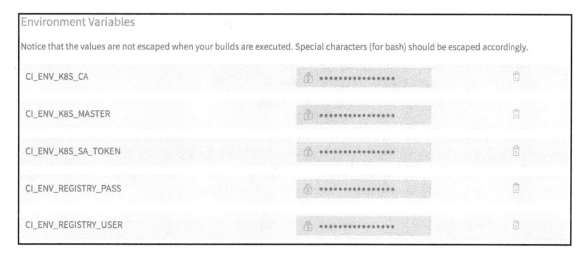

Every CI tool has own best practices to deal with secrets. For instance, some CI tools also allow us to save variables in the CI server, but they would still be printed in the building logs, so we're unlikely to save secrets in the CI server in such cases.

script

This section is where we run builds and tests:

```
docker build -t my-app .
docker run --rm --name app -dp 5000:5000 my-app
sleep 10
CODE=$(curl -IXGET -so /dev/null -w "%{http_code}" localhost:5000)
'[ ${CODE} -eq 200 ] && echo "Image is OK"'
docker stop app
```

As we're on Docker, the build is only one line of script. Our test is quite simple as well-- launching a container with the built image and making some requests against it to determine its correctness and integrity. Definitely, we can do everything such as adding unit tests, doing the multi-stage build, or running an automated integration test to better the resultant artifacts in this stage.

after_success

This block is executed only if the previous stage ends without any error. Once it comes here, we are good to publish our image:

```
docker login -u ${CI_ENV_REGISTRY_USER} -p "${CI_ENV_REGISTRY_PASS}"
docker tag my-app ${BUILD_IMAGE_PATH}
docker push ${BUILD_IMAGE_PATH}
if [[ ${TRAVIS_TAG} =~ ^rel.*$ ]]; then
  docker tag my-app ${RELEASE_IMAGE_PATH}
  docker push ${RELEASE_IMAGE_PATH}
fi
```

Our image tag trivially uses the build number on Travis CI, but using the hash of a commit, or version numbers to tag an image is common, too. However, using the default tag `latest` is strongly discouraged as it could result in version confusion such as running two different images but they have the same name. The last conditional block is publishing the image on certain branch tags, and it's not actually needed, for we just want to keep building and releasing on a separate track. Remember to authenticate to Docker Hub before pushing an image.

> Kubernetes decides whether the image should be pulled by the `imagePullPolicy`:
> https://kubernetes.io/docs/concepts/containers/images/#updating-images.

Because we set our project deploys to actual machines only on a release, a build may stop and be returned at that moment. Let's see the log of this build: https://travis-ci.org/DevOps-with-Kubernetes/my-app/builds/268053332. The log retains scripts that Travis CI executed and outputs from every line of the script:

```
 514    $ docker login -u ${CI_ENV_REGISTRY_USER} -p "${CI_ENV_REGISTRY_PASS}"     after_success.1   0.43s
 517    $ docker tag my-app ${BUILD_IMAGE_PATH}                                     after_success.2   0.03s
 519    $ docker push ${BUILD_IMAGE_PATH}                                           after_success.3   4.16s
 536    $ if [[ ${TRAVIS_TAG} =~ ^rel.*$ ]]; then                                   after_success.4   0.00s
 542    Skipping a deployment with the script provider because a custom condition was not met
 543    Skipping a deployment with the script provider because this is not a tagged commit
 544
        Done. Your build exited with 0.
                                                                                                      Top ▲
```

As we can see, our build is successful, so the image is then published here:

https://hub.docker.com/r/devopswithkubernetes/my-app/tags/.

The build refers to tag `b1`, and we can run it outside the CI server now:

```
$ docker run --name test -dp 5000:5000 devopswithkubernetes/my-app:b1
72f0ef501dc4c86786a81363e278973295a1f67555eeba102a8d25e488831813
$ curl localhost:5000
OK
```

deploy

Although we can achieve a fully automated pipeline from end to end, we'd often encounter situations to hold up deploying builds due to business reasons. As such, we tell Travis CI to run deployment scripts only when we release a new version.

To manipulate resources in our Kubernetes cluster from Travis CI, we'll need to grant Travis CI sufficient permissions. Our example uses a service account `cd-agent` under RBAC mode to create and update our deployments on behalf of us. Later chapters will have more descriptions on RBAC. The templates for creating the account and permissions are at: `https://github.com/DevOps-with-Kubernetes/examples/tree/master/chapter7/7-2_service-account-for-ci-tool`. The account is created under namespace `cd`, and it's authorized to create and modify most kinds of resources across namespaces.

Here we use a service account that is able to read and modify most resources across namespaces, including secrets of the whole cluster. Due to security concerns, its always encouraged to restrict permissions of a service account to resources the account actually used, or it could be a potential vulnerability.

Because Travis CI sits outside our cluster, we have to export credentials from Kubernetes so that we can configure our CI job to use them. Here we provide a simple script to help export those credentials. The script is at: `https://github.com/DevOps-with-Kubernetes/examples/blob/master/chapter7/get-sa-token.sh`.

```
$ ./get-sa-token.sh --namespace cd --account cd-agent
API endpoint:
https://35.184.53.170
ca.crt and sa.token exported
$ cat ca.crt | base64
LS0tLS1C...
$ cat sa.token
eyJhbGci...
```

Corresponding variables of exported API endpoint, `ca.crt`, and `sa.token` are `CI_ENV_K8S_MASTER`, `CI_ENV_K8S_CA`, and `CI_ENV_K8S_SA_TOKEN` respectively. The client certificate (`ca.crt`) is encoded to base64 for portability, and it will be decoded at our deployment script.

The deployment script (`https://github.com/DevOps-with-Kubernetes/my-app/blob/master/deployment/deploy.sh`) downloads `kubectl` first, and configures `kubectl` with environment variables accordingly. Afterwards, the image path of the current build is filled in the deployment template, and the templates are applied. Finally, after the rollout is finished, our deployment is done.

Let's see the entire flow in action.

As soon as we publish a release at GitHub:

`https://github.com/DevOps-with-Kubernetes/my-app/releases/tag/rel.0.3`

Travis CI starts to build our job right after that:

The built image is pushed onto Docker Hub after a while:

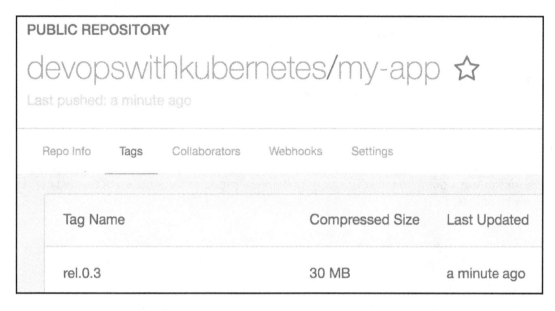

At this point, Travis CI should start to run deployment tasks, let's see the building log to know the status of our deployment:

```
https://travis-ci.org/DevOps-with-Kubernetes/my-app/builds/268107714
```

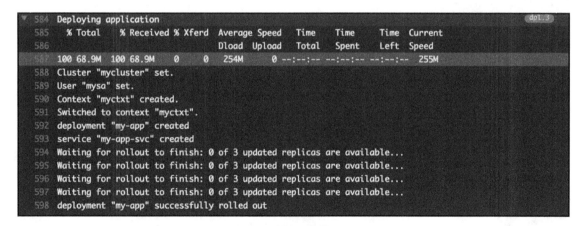

As we can see, our application has rolled out successfully, and it should start to welcome everyone with `OK`:

```
$ kubectl get deployment
NAME       DESIRED    CURRENT    UP-TO-DATE    AVAILABLE    AGE
my-app     3          3          3             3            30s
$ kubectl proxy &
$ curl localhost:8001/api/v1/namespaces/default/services/my-app-
svc:80/proxy/
OK
```

The pipeline we built and demonstrated in this section is a classical flow to deliver codes continuous in Kubernetes. Nonetheless, as the work style and cultures vary from team to team, designing a tailor-made continuously delivery pipeline for your team rewards efficiency boosts.

Gaining deeper understanding of pods

Although the birth and the death are merely a wink during a pod's lifetime, they are the most fragile point of a service. Common situations in the real world such as routing requests to an unready box, or brutally cutting all in-flight connections to a terminating machine, are all what we want to avoid. As a result, even Kubernetes takes care of most things for us, and we should know how to configure it correctly to gain more confident in deploying.

Starting a pod

By default, Kubernetes transfers a pod's state to **Running** as soon as a pod launches. If the pod is behind a service, the endpoint controller registers an endpoint to Kubernetes immediately. Later on kube-proxy observes the change of endpoints and add rules to iptables accordingly. Requests from the outside world now go to pods. Kubernetes makes the pod registration lightning fast, so the changes are that the request goes to pods prior to an application's readiness, especially on bulky software. On the other hand, if a pod fails while running, we should have an automatic way to remove it instantly.

 The `minReadySeconds` field of Deployment and other controllers doesn't postpone a pod from becoming ready. Instead, it delays a pod from becoming **available**, which is meaningful during a rollout process: a rollout is successful only when all pods are available.

Liveness and readiness probes

A probe is an indicator to a container's health. It judges the health through periodically performing a diagnostic action against a container via kubelet:

- **Liveness probe**: Indicates whether a container is alive or not. If a container fails on this probe, kubelet kills it and may restart it based on the `restartPolicy` of a pod.
- **Readiness probe**: Indicates whether a container is ready for incoming traffic. If a pod behind a service is not ready, its endpoint won't be created until the pod is ready.

 `retartPolicy` tells how Kubernetes treats a pod on failures or terminations. It has three modes: `Always`, `OnFailure`, or `Never`. Default is set to `Always`.

Three kinds of action handlers can be configured to perform against a container:

- `exec`: Executes a defined command inside the container. Considered to be successful if the exit code is `0`.
- `tcpSocket`: Tests a given port via TCP, successful if the port is opened.
- `httpGet`: Performs an `HTTP GET` to the IP address of target container. Headers in the request to be sent is customizable. This check is considered to be healthy if the status code satisfies: `400 > CODE >= 200`.

Additionally, there are five parameters to define a probe's behavior:

- `initialDelaySeconds`: How long kubelet should be waiting for before the first probing.
- `successThreshold`: A container is considered to be healthy when getting consecutive times of probing successes passed this threshold.
- `failureThreshold`: Same as preceding but defines the negative side.
- `timeoutSeconds`: The time limitation of a single probe action.
- `periodSeconds`: Intervals between probe actions.

The following code snippet demonstrates the usage of a readiness probe, the full template is here: https://github.com/DevOps-with-Kubernetes/examples/blob/master/chapter7/7-3_on_pods/probe.yml

```
    ...
        containers:
          - name: main
            image: devopswithkubernetes/my-app:b5
            readinessProbe:
              httpGet:
                path: /
                port: 5000
              periodSeconds: 5
              initialDelaySeconds: 10
              successThreshold: 2
              failureThreshold: 3
              timeoutSeconds: 1
            command:
    ...
```

How the probe behaves is illustrated in the following diagram:

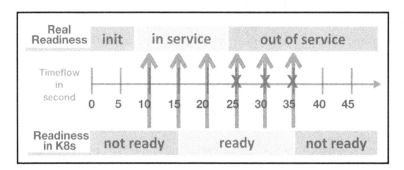

The upper timeline is a pod's real readiness, and another line below is its readiness from Kubernetes' view. The first probing executes 10 seconds after the pod is created, and the pod is regarded as ready after 2 probing successes. A few seconds later, the pod goes out of service due to an unknown reason, and it becomes unready after the next three failures. Try to deploy the preceding example and observe its output:

```
...
Pod is created at 1505315576
starting server at 1505315583.436334
1505315586.443435 - GET / HTTP/1.1
1505315591.443195 - GET / HTTP/1.1
1505315595.869020 - GET /from-tester
1505315596.443414 - GET / HTTP/1.1
```

```
1505315599.871162 - GET /from-tester
stopping server at 1505315599.964793
1505315601 readiness test fail#1
1505315606 readiness test fail#2
1505315611 readiness test fail#3
...
```

In our example file, there is another pod `tester` which is constantly making requests to our service, and the log entries `/from-tester` in our service is caused by the tester thereof. From tester's activity logs, we can observe that the traffic from the `tester` is stopped after our service becomes unready:

```
$ kubectl logs tester
1505315577 - nc: timed out
1505315583 - nc: timed out
1505315589 - nc: timed out
1505315595 - OK
1505315599 - OK
1505315603 - HTTP/1.1 500
1505315607 - HTTP/1.1 500
1505315612 - nc: timed out
1505315617 - nc: timed out
1505315623 - nc: timed out
...
```

Since we didn't configure the liveness probe in our service, the unhealthy container wouldn't be restarted unless we kill it manually. Therefore, in general, we would use both probes together so as to make the healing process automated.

Init containers

Even though `initialDelaySeconds` allows us to block a pod for some time prior to receiving traffic, it's still limited. Imagine that if our application is serving a file that fetches from somewhere upon initializing, the ready time might differ a lot depending on the file size. Hence, the Init containers come in handy here.

Init containers are one or more containers that start prior to application containers and run one by one to completion in order. If any container fails, it's subject to the `restartPolicy` of a pod and starts over again, till all containers exited with code `0`.

Defining Init containers is akin to regular containers:

```
...
spec:
  containers:
  - name: my-app
    image: <my-app>
  initContainers:
  - name: init-my-app
    image: <init-my-app>
  ...
```

They only differ in:

- Init containers don't have readiness probes as they'd run to completion
- The port defined in init containers wouldn't be captured by the service in front of the pod
- The request/limit of resources are calculated with `max(sum(regular containers), max(init containers))`, which means if one of init containers sets a higher resource limit than other init containers as well as the sum of resource limit of all regular containers, Kubernetes schedules the pod according to the init container's resource limit

The usefulness of init containers is more than blocking the application containers. For instance, we can utilize them to configure an image by sharing an `emptyDir` volume to Init containers and application containers, instead of building another image that only runs `awk/sed` on the base image, mounts and consume secrets in an Init container rather than in application containers.

Terminating a pod

The sequence of shutdown events is similar to events while starting a pod. After receiving a deletion invocation, Kubernetes sends `SIGTERM` to the pod to be deleted, and the pod's state becomes **Terminating**. Meanwhile, Kubernetes removes the endpoint of that pod to stop further requests if the pod is backing a service. Occasionally, there are pods that aren't quitting at all. It could be the pods don't honor `SIGTERM`, or simply because their tasks aren't completed. Under such circumstances, Kubernetes would send a `SIGKILL` to forcibly kill those pods after the termination periods. The period length is set at `.spec.terminationGracePeriodSeconds` under pod specification. Nonetheless, even though Kubernetes has mechanisms to reclaim such pods anyway, we still should make sure our pods can be closed properly.

Besides, like in starting a pod, here we also need to take care of a case that might affect our service, that is, the process which is serving requests in a pod closed prior to the corresponding iptables rules are entirely removed.

Handling SIGTERM

Graceful termination is not a new idea, it's a common practice in programming, and especially important for business- critical missions.

The implementation principally includes three steps:

1. Add a handler to capture termination signals.
2. Do everything required in the handler, such as returning resources, releasing distribution locks, or closing connections.
3. Program shutdown. Our previous example demonstrates the idea: closing the controller thread on `SIGTERM` in the handler `graceful_exit_handler`. The code can be found here (`https://github.com/DevOps-with-Kubernetes/my-app/blob/master/app.py`).

As a matter of fact, common pitfalls that fail a graceful exit are not on the program side:

SIGTERM is not forwarded to the container process

In `Chapter 2`, *DevOps with Container*, we've learned that there are two forms to invoke our program when writing a Dockerfile, namely the shell form and the exec form, and the shell to run the shell form commands is default to `/bin/sh` on Linux containers. Let's see the following example (`https://github.com/DevOps-with-Kubernetes/examples/tree/master/chapter7/7-3_on_pods/graceful_docker`):

```
--- Dockerfile.shell-sh ---
FROM python:3-alpine
EXPOSE 5000
ADD app.py .
CMD python -u app.py
```

We know that the signal sent to a container would be caught by the `PID 1` process inside the container, so let's build and run it.

```
$ docker run -d --rm --name my-app my-app:shell-sh
8962005f3722131f820e750e72d0eb5caf08222bfbdc5d25b6f587de0f6f5f3f
$ docker logs my-app
starting server at 1503839211.025133
$ docker kill --signal TERM my-app
```

```
my-app
$ docker ps --filter name=my-app --format '{{.Names}}'
my-app
```

Our container is still there. Let's see what happened inside the container:

```
$ docker exec my-app ps
PID    USER       TIME      COMMAND
1      root       0:00      /bin/sh -c python -u app.py
5      root       0:00      python -u app.py
6      root       0:00      ps
```

The PID 1 process is the shell itself, and it doesn't forward our signal to the sub process apparently. In this example, we're using Alpine as the base image which uses ash as the default shell. If we execute anything with /bin/sh, it's linked to ash actually. Similarly, the default shell in Debian family is dash, which doesn't forward signals as well. There is still a shell that forwards signals, such as bash. To leverage bash, we can either install an extra shell, or switch the base image to distributions that use bash. But both of them are rather cumbersome.

Instead, there are still options to fix the signal problem without using bash. One is running our program with exec in the shell form:

```
CMD exec python -u app.py
```

Our process will replace the shell process and thus become the PID 1 process. Another choice and also the recommended one is writing Dockerfile in EXEC form:

```
CMD [ "python", "-u", "app.py" ]
```

Let's try the example again with the one in EXEC form:

```
---Dockerfile.exec-sh---
FROM python:3-alpine
EXPOSE 5000
ADD app.py .
CMD [ "python", "-u", "app.py" ]
---
$ docker run -d --rm --name my-app my-app:exec-sh
5114cabae9fcec530a2f68703d5bc910d988cb28acfede2689ae5eebdfd46441
$ docker exec my-app ps
PID    USER       TIME      COMMAND
1      root       0:00      python -u app.py
5      root       0:00      ps
$ docker kill --signal TERM my-app && docker logs -f my-app
my-app
starting server at 1503842040.339449
```

```
stopping server at 1503842134.455339
```

The EXEC form works like a charm. As we can see, the processes in the container is what we would anticipate, and our handler now receives SIGTERM correctly.

SIGTERM doesn't invoke the termination handler

In some cases, the termination handler of a process is not triggered by SIGTERM. For instance, sending a SIGTERM to nginx actually causes a fast shutdown. To gracefully close a nginx controller, we have to send SIGQUIT with `nginx -s quit` instead.

 The full list of supported actions on the signal of nginx is listed here: `http://nginx.org/en/docs/control.html`.

Now another problem arises--how do we send signals other than SIGTERM to a container on deleting a pod? We can modify the behavior of our program to trap SIGTERM, but there's nothing we can do about a popular tool like nginx. For such a situation, the life cycle hook is capable of solving the problem.

Container lifecycle hooks

Lifecycle hooks are event-aware actions performs against a container. They work like a single Kubernetes probing action, but they'll only be fired at least once per event during a container's lifetime. Right now, there are two events supported:

- `PostStart`: Executes right after a container is created. Since this hook and the entry point of a container are fired asynchronously, there is no guarantee that the hook would be executed before the container starts. As such, we're unlikely to use it to initialize resources for a container.
- `PreStop`: executes right before sending SIGTERM to a container. One difference to `PostStart` hook is that the `PreStop` hook is a synchronous call, in other words, SIGTERM is only sent after a `PreStop` hook exited.

So, our nginx shutdown problem is able to be trivially solved with a `PreStop` hook:

```
. . .
    containers:
    - name: main
      image: nginx
      lifecycle:
```

```
preStop:
 exec:
  command: [ "nginx", "-s", "quit" ]
...
```

Additionally, an important property of hooks is they could affect the state of a pod in certain ways: a pod won't be running unless its `PostStart` hook exited successfully; a pod is set to terminating immediately on deletion, but `SIGTERM` won't be sent unless the `PreStop` hook exited successfully. Therefore, for the case we mentioned earlier, the container quits before its iptables rules are removed, we can resolve it by the `PreStop` hook. The following figure illustrates how to use the hook to eliminate the unwanted gap:

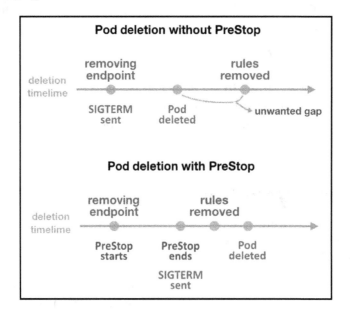

The implementation is just adding a hook that sleeps for few seconds:

```
...
    containers:
    - name: main
      image: my-app
      lifecycle:
       preStop:
        exec:
          command: [ "/bin/sh", "-c", "sleep 5" ]
...
```

Placing pods

Most of time we don't really care about which node our pods is running on as scheduling pods is a fundamental feature of Kubernetes. Nevertheless, Kubernetes is not aware of factors such as geographical location of a node, availability zones, or machine types when scheduling a pod. Moreover, at times we'd like to deploy pods that run testing builds in an isolated instance group. As such, to complete the scheduling, Kubernetes provides different levels of affinities that allows us to actively assign pods to certain nodes.

The node selector of a pod is the simplest way to place pods manually. It's similar to pod selectors of service. A pod would only be put on nodes with matching labels. The field is set at `.spec.nodeSelector`. For example, the following snippet of a pod `spec` schedules the pod to nodes with label `purpose=sandbox,disk=ssd`.

```
. . .
    spec:
      containers:
      - name: main
        image: my-app
      nodeSelector:
        purpose: sandbox
        disk: ssd
. . .
```

Checking labels on nodes is the same as how we check other resources in Kubernetes:

```
$ kubectl describe node gke-my-cluster-ins-49e8f52a-1z41
Name:         gke-my-cluster-ins-49e8f52a-1z41
Role:
Labels:       beta.kubernetes.io/arch=amd64
              beta.kubernetes.io/fluentd-ds-ready=true
              beta.kubernetes.io/instance-type=g1-small
              beta.kubernetes.io/os=linux
              cloud.google.com/gke-nodepool=ins
              failure-domain.beta.kubernetes.io/region=us-
              central1
              failure-domain.beta.kubernetes.io/zone=us-
              central1-b
              kubernetes.io/hostname=gke-my-cluster-ins-
              49e8f52a-1z41
. . .
```

As we can see, there are already labels on our node. Those labels are set by default, and the default labels are as follows:

- `kubernetes.io/hostname`
- `failure-domain.beta.kubernetes.io/zone`
- `failure-domain.beta.kubernetes.io/region`
- `beta.kubernetes.io/instance-type`
- `beta.kubernetes.io/os`
- `beta.kubernetes.io/arch`

If we'd like to label a node to make our example pods scheduled, we can either update the manifest of the node or use the shortcut command `kubectl label`:

```
$ kubectl label node gke-my-cluster-ins-49e8f52a-lz41 \
  purpose=sandbox disk=ssd
node "gke-my-cluster-ins-49e8f52a-lz41" labeled
$ kubectl get node --selector purpose=sandbox,disk=ssd
NAME                                STATUS    AGE       VERSION
gke-my-cluster-ins-49e8f52a-lz41    Ready     5d        v1.7.3
```

Aside from placing pods to a node, a node is able to reject pods as well, that is, *taints and tolerations*, and we will learn it at the next chapter.

Summary

In this chapter, we've discussed topics not only on building a continuous delivery pipeline, but also on techniques to strengthen our every deployment task. The rolling update of pods is a powerful tool that performs updates in a controlled fashion. To trigger a rolling update, what we need to do is update the pod's specification. Although the update is managed by Kubernetes, we can still control it with `kubectl rollout`.

Later on, we fabricated an extensible continuous delivery pipeline by `GitHub/DockerHub/Travis-CI`. Next, we moved our steps to learn more about the life of pods to prevent any possible failure, including using the readiness and liveness probe to protect a pod, initializing a pod with Init containers, handling `SIGTERM` properly by writing `Dockerfile` in the exec form, leveraging life cycle hooks to stall a pod's readiness as well as its termination for the iptables rules to be removed at the right timing, and assigning pods to specific nodes with node selectors.

In the next chapter, we'll learn how to segment our cluster with logical boundaries to share resource more stable and secure in Kubernetes.

8
Cluster Administration

We've learned most of our basic DevOps skills with Kubernetes in previous chapters, from how to containerize our application to deploying our containerized software into Kubernetes seamlessly via continuous deployment. Now, it's time to have a deeper insight into how to administer a Kubernetes cluster.

In this chapter, we'll learn:

- How to utilize namespaces to set administrative boundaries
- Using kubeconfig to switch between multiple clusters
- Kubernetes authentication
- Kubernetes authorization

While minikube is a fairly simple environment, we will use the **Google Container Engine** (**GKE**) and self-hosted cluster in AWS as the example, instead of minikube in this chapter. For the detailed setting, please refer to Chapter 9, *Kubernetes on AWS*, and Chapter 10, *Kubernetes on GCP*.

Kubernetes namespaces

Kubernetes has a namespace concept to divide the resources from a physical cluster to multiple virtual clusters. In this way, different groups could share the same physical cluster with isolation. Each namespace provides:

- A scope of names; object name in each namespace is unique
- Policies to ensure trusted authentication
- Ability to set up resource quotas for resource management

Namespaces are ideal for different teams or projects in the same company, so different groups can have their own virtual clusters, which have the resource isolation but share the same physical cluster. Resources in one namespace are invisible from other namespaces. Different resource quotas could be set to different namespaces and provide different levels of QoS. Note that not all objects are in a namespace, such as nodes and Persistent Volumes, which belong to entire clusters.

Default namespaces

By default, Kubernetes has three namespaces: `default`, `kube-system` and `kube-public`. The `default` namespace contains the objects which are created without specifying any namespace, and `kube-system` contains the objects which are created by Kubernetes systems, usually used by the system components, such as Kubernetes dashboard or Kubernetes DNS. The `kube-public` is newly introduced in 1.6, which intends to locate the resources that everybody can access. It mainly focuses on public ConfigMap now, such as cluster info.

Create a new namespace

Let's see how to create a namespace. A namespace is also a Kubernetes object. We could just specify the kind as a namespace like other objects. Below is the example to create one namespace, `project1`:

```
// configuration file of namespace
# cat 8-1-1_ns1.yml
apiVersion: v1
kind: Namespace
metadata:
name: project1

// create namespace for project1
# kubectl create -f 8-1-1_ns1.yml
namespace "project1" created

// list namespace, the abbreviation of namespaces is ns. We could use
`kubectl get ns` to list it as well.
# kubectl get namespaces
NAME            STATUS    AGE
default         Active    1d
kube-public     Active    1d
kube-system     Active    1d
project1        Active    11s
```

Then let's try to start two nginx containers via deployment in `project1` namespace:

```
// run a nginx deployment in project1 ns
# kubectl run nginx --image=nginx:1.12.0 --replicas=2 --port=80 --
namespace=project1
```

When we list pods by `kubectl get pods`, we'll see nothing in our cluster. Why? Because Kubernetes uses the current context to decide which namespace is current. If we don't explicitly specify namespace in the context or `kubectl` command line, the `default` namespace will be used:

```
// We'll see the Pods if we explicitly specify --namespace
# kubectl get pods --namespace=project1
NAME                     READY     STATUS     RESTARTS     AGE
nginx-3599227048-gghvw   1/1       Running    0            15s
nginx-3599227048-jz31g   1/1       Running    0            15s
```

 You could use `--namespace <namespace_name>`, `--namespace=<namespace_name>`, `-n <namespace_name>` or `-n=<namespace_name>` to specify the namespace for a command. To list the resources across namespaces, use `--all-namespaces` parameter.

Another way is changing the current context to point to the desired namespace rather than the default namespace.

Context

Context is a concept of the combination of cluster information, a user for authentication and a namespace. For example, the following is the context information for one of our clusters in GKE:

```
- context:
cluster: gke_devops-with-kubernetes_us-central1-b_cluster
user: gke_devops-with-kubernetes_us-central1-b_cluster
name: gke_devops-with-kubernetes_us-central1-b_cluster
```

We could use the `kubectl config current-context` command to see the current context:

```
# kubectl config current-context
gke_devops-with-kubernetes_us-central1-b_cluster
```

To list all config info including contexts, you could use the `kubectl config view` command; to checkout what context is currently in use, use `kubectl config get-contexts` command.

Create a context

The next step is to create a context. As in the preceding example, we'll need to set a user and cluster name for the context. If we don't specify those, the empty value will be set. The command to create a context is:

```
$ kubectl config set-context <context_name> --namespace=<namespace_name> --cluster=<cluster_name> --user=<user_name>
```

Multiple contexts could be created in the same cluster. The following is an example of how to create a context for `project1` in my GKE cluster `gke_devops-with-kubernetes_us-central1-b_cluster`:

```
// create a context with my GKE cluster
# kubectl config set-context project1 --namespace=project1 --cluster=gke_devops-with-kubernetes_us-central1-b_cluster --user=gke_devops-with-kubernetes_us-central1-b_cluster
Context "project1" created.
```

Switch the current context

Then we could switch the context by the `use-context` sub-command:

```
# kubectl config use-context project1
Switched to context "project1".
```

After the context is switched, every command we invoke via `kubectl` is under the `project1` context. We don't need to explicitly specify the namespace to see our pods:

```
// list pods
# kubectl get pods
NAME                        READY     STATUS     RESTARTS   AGE
nginx-3599227048-gghvw      1/1       Running    0          3m
nginx-3599227048-jz31g      1/1       Running    0          3m
```

ResourceQuota

By default, pods in Kubernetes are resource-unbounded. Then the running pods might use up all the compute or storage resources in a cluster. ResourceQuota is a resource object that allows us to restrict the resource consumption that a namespace could use. By setting up the resource limit, we could reduce the noisy neighbor symptom. The team working for `project1` won't use up all the resources in the physical cluster.

Then we can ensure the quality of service for other teams working in other projects which share the same physical cluster. There are three kinds of resource quotas supported in Kubernetes 1.7. Each kind includes different resource names, (`https://kubernetes.io/docs/concepts/policy/resource-quotas`):

- Compute resource quota (CPU, memory)
- Storage resource quota (requested storage, Persistent Volume Claims)
- Object count quotas (pods, RCs, ConfigMaps, services, LoadBalancers)

Created resources won't be affected by newly created resource quotas. If the resource creation request exceeds the specified ResourceQuota, the resources won't be able to start up.

Create a ResourceQuota for a namespace

Now, let's learn the syntax of `ResourceQuota`. Below is one example:

```
# cat 8-1-2_resource_quota.yml
apiVersion: v1
kind: ResourceQuota
metadata:
  name: project1-resource-quota
spec:
  hard:# the limits of the sum of memory request
    requests.cpu: "1"              # the limits of the sum
    of requested CPU
    requests.memory: 1Gi           # the limits of the sum
    of requested memory
    limits.cpu: "2"          # the limits of total CPU
    limits
    limits.memory: 2Gi          # the limits of total memory
    limit
    requests.storage: 64Gi     # the limits of sum of
    storage requests across PV claims
    pods: "4"                  # the limits of pod number
```

The template is like other objects, just this kind becomes `ResourceQuota`. The quota we specified is valid across the pods which are in a succeeded or failed state (that is, non-terminal state). There are several resource constraints that are supported. In the preceding example, we demonstrate how to set compute ResourceQuota, storage ResourceQuota and object CountQuota. Any time, we could still use the `kubectl` command to check the quota we set: `kubectl describe resourcequota <resource_quota_name>`.

Right now let's modify our existing nginx Deployment by the command `kubectl edit deployment nginx`, changing replica from 2 to 4 and save. Let's list the state now.

```
# kubectl describe deployment nginx
Replicas:          4 desired | 2 updated | 2 total | 2 available | 2
unavailable
Conditions:
  Type                Status      Reason
  ----                ------      ------
  Available                   False MinimumReplicasUnavailable
  ReplicaFailure  True  FailedCreate
```

It indicates some pods failed on creation. If we check the corresponding ReplicaSet, we could find out the reason:

```
# kubectl describe rs nginx-3599227048
...
Error creating: pods "nginx-3599227048-" is forbidden: failed quota:
project1-resource-quota: must specify
limits.cpu,limits.memory,requests.cpu,requests.memory
```

Since we've specified the request limits on memory and CPU, Kubernetes doesn't know the default request limits on the newly desired three pods. We could see the original two pods are still up and running, since the resource quota doesn't apply to existing resources. We now then use `kubectl edit deployment nginx` to modify container specs as follows:

```
spec:
  containers:
  - image: nginx:1.12.0
    imagePullPolicy: IfNotPresent
    name: nginx
    ports:
    - containerPort: 80
      protocol: TCP
    resources:
      limits:
        memory: "300Mi"
        cpu: "300m"
      requests:
        memory: "150Mi"
        cpu: "100m"
    terminationMessagePath: /dev/termination-log
    terminationMessagePolicy: File
```

Here, we specify the requests and limits for CPU and memory in the pod spec. It indicates the pod can't exceed the specified quota, otherwise it will be unable to start:

```
// check the deployment state
# kubectl get deployment
NAME      DESIRED   CURRENT   UP-TO-DATE   AVAILABLE   AGE
nginx     4         3         2            3           2d
```

Available pods become four instead of two, but still not equal to our desired four. What went wrong? If we take a step back and check our resource quota, we can find we've used all the quota of pods. Since Deployments use the rolling update deployment mechanism by default, it'll require pod numbers larger than four, which is exact object limit we set earlier:

```
# kubectl describe resourcequota project1-resource-quota
Name:             project1-resource-quota
Namespace:        project1
Resource          Used   Hard
--------          ----   ----
limits.cpu        900m   4
limits.memory     900Mi  4Gi
pods              4      4
requests.cpu      300m   4
requests.memory   450Mi  16Gi
requests.storage  0      64Gi
```

After modifying the pods quota from 4 to 8 by `kubectl edit resourcequota project1-resource-quota` command, the Deployment has sufficient resource to launch the pods. Once the `Used` quota exceeds the `Hard` quota, the request will be rejected by the ResourceQuota admission controller, otherwise, the resource quota usage will be updated to ensure sufficient resource allocation.

Since ResourceQuota won't affect already created resources, sometimes we might need to tweak the failed resources, such as deleting an empty change set of RS or scale up and down Deployment, in order to let Kubernetes create new pods or RS which will soak the latest quota limits.

Request pods with default compute resource limits

We could also specify default resource requests and limits for a namespace. Default setting will be used if we don't specify the requests and limits during pod creation. The trick is using `LimitRange` resource object. A `LimitRange` object contains a set of `defaultRequest` (request) and `default` (limits).

LimitRange is controlled by the LimitRanger admission controller plugin. Be sure you enable it if you launch a self-hosted solution. For more information, check out the admission controller section in this chapter.

Below is an example where we set `cpu.request` as 250m and `limits` as 500m, `memory.request` as 256Mi and `limits` as 512Mi:

```
# cat 8-1-3_limit_range.yml
apiVersion: v1
kind: LimitRange
metadata:
  name: project1-limit-range
spec:
  limits:
  - default:
      cpu: 0.5
      memory: 512Mi
    defaultRequest:
      cpu: 0.25
      memory: 256Mi
    type: Container

// create limit range
# kubectl create -f 8-1-3_limit_range.yml
limitrange "project1-limit-range" created
```

When we launch pods inside this namespace, we don't need to specify the `cpu` and `memory` requests and `limits` anytime, even if we have a total limitation set inside ResourceQuota.

The unit of CPU is core, which is an absolute quantity. It can be an AWS vCPU, a GCP core or a hyperthread on a machine with hyperthreading processor equipped. The unit of memory is a byte. Kubernetes uses the first alphabet or power-of-two equivalents. For example, 256M would be written as 256,000,000, 256 M or 244 Mi.

Additionally, we can set minimum and maximum CPU and memory values for a pod in LimitRange. It acts differently as default values. Default values are only used if a pod spec doesn't contain any requests and limits. The minimum and maximum constraint is used for verifying if a pod requests too much resource. The syntax is `spec.limits[].min` and `spec.limits[].max`. If the request exceeds the minimum and maximum values, forbidden will be thrown from the server.

```
limits:
   - max:
       cpu: 1
       memory: 1Gi
     min:
       cpu: 0.25
       memory: 128Mi
     type: Container
```

Quality of service for pods: There are three QoS classes for pods in Kubernetes: Guaranteed, Burstable and BestEffort. It's tied together with the namespace and resource management concept we learned above. We also learned QoS in `Chapter 4`, *Working with Storage and Resources*. Please refer to the last section *Kubernetes Resource Management* in `Chapter 4`, *Working with Storage and Resources* for recap.

Delete a namespace

Just like any other resources, deleting a namespace is `kubectl delete namespace` `<namespace_name>`. Please be aware that if a namespace is deleted, all the resources associated with that namespace will be evicted.

Kubeconfig

Kubeconfig is a file that you can use to switch multiple clusters by switching context. We can use `kubectl config view` to view the setting. The following is an example of a minikube cluster in a `kubeconfig` file.

```
# kubectl config view
apiVersion: v1
clusters:
- cluster:
    certificate-authority: /Users/k8s/.minikube/ca.crt
    server: https://192.168.99.100:8443
  name: minikube
contexts:
- context:
    cluster: minikube
    user: minikube
  name: minikube
current-context: minikube
kind: Config
preferences: {}
users:
- name: minikube
  user:
    client-certificate: /Users/k8s/.minikube/apiserver.crt
    client-key: /Users/k8s/.minikube/apiserver.key
```

Just like what we learned previously. We could use `kubectl config use-context` to switch the cluster to manipulate. We could also use `kubectl config --kubeconfig=<config file name>` to specify which `kubeconfig` file we'd like to use. Only the specified file will be used. We could also specify `kubeconfig` files by the environment variable `$KUBECONFIG`. In this way, config files could be merged. For example, the following command will merge `kubeconfig-file1` and `kubeconfig-file2`:

```
# export KUBECONFIG=$KUBECONFIG: kubeconfig-file1: kubeconfig-file2
```

You might find we didn't do any specific setting previously. Then where does the output of `kubectl config view` come from? By default, it exists under `$HOME/.kube/config`. This file will be loaded if none of the preceding are set.

Service account

Unlike normal users, **service account** is used by processes inside a pod to contact the Kubernetes API server. By default, a Kubernetes cluster creates different service accounts for different purposes. In GKE, there are bunch of service accounts that have been created:

```
// list service account across all namespaces
# kubectl get serviceaccount --all-namespaces
NAMESPACE       NAME                          SECRETS    AGE
default         default                       1          5d
kube-public     default                       1          5d
kube-system     namespace-controller          1          5d
kube-system     resourcequota-controller      1          5d
kube-system     service-account-controller    1          5d
kube-system     service-controller            1          5d
project1        default                       1          2h
...
```

Kubernetes will create a default service account in each namespace, which will be used if no service account is specified in pod spec during pod creation. Let's take a look at how the default service account acts for our `project1` namespace:

```
# kubectl describe serviceaccount/default
Name:          default
Namespace:     project1
Labels:             <none>
Annotations:        <none>
Image pull secrets:     <none>
Mountable secrets:      default-token-nsqls
Tokens:                 default-token-nsqls
```

We could see a service account is basically using mountable secrets as a token. Let's dig into what contents are inside the token:

```
// describe the secret, the name is default-token-nsqls here
# kubectl describe secret default-token-nsqls
Name:          default-token-nsqls
Namespace:     project1
Annotations:   kubernetes.io/service-account.name=default
               kubernetes.io/service-account.uid=5e46cc5e-
               8b52-11e7-a832-42010af00267
```

```
Type: kubernetes.io/service-account-token
Data
====
ca.crt:      # the public CA of api server. Base64 encoded.
namespace:   # the name space associated with this service account. Base64
encoded
token:       # bearer token. Base64 encoded
```

The secret will be automatically mounted to the directory
`/var/run/secrets/kubernetes.io/serviceaccount`. When the pod accesses the API
server, the API server will check the cert and token to do the authentication. The concept of
a service account will be with us in the following sections.

Authentication and authorization

Authentication and authorization are important from DevOps' point of view.
Authentication verifies users and checks if the users are really who they represent
themselves to be. Authorization, on the other hand, checks what permission levels users
have. Kubernetes supports different authentication and authorization modules.

The following is an illustration that shows how the Kubernetes API server processes the
access control when it receives a request.

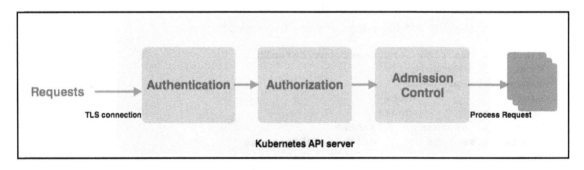

Access control in API server

When the request comes to API server, firstly, it establishes a TLS connection by validating the clients' certificate with the **certificate authority (CA)** in the API server. The CA in the API server is usually at `/etc/kubernetes/`, and the clients' certificate is usually at `$HOME/.kube/config`. After the handshake, it goes to the authentication stage. In Kuberentes, authentication module are chain-based. We could use more than one authentication and authorization modules. When the request comes, Kubernetes will try all the authenticators one by one until it succeeds. If the request fails on all authentication modules, it will be rejected as **HTTP 401 Unauthorized**. Otherwise, one of the authenticators verifies the user's identity and the requests are authenticated. Then Kubernetes authorization modules will come into play. It will verify if the user has the permission to do the action that they request to do by a set of policies. Authorization modules are also chain-based. It keeps trying every module until it succeeds. If the request fails on all the modules, it'll get a **HTTP 403 Forbidden** response. Admission control is a set of configurable plugins in an API server that determine if a request is admitted or denied. At this stage, if the request doesn't pass through one of the plugins, then the request is denied immediately.

Authentication

By default, a service account is token-based. When you create a service account or a namespace with default service account, Kubernetes creates the token and stores it as a secret which is encoded by base64, and mounts the secret as a volume into the pod. Then the processes inside the pod have the ability to talk to the cluster. The user account, on the other hand, represents a normal user, who might use `kubectl` to manipulate the resource directly.

Service account authentication

When we create a service account, a signed bearer token will be created automatically by the Kubernetes service account admission controller plugin.

In `Chapter 7`, *Continuous Delivery*, in the example that we demonstrated how to do the deployment of `my-app`, we created a namespace named `cd`, and we used the script `get-sa-token.sh` (`https://github.com/DevOps-with-Kubernetes/examples/blob/master/chapter7/get-sa-token.sh`) to export the token for us. Then we create a user `mysa` via `kubectl config set-credentials <user> --token=$TOKEN` command:

```
# kubectl config set-credentials mysa --token=${CI_ENV_K8S_SA_TOKEN}
```

Next, we set the context to bind with user and namespace:

```
# kubectl config set-context myctxt --cluster=mycluster --user=mysa
```

Finally, we set our context `myctxt` as default context:

```
# kubectl config use-context myctxt
```

When the service account sends a request, the token will be verified by the API server to check if the requester is eligible and it is what it claims to be.

User account authentication

There are several implementations for user account authentication. From client certificates, bearer tokens, static files to OpenID connect tokens. You can choose more than one as authentication chains. Here, we'll demonstrate how client certificates works.

In `Chapter 7`, *Continuous Delivery* we've learned how to export cert and token for service account. Now, let's learn how to do it for a user. Assume we are still inside `project1` namespace, and we want to create a user for our new DevOps member Linda, who will help us to do the Deployment for my-app.

First, we'll generate a private key by OpenSSL (`https://www.openssl.org`):

```
// generate a private key for Linda
# openssl genrsa -out linda.key 2048
```

Next, we'll create a certificate sign request (`.csr`) for Linda:

```
// making CN as your username
# openssl req -new -key linda.key -out linda.csr -subj "/CN=linda"
```

Now, `linda.key` and `linda.csr` should be located in the current folder. For approving the sign request, we'll need to locate the CA of our Kubernetes cluster.

In minikube, it's under `~/.minikube/`. For other self-hosted solutions, normally it's under `/etc/kubernetes/`. If you use kops to deploy the cluster, the location is under `/srv/kubernetes`, where you could find the path in `/etc/kubernetes/manifests/kube-apiserver.manifest` file.

Assume we have `ca.crt` and `ca.key` under the current folder, we could generate the cert by our sign request. Using the `-days` parameter we could define the expired date:

```
// generate the cert for Linda, this cert is only valid for 30 days.
# openssl x509 -req -in linda.csr -CA ca.crt -CAkey ca.key -CAcreateserial -out linda.crt -days 30
Signature ok
subject=/CN=linda
Getting CA Private Key
```

After we have cert signed by our cluster, we could set a user in the cluster.

```
# kubectl config set-credentials linda --client-certificate=linda.crt --client-key=linda.key
User "linda" set.
```

Remember the concept of context: it's the combination of cluster information, a user for authentication and a namespace. Now, we'll set a context entry in `kubeconfig`. Remember to replace your cluster name, namespace and user from the following example:

```
# kubectl config set-context devops-context --cluster=k8s-devops.net --namespace=project1 --user=linda
Context "devops-context" modified.
```

Now, Linda should have zero permission:

```
// test for getting a pod
# kubectl --context=devops-context get pods
Error from server (Forbidden): User "linda" cannot list pods in the namespace "project1". (get pods)
```

Linda now passes the authentication stage while Kubernetes knows she is Linda. However, to make Linda have the permission to do the Deployment, we need to set up the polices in authorization modules.

Authorization

Kubernetes supports several authorization modules. At the time we're writing, it supports:

- ABAC
- RBAC
- Node authorization
- Webhook
- Custom modules

Attribute-based access control (**ABAC**) was the major authorization mode before **role-based access control** (**RBAC**) was introduced. Node authorization is used by kubelet to make a request to the API server. Kubernetes supports webhook authorization mode to establish a HTTP callback with an external RESTful service. It'll do a POST whenever it faces an authorization decision. Another common way is you could implement your in-house module by following along the pre-defined authorizer interface. For more implementation information, refer to `https://kubernetes.io/docs/admin/authorization/#custom-modules`. In this section, we'll describe more details for ABAC and RBAC.

Attribute-based access control (ABAC)

ABAC allows admin to define a set of user authorization polices into a file with one JSON per line format. The major drawback of ABAC mode is the policy file has to exist when launching the API server. Any change in the file requires restarting the API server with `--authorization-policy-file=<policy_file_name>` command. Another authorization method RBAC was introduced since Kubernetes 1.6. which is more flexible and doesn't require restarting the API server. RBAC has now become the most common authorization mode.

The following is an example of how ABAC works. The format of the policy file is one JSON object per line. The configuration file of the policy is similar to our other configuration files. Just with different syntax in spec. There are four main properties in ABAC:

Properties type	Supported values
Subject-matching	user, group
Resource-matching	`apiGroup`, namespace, and resource
Non-resource-matching	Used for non-resource type requests, such as `/version`, `/apis`, `/cluster`
readonly	true or false

The following are some examples:

```
{"apiVersion": "abac.authorization.kubernetes.io/v1beta1", "kind":
"Policy", "spec": {"user":"admin", "namespace": "*", "resource": "*",
"apiGroup": "*"}}
{"apiVersion": "abac.authorization.kubernetes.io/v1beta1", "kind":
"Policy", "spec": {"user":"linda", "namespace": "project1", "resource":
"deployments", "apiGroup": "*", "readonly": true}}
{"apiVersion": "abac.authorization.kubernetes.io/v1beta1", "kind":
```

```
"Policy", "spec": {"user":"linda", "namespace": "project1", "resource":
"replicasets", "apiGroup": "*", "readonly": true}}
```

In the preceding example, we have a user admin who could access everything. Another user named `linda` who can only read the Deployment and ReplicaSets in the namespace `project1`.

Role-based access control (RBAC)

RBAC was in beta in Kubernetes 1.6, which is enabled by default. In RBAC, admin creates several `Roles` or `ClusterRoles`, which define the fine-grained permissions that specifies a set of resources and actions (verbs) that roles could access and manipulate. After that, admin grants the `Role` permission to users by `RoleBinding` or `ClusterRoleBindings`.

> If you're running a minikube, add `--extra-config=apiserver.Authorization.Mode=RBAC` when doing `minikube start`. If you're running self-hosted cluster on AWS via kops, adding `--authorization=rbac` when launching the cluster. Kops launches API server as a pod; using `kops edit cluster` command could modify the spec of the containers.

Roles and ClusterRoles

A `Role` in Kubernetes is bound within a namespace, a `ClusterRole`, on the other hand, is cluster-wide. The following is an example of `Role`, which could do all the operations, including `get`, `watch`, `list`, `create`, `update`, `delete`, `patch` to the resources Deployment, ReplicaSet and pods.

```
# cat 8-5-2_role.yml
kind: Role
apiVersion: rbac.authorization.k8s.io/v1beta1
metadata:
  namespace: project1
  name: devops-role
rules:
- apiGroups: ["", "extensions", "apps"]
  resources:
    - "deployments"
    - "replicasets"
    - "pods"
  verbs: ["*"]
```

The `apiVersion` is still `v1beta1` at the time we wrote the book. If it happens that the API version changes, Kubernetes will throw the error and remind you to change. In `apiGroups`, an empty string indicates the core API group. The API group is part of the RESTful API call. The core indicates original API call path, such as `/api/v1`. The newer REST path has the group name and API version in it, such as `/apis/$GROUP_NAME/$VERSION`; for looking up API groups you'd like to use, check out API References at `https://kubernetes.io/docs/reference`. Under resources you could add the resources you'd like to grant the access to, and under verbs lists an array of actions that this role could perform. Let's get into a more advanced example for `ClusterRoles`, which we used in previous chapter as Continuous Delivery role:

```
# cat cd-clusterrole.yml
apiVersion: rbac.authorization.k8s.io/v1beta1
kind: ClusterRole
metadata:
  name: cd-role
rules:
- apiGroups: ["extensions", "apps"]
  resources:
  - deployments
  - replicasets
  - ingresses
  verbs: ["*"]
 - apiGroups: [""]
  resources:
  - namespaces
  - events
  verbs: ["get", "list", "watch"]
 - apiGroups: [""]
  resources:
  - pods
  - services
  - secrets
  - replicationcontrollers
  - persistentvolumeclaims
  - jobs
  - cronjobs
  verbs: ["*"]
```

`ClusterRole` is cluster-wide. Some resources don't belong to any namespace, such as nodes, only could be controlled by `ClusterRole`. The namespaces it could access depends on the `namespaces` field in `ClusterRoleBinding` it associates with. We could see we grant the permission to allow this role read and write Deployments, ReplicaSets and ingresses in both extensions and apps groups. In the core API group, we grant only access for namespace and events, and all permission for other resources, such as pods and services.

RoleBinding and ClusterRoleBinding

A `RoleBinding` is used to bind a `Role` or `ClusterRole` to a list of users or service accounts. If a `ClusterRole` is bound with a `RoleBinding` instead of a `ClusterRoleBinding`, it'll be only granted the permissions within the namespace that `RoleBinding` specified. The following is an example of `RoleBinding` spec:

```
# cat 8-5-2_rolebinding_user.yml
kind: RoleBinding
apiVersion: rbac.authorization.k8s.io/v1beta1
metadata:
  name: devops-role-binding
  namespace: project1
subjects:
- kind: User
  name: linda
  apiGroup: [""]
roleRef:
  kind: Role
  name: devops-role
  apiGroup: [""]
```

In this example, we bind a `Role` with a user by `roleRef`. Kubernetes supports different kind of `roleRef`; we could replace the kind from `Role` to `ClusterRole` here:

```
roleRef:
kind: ClusterRole
name: cd-role
apiGroup: rbac.authorization.k8s.io
```

Then `cd-role` can only access the resources in namespace `project1`.

On the other hand, a `ClusterRoleBinding` is used to grant permission in all namespace. Let's review what we did in Chapter 7, *Continuous Delivery*. We first created a service account named `cd-agent`, then create a `ClusterRole` named `cd-role`. At the end, we created a `ClusterRoleBinding` for `cd-agent` and `cd-role`. We then used `cd-agent` to do the Deployment on our behalf:

```
# cat cd-clusterrolebinding.yml
apiVersion: rbac.authorization.k8s.io/v1beta1
kind: ClusterRoleBinding
metadata:
  name: cd-agent
roleRef:
  apiGroup: rbac.authorization.k8s.io
  kind: ClusterRole
   name: cd-role
subjects:
- apiGroup: rbac.authorization.k8s.io
  kind: User
  name: system:serviceaccount:cd:cd-agent
```

The `cd-agent` is bound with a `ClusterRole` via `ClusterRoleBinding`, so it can have the permission specified in `cd-role` across namespaces. Since a service account is created in a namespace, we'll need to specify its full name including namespace:

```
system:serviceaccount:<namespace>:<serviceaccountname>
```

Let's launch the `Role` and `RoleBinding` via `8-5-2_role.yml` and `8-5-2_rolebinding_user.yml`:

```
# kubectl create -f 8-5-2_role.yml
role "devops-role" created
# kubectl create -f 8-5-2_rolebinding_user.yml
rolebinding "devops-role-binding" created
```

Now, we don't get forbidden anymore:

```
# kubectl --context=devops-context get pods
No resources found.
```

What about if Linda wants to list namespaces, is it allowed?:

```
# kubectl --context=devops-context get namespaces
Error from server (Forbidden): User "linda" cannot list namespaces at the
cluster scope. (get namespaces)
```

The answer is no, since Linda is not granted permission for listing namespaces.

Admission control

Admission control takes place before Kubernetes processes the request and after authentication and authorization are passed. It's enabled when launching API server by adding `--admission-control` parameter. Kubernetes recommends officially to have the following plugins with the cluster if the cluster version is >= 1.6.0.

```
--admission-
control=NamespaceLifecycle,LimitRanger,ServiceAccount,PersistentVolumeLabel
,DefaultStorageClass,DefaultTolerationSeconds,ResourceQuota
```

The following introduces the usage of these plugins, and why should we need them. For more latest information about supported admission control plugins, please visit official document `https://kubernetes.io/docs/admin/admission-controllers`.

Namespace life cycle

As we learned earlier, when a namespace is deleted, all objects in that namespace will be evicted as well. This plugin ensures no new object creation requests could be made in the namespace that is terminating or non-existed. It also prevents Kubernetes native namespaces from deletion.

LimitRanger

This plugin ensures `LimitRange` could work properly. With `LimitRange`, we could set default requests and limits in a namespace, which will be used when launching a pod without specifying the requests and limits.

Service account

The service account plugin must be added if you use service account objects. For more information about service account, revisit again service account section in this chapter.

PersistentVolumeLabel

`PersistentVolumeLabel` adds labels to newly-created PV, based on the labels provided by the underlying cloud provider. This admission controller has been deprecated from 1.8.

DefaultStorageClass

This plugin ensures default storage classes could work expectedly if no `StorageClass` is set in a Persistent Volume Claim. Different provisioning tools with different cloud providers will leverage `DefaultStorageClass` (such as GKE uses Google Cloud Persistent Disk). Be sure you have this enabled.

ResourceQuota

Just like the `LimitRange`, if you're using the `ResourceQuota` object to administer different level of QoS, this plugin must be enabled. The ResourceQuota should be always be put at the end of the admission control plugin list. As we mentioned in the ResourceQuota section, if used quota is less than hard quota, resource quota usage will be updated to ensure cluster have the sufficient resource for accepting request. Putting it into the end of admission controller list could prevent the request from increasing quota usage prematurely if it eventually gets rejected by the following controllers.

DefaultTolerationSeconds

Before introducing this plugin, we have to learn what **taints** and **tolerations** are.

Taints and tolerations

Taints and toleration are used to prevent a set of pods from scheduling running on some nodes. Taints are applied to nodes, while tolerations are specified to pods. The value of taints could be `NoSchedule` or `NoExecute`. If pods running one tainted node have no matching toleration, the pods will be evicted.

Let's say we have two nodes:

```
# kubectl get nodes
NAME                         STATUS   AGE       VERSION
ip-172-20-56-91.ec2.internal Ready 6h v1.7.2
ip-172-20-68-10.ec2.internal Ready 29m v1.7.2
```

Let's run a nginx pod now by `kubectl run nginx --image=nginx:1.12.0 --replicas=1 --port=80` command.

The pod is running on the first node `ip-172-20-56-91.ec2.internal`:

```
# kubectl describe pods nginx-4217019353-s9xrn
Name:         nginx-4217019353-s9xrn
Node:         ip-172-20-56-91.ec2.internal/172.20.56.91
Tolerations:    node.alpha.kubernetes.io/notReady:NoExecute for 300s
node.alpha.kubernetes.io/unreachable:NoExecute for 300s
```

By the pod description, we can see there are two default tolerations attached to the pod. It means if the node is not ready or unreachable yet, wait for 300 s before the pod is evicted from the node. These two tolerations are applied by DefaultTolerationSeconds admission controller plugin. We'll talk about this later. Next, we'll set a taint to the first node:

```
# kubectl taint nodes ip-172-20-56-91.ec2.internal
experimental=true:NoExecute
node "ip-172-20-56-91.ec2.internal" tainted
```

Since we set the action as `NoExecute`, and `experimental=true` doesn't match any tolerations on our pod, the pod will be removed from the node immediately and reschedule. Multi-taints could be applied to a node. The pods must match all the tolerations in order to run on that node. The following is an example that could pass the tainted node:

```
# cat 8-6_pod_tolerations.yml
apiVersion: v1
kind: Pod
metadata:
  name: pod-with-tolerations
spec:
  containers:
  - name: web
    image: nginx
  tolerations:
  - key: "experimental"
    value: "true"
    operator: "Equal"
    effect: "NoExecute"
```

Other than `Equal` operator, we could use `Exists` as well. In that case, we don't need to specify the value. As long as the key presents and effect matches, then the pod is eligible to run on that tainted node.

The `DefaultTolerationSeconds` plugin is used to set those pods without any toleration set. It will then apply for the default toleration for the taints `not ready:NoExecute` and `unreachable:NoExecute` for 300 s. If you don't want this behavior to occur in the cluster, disabling this plugin could work.

PodNodeSelector

This plugin is used to set `node-selector` annotation to the namespace. When the plugin is enabled, passing along a configuration file with `--admission-control-config-file` command using the following format:

```
podNodeSelectorPluginConfig:
  clusterDefaultNodeSelector: <default-node-selectors-
  labels>
  namespace1: <namespace-node-selectors-labels-1>
  namespace2: <namespace-node-selectors-labels-2>
```

Then the `node-selector` annotation will be applied to namespace. The pods on that namespace will then run on those matched nodes.

AlwaysAdmit

This always admits all the requests, its possible to use for test only.

AlwaysPullImages

Pull policy defines the behavior when kubelet pulling the images. The default pull policy is `IfNotPresent`, that is, it will pull the image if it is not present locally. If this plugin is enabled, the default pull policy will become `Always`, which is, always pull the latest image. This plugin also brings another benefit if your cluster is shared by different teams. Whenever a pod is scheduled, it'll always pull the latest image whether the image exists locally or not. Then we can ensure pod creation request always go through authorization check against the image.

AlwaysDeny

This always denies all the requests. It may only be used for testing only.

DenyEscalatingExec

This plugin denies any `kubectl exec` and `kubectl attach` command to be escalated privilege mode. Pods with privilege mode have the access of host namespace, which could become a security risk.

Other admission controller plugins

There are many more other admission controller plugins we could use, such as NodeRestriciton to limit kubelet's permission, ImagePolicyWebhook to establish a webhook to control the access of the images, SecurityContextDeny for controlling the privilege for a pod or a container. Please refer to official documents at (`https://kubernetes.io/docs/admin/admission-controllers`) to find out other plugins.

Summary

In this chapter, we learned what is namespace and context and how do they work, how to switch between physical cluster and virtual cluster by setting the context. We then learned about the important object—service account, which provides to identify the processes running within a pod. Then we get to know how to control access flow in Kubernetes. We learned what the difference are between authentication and authorization, and how they work in Kubernetes. We also learn how to leverage RBAC to have fine-grained permission to users. At the end, we learned a couple of admission controller plugins, which are the last goalkeepers in the access control flow.

AWS is the most major player in public IaaS providers. We've used it lots as self-hosted cluster examples in this chapter. In next chapter `Chapter 9`, *Kubernetes on AWS*, we'll finally learn how to deploy the cluster on AWS and basic concept when using AWS.

9

Kubernetes on AWS

Using Kubernetes on the public cloud is flexible and scalable for your application. AWS is one of the popular services in the public cloud industry. In this chapter, you will know what AWS is and how to set up Kubernetes on AWS along with the following topics:

- Understanding the public cloud
- Using and understanding AWS components
- Kubernetes setup and management by kops
- Kubernetes cloud provider

Introduction to AWS

When you run your application on the public network, you need an infrastructure such as networks, Virtual Machines, and storage. Obviously, companies borrow or build their own data center to prepare those infrastructures, and then hire data center engineers and operators to monitor and manage those resources.

However, purchasing and maintaining those assets need a large capital expense; you also need an operation expense for data center engineers/operators. You also need a read time to fully set up those infrastructures, such as buying a server, mounting to a data center rack, cabling a network, and then the initial configuration/installation of the OS, and so on.

Therefore, rapidly allocating an infrastructure with appropriate resource capacity is one of the important factors that dictates that success of your business.

To make infrastructure management easier and quicker, there is a lot of technology helps for data centers. Such as, for virtualization, **Software Defined Network (SDN)**, **Storage Area Network (SAN)**, and so on. But combining this technology has some sensitive compatibility issues and is difficult to stabilize; therefore it is required to hire experts in this industry, which makes operation costs higher eventually.

Public cloud

There are some companies that have provided an online infrastructure service. AWS is a well known service that provides online infrastructure, which is called cloud or public cloud. Back in the year 2006, AWS officially launched the Virtual Machine service, which was called **Elastic Computing Cloud (EC2)**, an online object store service, which was called **Simple Storage Service (S3)** and an online messaging queue service, which was called **Simple Queue Service (SQS)**.

These services are simple enough, but from a data center management point of view, they relieve infrastructure pre-allocation and reduce read time, because of pay-as-you-go pricing models (paying hourly or yearly for usage to AWS). Therefore, AWS is getting so popular that many companies have switched from their own data centers to the public cloud.

 An antonym of the public cloud, your own data center is called **on-premises**.

API and infrastructure as code

One of the unique benefits of using a public cloud instead of on-premises data centers that public cloud provides an API to control infrastructure. AWS provides command-line tools (**AWS CLI**) to control AWS infrastructure. For example, after signing up to AWS (https://aws.amazon.com/free/), then install AWS CLI (http://docs.aws.amazon.com/cli/latest/userguide/installing.html), then if you want to launch one Virtual Machine (EC2 instance), use AWS CLI as follows:

```
saito — ec2-user@ip-172-31-31-217:~ — ssh ec2-user@54.172.10.42 — 80×19
             ec2-user@ip-172-31-31-217:~ — ssh ec2-user@54.172.10.42                +
$ aws ec2 run-instances --image-id ami-a4c7edb2 --key-name my-key --instance-typ
e t2.nano --security-groups ssh-only > /dev/null
$ aws ec2 describe-instances | grep PublicIpAddress
                "PublicIpAddress": "54.172.10.42",
$ ssh ec2-user@54.172.10.42
The authenticity of host '54.172.10.42 (54.172.10.42)' can't be established.
ECDSA key fingerprint is SHA256:4/4exJT5PiRzcqXSg+mo2Q4de/DJrPEWR2cG+M92ojg.
Are you sure you want to continue connecting (yes/no)? yes
Warning: Permanently added '54.172.10.42' (ECDSA) to the list of known hosts.
Enter passphrase for key '/Users/saito/.ssh/id_rsa':

      __|  __|_  )
      _|  (     /   Amazon Linux AMI
     ___|\___|___|

https://aws.amazon.com/amazon-linux-ami/2017.03-release-notes/
2 package(s) needed for security, out of 6 available
Run "sudo yum update" to apply all updates.
[ec2-user@ip-172-31-31-217 ~]$
```

As you can see, it takes only just a few minutes to access your Virtual Machine after signing up to AWS. On the other hand, what if you set up your own on premise data center from scratch? The following diagram is a high-level comparison on if you use on premise data centers or if you use the public cloud:

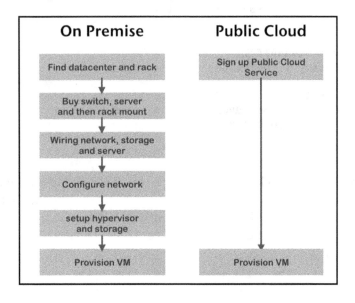

As you can see, the public cloud is too simple and quick; this is why public cloud is flexible and convenient for not only emerging, but also permanent usage.

AWS components

AWS has some components to configure network and storage. These are important to understand how the public cloud works and also important to know how to configure Kubernetes.

VPC and subnet

On AWS, first of all you need to create your own network; it is called **Virtual Private Cloud** (**VPC**) and uses a SDN technology. AWS allows you to create one or more VPC on AWS. Each VPC may connect with each other as required. When you create a VPC, just define one network CIDR block and AWS region. For example, CIDR `10.0.0.0/16` on `us-east-1`. No matter if you have access to a public network or not, you can define any network address range (between /16 to /28 netmask range). VPC creation is very quick, once done to create a VPC, and then you need to create one or more subnets within VPC.

In the following example, one VPC is created via the AWS command line:

```
//specify CIDR block as 10.0.0.0/16
//the result, it returns VPC ID as "vpc-66eda61f"
$ aws ec2 create-vpc --cidr-block 10.0.0.0/16
{
  "Vpc": {
   "VpcId": "vpc-66eda61f",
   "InstanceTenancy": "default",
   "Tags": [],
   "State": "pending",
   "DhcpOptionsId": "dopt-3d901958",
   "CidrBlock": "10.0.0.0/16"
  }
}
```

Subnet is a logical network block. It must belong to one VPC and in addition, belong to one availability zone. For example, VPC `vpc-66eda61f` and `us-east-1b`. Then the network CIDR must be within VPC's CIDR. For example, if VPC CIDR is `10.0.0.0/16` (`10.0.0.0` - `10.0.255.255`) then one subnet CIDR could be `10.0.1.0/24` (`10.0.1.0` - `10.0.1.255`).

In the following example, two subnets are created (`us-east-1a` and `us-east-1b`) onto `vpc-66eda61f`:

```
//1st subnet 10.0."1".0/24 on us-east-1"a" availability zone
$ aws ec2 create-subnet --vpc-id vpc-66eda61f --cidr-block 10.0.1.0/24 --
availability-zone us-east-1a
{
    "Subnet": {
      "VpcId": "vpc-66eda61f",
      "CidrBlock": "10.0.1.0/24",
      "State": "pending",
      "AvailabilityZone": "us-east-1a",
      "SubnetId": "subnet-d83a4b82",
      "AvailableIpAddressCount": 251
    }
}

//2nd subnet 10.0."2".0/24 on us-east-1"b"
$ aws ec2 create-subnet --vpc-id vpc-66eda61f --cidr-block 10.0.2.0/24 --
availability-zone us-east-1b
{
    "Subnet": {
      "VpcId": "vpc-66eda61f",
      "CidrBlock": "10.0.2.0/24",
      "State": "pending",
      "AvailabilityZone": "us-east-1b",
      "SubnetId": "subnet-62758c06",
      "AvailableIpAddressCount": 251
    }
}
```

Let's make the first subnet a public facing subnet and the second subnet a private subnet. This means the public facing subnet can be accessible from the internet, which allows it to have a public IP address. On the other hand, a private subnet can't have a public IP address. To do that, you need to set up gateways and routing tables.

In order to make high availability for public networks and private networks, it is recommended to create at least four subnets (two public and two private on different availability zones).
But to simplify examples that are easy to understand, these examples create one public and one private subnet.

Internet gateway and NAT-GW

In most cases, your VPC needs to have a connection with the public internet. In this case, you need to create an **IGW** (**internet gateway**) to attach to your VPC.

In the following example, an IGW is created and attached to `vpc-66eda61f`:

```
//create IGW, it returns IGW id as igw-c3a695a5
$ aws ec2 create-internet-gateway
{
    "InternetGateway": {
        "Tags": [],
        "InternetGatewayId": "igw-c3a695a5",
        "Attachments": []
    }
}


//attach igw-c3a695a5 to vpc-66eda61f
$ aws ec2 attach-internet-gateway --vpc-id vpc-66eda61f --internet-gateway-
id igw-c3a695a5
```

Once the IGW is attached, then set a routing table (default gateway) for a subnet that points to the IGW. If a default gateway points to an IGW, this subnet is able to have a public IP address and access from/to the internet. Therefore, if the default gateway doesn't point to IGW, it is determined as a private subnet, which means no public access.

In the following example, a routing table is created that points to IGW and is set to the first subnet:

```
//create route table within vpc-66eda61f
//it returns route table id as rtb-fb41a280
$ aws ec2 create-route-table --vpc-id vpc-66eda61f
{
  "RouteTable": {
   "Associations": [],
   "RouteTableId": "rtb-fb41a280",
   "VpcId": "vpc-66eda61f",
   "PropagatingVgws": [],
   "Tags": [],
   "Routes": [
     {
       "GatewayId": "local",
       "DestinationCidrBlock": "10.0.0.0/16",
        "State": "active",
        "Origin": "CreateRouteTable"
     }
   ]
```

```
    }
}


//then set default route (0.0.0.0/0) as igw-c3a695a5
$ aws ec2 create-route --route-table-id rtb-fb41a280 --gateway-id igw-
c3a695a5 --destination-cidr-block 0.0.0.0/0
{
    "Return": true
}


//finally, update 1ˢᵗ subnet (subnet-d83a4b82) to use this route table
$ aws ec2 associate-route-table --route-table-id rtb-fb41a280 --subnet-id
subnet-d83a4b82
{
    "AssociationId": "rtbassoc-bf832dc5"
}


//because 1ˢᵗ subnet is public, assign public IP when launch EC2
$ aws ec2 modify-subnet-attribute --subnet-id subnet-d83a4b82 --map-public-
ip-on-launch
```

On the other hand, the second subnet, although a private subnet, does not need a public IP address, however, a private subnet sometimes needs to access the internet. For example, download some packages and access the AWS service access. In this case, we still have an option to connect to the internet. It is called **Network Address Translation Gateway (NAT-GW)**.

NAT-GW allows private subnets to access the public internet through NAT-GW. Therefore, NAT-GW must be located at a public subnet, and the private subnet routing table points to NAT-GW as a default gateway. Note that in order to access NAT-GW on the public network, it needs **Elastic IP (EIP)** attached to the NAT-GW.

In the following example, a NAT-GW is created:

```
//allocate EIP, it returns allocation id as eipalloc-56683465
$ aws ec2 allocate-address
{
    "PublicIp": "34.233.6.60",
    "Domain": "vpc",
    "AllocationId": "eipalloc-56683465"
}


//create NAT-GW on 1ˢᵗ public subnet (subnet-d83a4b82)
//also assign EIP eipalloc-56683465
$ aws ec2 create-nat-gateway --subnet-id subnet-d83a4b82 --allocation-id
eipalloc-56683465
```

```
{
  "NatGateway": {
    "NatGatewayAddresses": [
      {
        "AllocationId": "eipalloc-56683465"
      }
    ],
    "VpcId": "vpc-66eda61f",
    "State": "pending",
    "NatGatewayId": "nat-084ff8ba1edd54bf4",
    "SubnetId": "subnet-d83a4b82",
    "CreateTime": "2017-08-13T21:07:34.000Z"
  }
}
```

Unlike an IGW, AWS charges you an additional hourly cost for Elastic IP and NAT-GW. Therefore, if you wish to save costs, launch an NAT-GW only while accessing the internet.

Creating NAT-GW takes a few minutes, then once NAT-GW is created, update a private subnet routing table that point to NAT-GW, and then any EC2 instances are able to access the internet, but again, due to no public IP address on the private subnet, there is no chance of access from the public internet to the private subnet EC2 instances.

In the following example, an update routing table for the second subnet points to NAT-GW as the default gateway:

```
//as same as public route, need to create a route table first
$ aws ec2 create-route-table --vpc-id vpc-66eda61f
{
  "RouteTable": {
    "Associations": [],
    "RouteTableId": "rtb-cc4cafb7",
    "VpcId": "vpc-66eda61f",
    "PropagatingVgws": [],
    "Tags": [],
    "Routes": [
      {
        "GatewayId": "local",
        "DestinationCidrBlock": "10.0.0.0/16",
        "State": "active",
        "Origin": "CreateRouteTable"
      }
    ]
  }
}
```

```
//then assign default gateway as NAT-GW
$ aws ec2 create-route --route-table-id rtb-cc4cafb7 --nat-gateway-id
nat-084ff8ba1edd54bf4 --destination-cidr-block 0.0.0.0/0
{
    "Return": true
}

//finally update 2nd subnet that use this routing table
$ aws ec2 associate-route-table --route-table-id rtb-cc4cafb7 --subnet-id
subnet-62758c06
{
    "AssociationId": "rtbassoc-2760ce5d"
}
```

Overall, there are two subnets that have been configured as public subnet and private subnet. Each subnet has a default route to use IGW and NAT-GW as follows. Note that ID varies because AWS assigns a unique identifier:

Types of subnet	CIDR block	Subnet ID	Route table ID	Default gateway	Assign Public IP while EC2 launches
Public	10.0.1.0/24	subnet-d83a4b82	rtb-fb41a280	igw-c3a695a5 (IGW)	Yes
Private	10.0.2.0/24	subnet-62758c06	rtb-cc4cafb7	nat-084ff8ba1edd54bf4 (NAT-GW)	No (default)

> Technically, you can still assign a public IP to private subnet EC2 instance, but there is no default gateway to the internet (IGW). Therefore, a public IP will just be wasted and absolutely not have connectivity from the internet.

Now if you launch an EC2 instance on the public subnet, it becomes public facing, so you can serve your application from this subnet.

On the other hand, if you launch an EC2 instance on the private subnet, it can still access to the internet through NAT-GW, but there will be no access from the internet. However, it can still access it from the public subnet's EC2 instances. So you can deploy internal services such as database, middleware, and monitoring tools.

Security group

Once VPC and subnets with related gateways/routes are ready, you can create EC2 instances. However, at least one access control needs to be created beforehand, which is called a **security group**. It can define a firewall rule that ingress (incoming network access) and egress (outgoing network access).

In the following example, a security group and a rule for public subnet hosts are created that allows ssh from your machine's IP address, as well as open HTTP(80/tcp) world-wide:

 When you define a security group for public subnet, it is highly recommended it to be reviewed by a security expert. Because once you deploy an EC2 instance onto the public subnet, it has a public IP address and then everyone including crackers and bots are able to access your instances directly.

```
//create one security group for public subnet host on vpc-66eda61f
$ aws ec2 create-security-group --vpc-id vpc-66eda61f --group-name public -
-description "public facing host"
{
   "GroupId": "sg-7d429f0d"
}


//check your machine's public IP (if not sure, use 0.0.0.0/0 as temporary)
$ curl ifconfig.co
107.196.102.199


//public facing machine allows ssh only from your machine
$ aws ec2 authorize-security-group-ingress --group-id sg-7d429f0d --
protocol tcp --port 22 --cidr 107.196.102.199/32


//public facing machine allow HTTP access from any host (0.0.0.0/0)
$ aws ec2 authorize-security-group-ingress --group-id sg-d173aea1 --
protocol tcp --port 80 --cidr 0.0.0.0/0
```

Next, create a security group for a private subnet host, that allows ssh from the public subnet host. In this case, specifing a public subnet security group ID (sg-7d429f0d) instead of a CIDR block is convenient:

```
//create security group for private subnet
$ aws ec2 create-security-group --vpc-id vpc-66eda61f --group-name private
--description "private subnet host"
{
    "GroupId": "sg-d173aea1"
}
```

```
//private subnet allows ssh only from ssh bastion host security group
//it also allows HTTP (80/TCP) from public subnet security group
$ aws ec2 authorize-security-group-ingress --group-id sg-d173aea1 --
protocol tcp --port 22 --source-group sg-7d429f0d

//private subnet allows HTTP access from public subnet security group too
$ aws ec2 authorize-security-group-ingress --group-id sg-d173aea1 --
protocol tcp --port 80 --source-group sg-7d429f0d
```

Overall, there are two security groups that have been created as follows:

Name	Security group ID	Allow ssh (22/TCP)	Allow HTTP (80/TCP)
Public	sg-7d429f0d	Your machine (107.196.102.199)	0.0.0.0/0
Private	sg-d173aea1	public sg (sg-7d429f0d)	public sg (sg-7d429f0d)

EC2 and EBS

EC2 is one important service in AWS that you can launch a VM on your VPC. Based on hardware spec (CPU, memory, and network), there are several types of EC2 instances that are available on AWS. When you launch an EC2 instance, you need to specify VPC, subnet, security group, and ssh keypair. Therefore, all of these must be created beforehand.

Because of previous examples, the only last step is ssh keypair. Let's make an ssh keypair:

```
//create keypair (internal_rsa, internal_rsa.pub)
$ ssh-keygen
Generating public/private rsa key pair.
Enter file in which to save the key (/Users/saito/.ssh/id_rsa):
/tmp/internal_rsa
Enter passphrase (empty for no passphrase):
Enter same passphrase again:
Your identification has been saved in /tmp/internal_rsa.
Your public key has been saved in /tmp/internal_rsa.pub.

//register internal_rsa.pub key to AWS
$ aws ec2 import-key-pair --key-name=internal --public-key-material "`cat
/tmp/internal_rsa.pub`"
{
    "KeyName": "internal",
    "KeyFingerprint":
 "18:e7:86:d7:89:15:5d:3b:bc:bd:5f:b4:d5:1c:83:81"
}
```

```
//launch public facing host, using Amazon Linux on us-east-1 (ami-a4c7edb2)
$ aws ec2 run-instances --image-id ami-a4c7edb2 --instance-type t2.nano --
key-name internal --security-group-ids sg-7d429f0d --subnet-id subnet-
d83a4b82

//launch private subnet host
$ aws ec2 run-instances --image-id ami-a4c7edb2 --instance-type t2.nano --
key-name internal --security-group-ids sg-d173aea1 --subnet-id
subnet-62758c06
```

After a few minutes, check the EC2 instances status on the AWS web console; it shows a public subnet host that has a public IP address. On the other hand, a private subnet host doesn't have a public IP address:

Instance ID	Availability :	IPv4 Public IP	Key Name	VPC ID	Subnet ID	Private IP Add
i-0b51f497f831fab28	us-east-1b	-	internal	vpc-66eda61f	subnet-62758c06	10.0.2.98
i-0db344916c90fae61	us-east-1a	54.227.197.56	internal	vpc-66eda61f	subnet-d83a4b82	10.0.1.24

```
//add private keys to ssh-agent
$ ssh-add -K /tmp/internal_rsa
Identity added: /tmp/internal_rsa (/tmp/internal_rsa)
$ ssh-add -l
2048 SHA256:AMkdBxkVZxPz0gBTzLPCwEtaDqou4XyiRzTTG4vtqTo /tmp/internal_rsa
(RSA)

//ssh to the public subnet host with -A (forward ssh-agent) option
$ ssh -A ec2-user@54.227.197.56
The authenticity of host '54.227.197.56 (54.227.197.56)' can't be
established.
ECDSA key fingerprint is
SHA256:ocI7Q60RB+k2qbU90H09Or0FhvBEydVI2wXIDzOacaE.
Are you sure you want to continue connecting (yes/no)? yes
Warning: Permanently added '54.227.197.56' (ECDSA) to the list of known
hosts.
          __|  __|_  )
          _|  (     /    Amazon Linux AMI
         ___|\___|___|
    https://aws.amazon.com/amazon-linux-ami/2017.03-release-notes/
    2 package(s) needed for security, out of 6 available
    Run "sudo yum update" to apply all updates.
```

Now you are in the public subnet host (54.227.197.56), but this host also has an internal (private) IP address, because this host is deployed in the 10.0.1.0/24 subnet (subnet-d83a4b82), therefore the private address range must be 10.0.1.1 - 10.0.1.254:

```
$ ifconfig eth0
eth0      Link encap:Ethernet  HWaddr 0E:8D:38:BE:52:34
          inet addr:10.0.1.24  Bcast:10.0.1.255
          Mask:255.255.255.0
```

Let's install nginx web server on the public host as follows:

```
$ sudo yum -y -q install nginx
$ sudo /etc/init.d/nginx start
Starting nginx:                                          [  OK  ]
```

Then, go back to your machine and check the website for 54.227.197.56:

```
$ exit
logout
Connection to 52.227.197.56 closed.

//from your machine, access to nginx
$ curl -I 54.227.197.56
HTTP/1.1 200 OK
Server: nginx/1.10.3
...
Accept-Ranges: bytes
```

In addition, within the same VPC, there is reachability for other availability zones, therefore you can ssh from this host to the private subnet host (10.0.2.98). Note that we are using the ssh -A option that forwards a ssh-agent, so there is no need to create a ~/.ssh/id_rsa file:

```
[ec2-user@ip-10-0-1-24 ~]$ ssh 10.0.2.98
The authenticity of host '10.0.2.98 (10.0.2.98)' can't be established.
ECDSA key fingerprint is 1a:37:c3:c1:e3:8f:24:56:6f:90:8f:4a:ff:5e:79:0b.
Are you sure you want to continue connecting (yes/no)? yes
    Warning: Permanently added '10.0.2.98' (ECDSA) to the list of known
 hosts.
           __|  __|_  )
           _|  (     /    Amazon Linux AMI
          ___|\___|___|
https://aws.amazon.com/amazon-linux-ami/2017.03-release-notes/
2 package(s) needed for security, out of 6 available
Run "sudo yum update" to apply all updates.
[ec2-user@ip-10-0-2-98 ~]$
```

In addition to EC2, there is an important functionality, which is disk management. AWS provides a flexible disk management service called **Elastic Block Store** (**EBS**). You may create one or more persistent data storage that can attach to an EC2 instance. From an EC2 point of view, EBS is one of HDD/SSD. Once you terminate (delete) an EC2 instance, EBS and its contents may remain and then reattach to another EC2 instance.

In the following example, one volume that has 40 GB capacity is created; and then attached to a public subnet host (instance ID i-0db344916c90fae61):

```
//create 40GB disk at us-east-1a (as same as EC2 host instance)
$ aws ec2 create-volume --availability-zone us-east-1a --size 40 --volume-
type standard
{
    "AvailabilityZone": "us-east-1a",
    "Encrypted": false,
    "VolumeType": "standard",
    "VolumeId": "vol-005032342495918d6",
    "State": "creating",
    "SnapshotId": "",
    "CreateTime": "2017-08-16T05:41:53.271Z",
    "Size": 40
}

//attach to public subnet host as /dev/xvdh
$ aws ec2 attach-volume --device xvdh --instance-id i-0db344916c90fae61 --
volume-id vol-005032342495918d6
{
    "AttachTime": "2017-08-16T05:47:07.598Z",
    "InstanceId": "i-0db344916c90fae61",
    "VolumeId": "vol-005032342495918d6",
    "State": "attaching",
    "Device": "xvdh"
}
```

After attaching the EBS volume to the EC2 instance, the Linux kernel recognizes `/dev/xvdh` as specified, and then you need to do partitioning in order to use this device, as follows:

```
● ● ●          ⬆ saito — root@ip-10-0-1-24:~ — ssh ec2-user@54.227.197.56 — 79×41
                    root@ip-10-0-1-24:~ — ssh ec2-user@54.227.197.56                    +
[root@ip-10-0-1-24 ~]# ls /dev/xv*
/dev/xvda    /dev/xvda1    /dev/xvdh
[root@ip-10-0-1-24 ~]# fdisk /dev/xvdh
Welcome to fdisk (util-linux 2.23.2).

Changes will remain in memory only, until you decide to write them.
Be careful before using the write command.

Device does not contain a recognized partition table
Building a new DOS disklabel with disk identifier 0x4867ac2f.

Command (m for help): n
Partition type:
   p   primary (0 primary, 0 extended, 4 free)
   e   extended
Select (default p): p
Partition number (1-4, default 1):
First sector (2048-83886079, default 2048):
Using default value 2048
Last sector, +sectors or +size{K,M,G} (2048-83886079, default 83886079):
Using default value 83886079
Partition 1 of type Linux and of size 40 GiB is set

Command (m for help): p

Disk /dev/xvdh: 42.9 GB, 42949672960 bytes, 83886080 sectors
Units = sectors of 1 * 512 = 512 bytes
Sector size (logical/physical): 512 bytes / 512 bytes
I/O size (minimum/optimal): 512 bytes / 512 bytes
Disk label type: dos
Disk identifier: 0x4867ac2f

    Device Boot      Start         End      Blocks   Id  System
/dev/xvdh1            2048    83886079    41942016   83  Linux

Command (m for help): w
The partition table has been altered!

Calling ioctl() to re-read partition table.
Syncing disks.
[root@ip-10-0-1-24 ~]# ▮
```

In this example, we made one partition as /dev/xvdh1, so you can create a filesystem as ext4 format on /dev/xvdh1 and then you can mount to use this device on an EC2 instance:

```
[root@ip-10-0-1-24 ~]# mkfs.ext4 /dev/xvdh1
mke2fs 1.42.12 (29-Aug-2014)
Creating filesystem with 10485504 4k blocks and 2621440 inodes
Filesystem UUID: 5cc5edff-d667-420c-a189-4d2b1e966607
Superblock backups stored on blocks:
        32768, 98304, 163840, 229376, 294912, 819200, 884736, 1605632, 2654208,

        4096000, 7962624

Allocating group tables: done
Writing inode tables: done
Creating journal (32768 blocks): done
Writing superblocks and filesystem accounting information: done

[root@ip-10-0-1-24 ~]#
[root@ip-10-0-1-24 ~]# mount /dev/xvdh1 /mnt
[root@ip-10-0-1-24 ~]# cd /mnt
[root@ip-10-0-1-24 mnt]# ls
lost+found
[root@ip-10-0-1-24 mnt]# df -h /mnt
Filesystem       Size   Used Avail Use% Mounted on
/dev/xvdh1        40G    48M   38G   1% /mnt
[root@ip-10-0-1-24 mnt]# touch hello
[root@ip-10-0-1-24 mnt]# cd /
[root@ip-10-0-1-24 /]# umount /mnt
```

After unmounting the volume, you can feel free to detach this volume and then re-attach it whenever needed:

```
//detach volume
$ aws ec2 detach-volume --volume-id vol-005032342495918d6
{
    "AttachTime": "2017-08-16T06:03:45.000Z",
    "InstanceId": "i-0db344916c90fae61",
    "VolumeId": "vol-005032342495918d6",
    "State": "detaching",
    "Device": "xvdh"
}
```

Route 53

AWS also provides a hosted DNS service called **Route 53**. Route 53 allows you to manage your own domain name and associated FQDN to an IP address. For example, if you want to have a domain name `k8s-devops.net`, you can order through Route 53 to register your DNS domain.

The following screenshot shows ordering a domain name `k8s-devops.net`; it may take a few hours to complete registration:

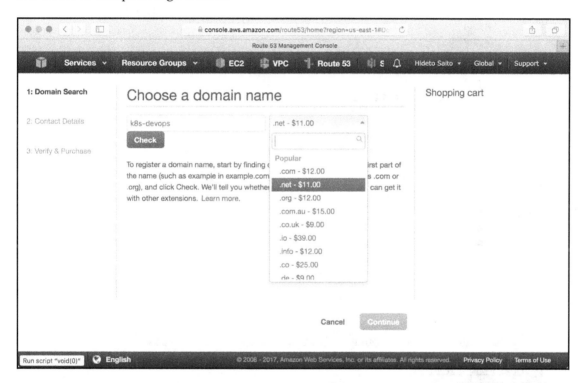

Once registration is completed, you may receive a notification email from AWS, and then you can control this domain name via the AWS command line or a web console. Let's add one record (FQDN to IP address) that associate `public.k8s-devops.net` with the public facing EC2 host public IP address `54.227.197.56`. To do that, get a hosted zone ID as follows:

```
$ aws route53 list-hosted-zones | grep Id
"Id": "/hostedzone/Z1CTVYM9SLEAN8",
```

Now you get a hosted zone id as `/hostedzone/Z1CTVYM9SLEAN8`, so let's prepare a JSON file to update the DNS record as follows:

```
//create JSON file
$ cat /tmp/add-record.json
{
  "Comment": "add public subnet host",
  "Changes": [
   {
     "Action": "UPSERT",
     "ResourceRecordSet": {
       "Name": "public.k8s-devops.net",
       "Type": "A",
       "TTL": 300,
       "ResourceRecords": [
         {
          "Value": "54.227.197.56"
         }
       ]
     }
   }
  ]
}

//submit to Route53
$ aws route53 change-resource-record-sets --hosted-zone-id
/hostedzone/Z1CTVYM9SLEAN8 --change-batch file:///tmp/add-record.json

//a few minutes later, check whether A record is created or not
$ dig public.k8s-devops.net
; <<>> DiG 9.8.3-P1 <<>> public.k8s-devops.net
;; global options: +cmd
;; Got answer:
;; ->>HEADER<<- opcode: QUERY, status: NOERROR, id: 18609
;; flags: qr rd ra; QUERY: 1, ANSWER: 1, AUTHORITY: 0, ADDITIONAL: 0
;; QUESTION SECTION:
;public.k8s-devops.net.        IN    A
;; ANSWER SECTION:
public.k8s-devops.net.  300   IN    A    54.227.197.56
```

Looks good, so now access the nginx through the DNS name `public.k8s-devops.net`:

```
$ curl -I public.k8s-devops.net
HTTP/1.1 200 OK
Server: nginx/1.10.3
...
```

ELB

AWS provides a powerful software based load balancer called **Elastic Load Balancer** (**ELB**). It allows you to load balance network traffic to one or multiple EC2 instances. In addition, ELB can offload SSL/TLS encryption/decryption and also supports multi-availability zone.

In the following example, an ELB is created and associated with a public subnet host nginx (80/TCP). Because ELB also needs a security group, create a new security group for ELB first:

```
$ aws ec2 create-security-group --vpc-id vpc-66eda61f --group-name elb --
description "elb sg"
{
   "GroupId": "sg-51d77921"
}


$ aws ec2 authorize-security-group-ingress --group-id sg-51d77921 --
protocol tcp --port 80 --cidr 0.0.0.0/0

$ aws elb create-load-balancer --load-balancer-name public-elb --listeners
Protocol=HTTP,LoadBalancerPort=80,InstanceProtocol=HTTP,InstancePort=80 --
subnets subnet-d83a4b82 --security-groups sg-51d77921
{
    "DNSName": "public-elb-1779693260.us-east-
    1.elb.amazonaws.com"
}


$ aws elb register-instances-with-load-balancer --load-balancer-name
public-elb --instances i-0db344916c90fae61

$ curl -I public-elb-1779693260.us-east-1.elb.amazonaws.com
HTTP/1.1 200 OK
Accept-Ranges: bytes
Content-Length: 3770
Content-Type: text/html
...
```

Let's update the Route 53 DNS record `public.k8s-devops.net` that points to ELB. In this case, ELB already has an `A` record, therefore use a `CNAME` (alias) that points to ELB FQDN:

```
$ cat change-to-elb.json
{
  "Comment": "use CNAME to pointing to ELB",
  "Changes": [
    {
      "Action": "DELETE",
      "ResourceRecordSet": {
        "Name": "public.k8s-devops.net",
        "Type": "A",
        "TTL": 300,
        "ResourceRecords": [
          {
            "Value": "52.86.166.223"
          }
        ]
      }
    },
    {
      "Action": "UPSERT",
      "ResourceRecordSet": {
        "Name": "public.k8s-devops.net",
        "Type": "CNAME",
        "TTL": 300,
        "ResourceRecords": [
          {
            "Value": "public-elb-1779693260.us-east-
1.elb.amazonaws.com"
          }
        ]
      }
    }
  ]
}

$ dig public.k8s-devops.net
; <<>> DiG 9.8.3-P1 <<>> public.k8s-devops.net
;; global options: +cmd
;; Got answer:
;; ->>HEADER<<- opcode: QUERY, status: NOERROR, id: 10278
;; flags: qr rd ra; QUERY: 1, ANSWER: 3, AUTHORITY: 0, ADDITIONAL: 0
;; QUESTION SECTION:
;public.k8s-devops.net.          IN      A
;; ANSWER SECTION:
public.k8s-devops.net.  300     IN      CNAME public-elb-1779693260.us-
east-1.elb.amazonaws.com.
```

```
public-elb-1779693260.us-east-1.elb.amazonaws.com. 60 IN A 52.200.46.81
public-elb-1779693260.us-east-1.elb.amazonaws.com. 60 IN A 52.73.172.171
;; Query time: 77 msec
;; SERVER: 10.0.0.1#53(10.0.0.1)
;; WHEN: Wed Aug 16 22:21:33 2017
;; MSG SIZE  rcvd: 134

$ curl -I public.k8s-devops.net
HTTP/1.1 200 OK
Accept-Ranges: bytes
Content-Length: 3770
Content-Type: text/html
...
```

S3

AWS provides a useful object data store service called **Simple Storage Service** (**S3**). It is not like EBS, no EC2 instance can mount as a file system. Instead, use AWS API to transfer a file to the S3. Therefore, AWS can make availability (99.999999999%) and multiple instances can access it at the same time. It is good to store non-throughput and random access sensitive files such as configuration files, log files, and data files.

In the following example, a file is uploaded from your machine to AWS S3:

```
//create S3 bucket "k8s-devops"
$ aws s3 mb s3://k8s-devops
make_bucket: k8s-devops

//copy files to S3 bucket
$ aws s3 cp add-record.json s3://k8s-devops/
upload: ./add-record.json to s3://k8s-devops/add-record.json
$ aws s3 cp change-to-elb.json s3://k8s-devops/
upload: ./change-to-elb.json to s3://k8s-devops/change-to-elb.json

//check files on S3 bucket
$ aws s3 ls s3://k8s-devops/
2017-08-17 20:00:21        319 add-record.json
2017-08-17 20:00:28        623 change-to-elb.json
```

Overall, we've discussed how to configure AWS components around VPC. The following diagram shows a major component and relationship:

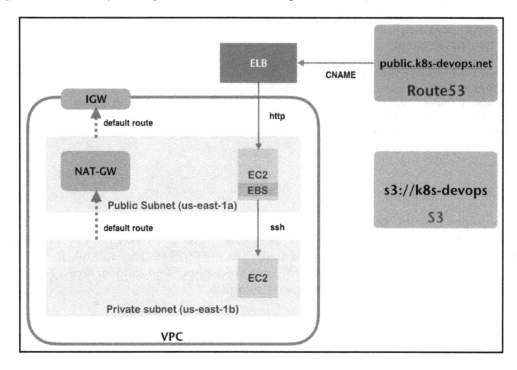

Setup Kubernetes on AWS

We've discussed some AWS components that are quite easy to set up networks, virtual machines, and storage. Therefore, there are a variety of ways to set up Kubernetes on AWS such as kubeadm (`https://github.com/kubernetes/kubeadm`), kops (`https://github.com/kubernetes/kops`), and kubespray (`https://github.com/kubernetes-incubator/kubespray`). One of the recommended ways to set up Kubernetes is using kops, which is a production grade setup tool and supports a lot of configuration. In this chapter, we will use kops to configure Kubernetes on AWS. Note that kops stands for Kubernetes operations.

Install kops

First of all, you need to install kops to your machine. Linux and macOS are supported. Kops is a single binary, so just copy the `kops` command to `/usr/local/bin` as recommended. After that, create an `IAM` user and role for kops that handles the kops operation. For details, follow the official documentation (`https://github.com/kubernetes/kops/blob/master/docs/aws.md`).

Run kops

Kops needs an S3 bucket that stores the configuration and status. In addition, use Route 53 to register the Kubernetes API server name, and etcd server name to the domain name system. Therefore, use S3 bucket and use the Route 53 that we've created in the previous section.

Kops supports a variety of configurations, such as deploying to public subnets, private subnets, using different types and number of EC2 instances, high availability, and overlaying networks. Let's configure Kubernetes with a similar configuration of network in the previous section as follows:

 Kops has an option to reuse existing VPC and subnets. However, it behaves tricky and may encounter some issues based on settings; it is recommended to create a new VPC by kops. For details, you may find a document at `https://github.com/kubernetes/kops/blob/master/docs/run_in_exist ing_vpc.md`.

Parameter	Value	Means
`--name`	`my-cluster.k8s-devops.net`	Set up `my-cluster` under `k8s-devops.net` domain
`--state`	`s3://k8s-devops`	Use k8s-devops S3 bucket
`--zones`	`us-east-1a`	Deploy on `us-east-1a` Availability Zone
`--cloud`	`aws`	Use AWS as cloud provider
`--network-cidr`	`10.0.0.0/16`	Create new VPC with CIDR 10.0.0.0/16

--master-size	t2.large	Use EC2 t2.large instance for master
--node-size	t2.medium	Use EC2 t2.medium instance for nodes
--node-count	2	Set up two nodes
--networking	calico	Use Calico for overlay network
--topology	private	Set up both public and private subnet, and deploy master and node to private
--ssh-puglic-key	/tmp/internal_rsa.pub	Use /tmp/internal_rsa.pub for bastion host
--bastion		Create ssh bastion server on public subnet
--yes		Immediately to execute

Therefore, run the following to run kops:

```
$ kops create cluster --name my-cluster.k8s-devops.net --state=s3://k8s-
devops --zones us-east-1a --cloud aws --network-cidr 10.0.0.0/16 --master-
size t2.large --node-size t2.medium --node-count 2 --networking calico --
topology private --ssh-public-key /tmp/internal_rsa.pub --bastion --yes
I0818 20:43:15.022735   11372 create_cluster.go:845] Using SSH public key:
/tmp/internal_rsa.pub
...
I0818 20:45:32.585246   11372 executor.go:91] Tasks: 78 done / 78 total; 0
can run
I0818 20:45:32.587067   11372 dns.go:152] Pre-creating DNS records
I0818 20:45:35.266425   11372 update_cluster.go:247] Exporting kubecfg for
cluster
Kops has set your kubectl context to my-cluster.k8s-devops.net
Cluster is starting.  It should be ready in a few minutes.
```

It may take around 5 to 10 minutes to fully complete after seeing the preceding messages. This is because it requires us to create the VPC, subnet, and NAT-GW, launch EC2s, then install Kubernetes master and node, launch ELB, and then update Route 53 as follows:

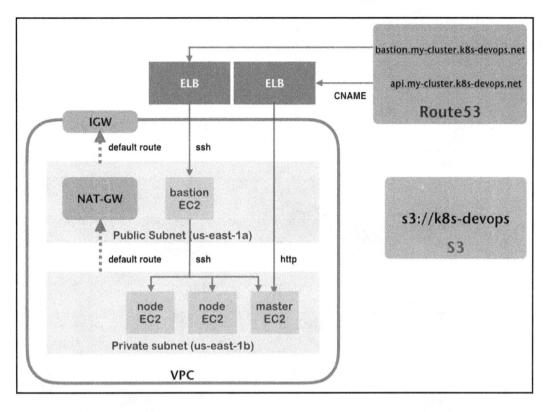

Once complete, `kops` updates `~/.kube/config` on your machine points to your
Kubernetes API Server. Kops creates an ELB and sets the corresponding FQDN record on
Route 53 as `https://api.<your-cluster-name>.<your-domain-name>/`, therefore,
you may run the `kubectl` command from your machine directly to see the list of nodes as
follows:

```
$ kubectl get nodes
NAME                           STATUS         AGE     VERSION
ip-10-0-36-157.ec2.internal    Ready,master   8m      v1.7.0
ip-10-0-42-97.ec2.internal     Ready,node     6m      v1.7.0
ip-10-0-42-170.ec2.internal    Ready,node     6m      v1.7.0
```

Hooray! It took just a few minutes to set up AWS Infrastructure and Kubernetes on the
AWS from scratch. Now you can deploy pod through the `kubectl` command. But you may
want to ssh to the master/node to see what is going on.

However, due to security reasons, if you specify `--topology private`, you can ssh to only the bastion host. Then ssh to master/node host using a private IP address. This is similar to the previous section that ssh to public subnet host, then ssh to the private subnet host using ssh-agent (`-A` option).

In the following example, we ssh to the bastion host (kops creates Route 53 entry as `bastion.my-cluster.k8s-devops.net`) and then ssh to master (`10.0.36.157`):

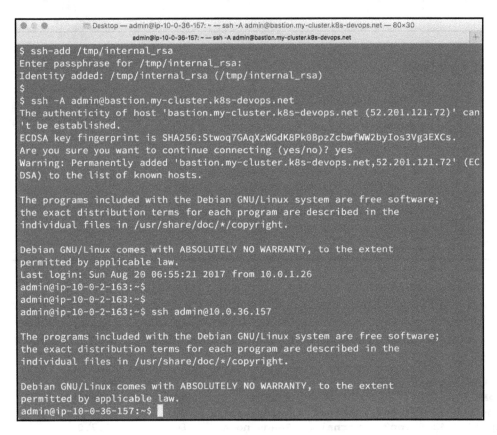

Kubernetes cloud provider

While setting up Kubernetes by kops, it also configures Kubernetes cloud provider as AWS. Which means when you use the Kubernetes service with LoadBalancer, it will use ELB. It also uses **Elastic Block Store** (**EBS**) as its `StorageClass`.

L4 LoadBalancer

When you make the Kubernetes service public to the external world, using ELB makes much more sense. Setting service type as LoadBalancer will invoke ELB creation and associate it with nodes:

```
$ cat grafana.yml
apiVersion: apps/v1beta1
kind: Deployment
metadata:
  name: grafana
spec:
  replicas: 1
  template:
   metadata:
    labels:
      run: grafana
    spec:
     containers:
      - image: grafana/grafana
        name: grafana
        ports:
         - containerPort: 3000
---
apiVersion: v1
kind: Service
metadata:
  name: grafana
spec:
  ports:
   - port: 80
     targetPort: 3000
  type: LoadBalancer
  selector:
    run: grafana


$ kubectl create -f grafana.yml
deployment "grafana" created
service "grafana" created

$ kubectl get service
NAME          CLUSTER-IP        EXTERNAL-IP        PORT(S)          AGE
grafana       100.65.232.120    a5d97c8ef8575...   80:32111/TCP     11s
kubernetes    100.64.0.1        <none>             443/TCP          13m

$ aws elb describe-load-balancers | grep a5d97c8ef8575 | grep DNSName
        "DNSName": "a5d97c8ef857511e7a6100edf846f38a-1490901085.us-
```

```
east-1.elb.amazonaws.com",
```

As you can see, ELB has been created automatically and the DNS is `a5d97c8ef857511e7a6100edf846f38a-1490901085.us-east-1.elb.amazonaws.com`, so now you can access Grafana at `http://a5d97c8ef857511e7a6100edf846f38a-1490901085.us-east-1.elb.amazonaws.com`.

You may use `awscli` to update Route 53 to assign a `CNAME` such as `grafana.k8s-devops.net`. Alternatively, the Kubernetes incubator project `external-dns` (`https://github.com/kubernetes-incubator/external-dns`) can automate to update Route 53 in this situation.

L7 LoadBalancer (ingress)

As of kops version 1.7.0, it doesn't set up the ingress controller out of the box yet. However, kops provides some add-ons
(`https://github.com/kubernetes/kops/tree/master/addons`) that expand the features of Kubernetes. One of the add-ons ingress-nginx
(`https://github.com/kubernetes/kops/tree/master/addons/ingress-nginx`) uses a combination of AWS ELB and nginx to achieve the Kubernetes ingress controller.

In order to install the `ingress-nginx` add-on, type the following command to set up the ingress controller:

```
$ kubectl create -f
https://raw.githubusercontent.com/kubernetes/kops/master/addons/ingress-ngi
nx/v1.6.0.yaml
namespace "kube-ingress" created
serviceaccount "nginx-ingress-controller" created
clusterrole "nginx-ingress-controller" created
role "nginx-ingress-controller" created
clusterrolebinding "nginx-ingress-controller" created
rolebinding "nginx-ingress-controller" created
service "nginx-default-backend" created
deployment "nginx-default-backend" created
configmap "ingress-nginx" created
service "ingress-nginx" created
deployment "ingress-nginx" created
```

After that, deploy nginx and echoserver using the NodePort service as follows:

```
$ kubectl run nginx --image=nginx --port=80
deployment "nginx" created
$
$ kubectl expose deployment nginx --target-port=80 --type=NodePort
service "nginx" exposed
$
$ kubectl run echoserver --image=gcr.io/google_containers/echoserver:1.4 --
port=8080
deployment "echoserver" created
$
$ kubectl expose deployment echoserver --target-port=8080 --type=NodePort
service "echoserver" exposed

// URL "/" point to nginx, "/echo" to echoserver
$ cat nginx-echoserver-ingress.yaml
apiVersion: extensions/v1beta1
kind: Ingress
metadata:
```

```
    name: nginx-echoserver-ingress
spec:
  rules:
  - http:
      paths:
      - path: /
        backend:
          serviceName: nginx
          servicePort: 80
      - path: /echo
        backend:
          serviceName: echoserver
          servicePort: 8080


//check ingress
$ kubectl get ing -o wide
NAME                             HOSTS       ADDRESS
PORTS       AGE
nginx-echoserver-ingress     *
a1705ab488dfa11e7a89e0eb0952587e-28724883.us-east-1.elb.amazonaws.com    80
1m
```

After a few minutes, the ingress controller associates the nginx service and echoserver service with the ELB. When you access the ELB server with URI "/" it shows the nginx screen as follows:

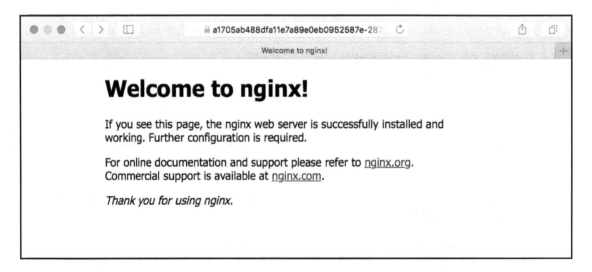

On the other hand, if you access the same ELB, but use the URI "/echo", it shows echoserver as follows:

Compared to the standard Kubernetes LoadBalancer service, one LoadBalancer service consumes one ELB. On the other hand, using the nginx-ingress addon, it can consolidate multiple Kubernetes NodePort services onto the single ELB. This will help to build your RESTful service easier.

StorageClass

As we discussed in `Chapter 4`, *Working with Storage and Resources*, there is a `StorageClass` that can dynamically allocate Persistent Volume. Kops sets up provisioner as `aws-ebs`, which uses EBS:

```
$ kubectl get storageclass
NAME             TYPE
default          kubernetes.io/aws-ebs
gp2 (default)    kubernetes.io/aws-ebs

$ cat pvc-aws.yml
apiVersion: v1
kind: PersistentVolumeClaim
metadata:
  name: pvc-aws-1
spec:
  storageClassName: "default"
  accessModes:
```

```
      - ReadWriteOnce
   resources:
    requests:
      storage: 10Gi

$ kubectl create -f pvc-aws.yml
persistentvolumeclaim "pvc-aws-1" created

$ kubectl get pv
NAME                                          CAPACITY   ACCESSMODES
RECLAIMPOLICY    STATUS    CLAIM               STORAGECLASS   REASON    AGE
pvc-94957090-84a8-11e7-9974-0ea8dc53a244   10Gi       RWO                   Delete
Bound      default/pvc-aws-1     default                  3s
```

This creates EBS volume automatically as follows:

```
$ aws ec2 describe-volumes --filter Name=tag-
value,Values="pvc-51cdf520-8576-11e7-a610-0edf846f38a6"
{
   "Volumes": [
     {
        "AvailabilityZone": "us-east-1a",
        "Attachments": [],
        "Tags": [
         {
...
     ],
        "Encrypted": false,
        "VolumeType": "gp2",
        "VolumeId": "vol-052621c39546f8096",
        "State": "available",
        "Iops": 100,
        "SnapshotId": "",
        "CreateTime": "2017-08-20T07:08:08.773Z",
        "Size": 10
        }
     ]
   }
```

Overall, the Kubernetes cloud provider for AWS is utilized to map ELB to Kubernetes services and also EBS to Kubernetes Persistent Volume. It is a great benefit to use AWS for Kubernetes as there is no need to pre-allocate or buy either a physical LoadBalancer or storage, just pay as you go; it creates flexibility and scalability for your business.

Maintenance Kubernetes cluster by kops

When you need to change the Kubernetes configuration, such as the number of nodes and even EC2 instance type, kops can support this kind of use case. For example, if you want to change Kubernetes node instance type from t2.medium to t2.micro, and also decrease number from 2 to 1 due to cost saving, you need to modify the kops node instance group (ig) setting as follows:

```
$ kops edit ig nodes --name my-cluster.k8s-devops.net --state=s3://k8s-
devops
```

It launches vi editor and you can change the setting for kops node instance group as follows:

```
apiVersion: kops/v1alpha2
kind: InstanceGroup
metadata:
 creationTimestamp: 2017-08-20T06:43:45Z
 labels:
  kops.k8s.io/cluster: my-cluster.k8s-devops.net
 name: nodes
spec:
 image: kope.io/k8s-1.6-debian-jessie-amd64-hvm-ebs-2017-
05-02
 machineType: t2.medium
 maxSize: 2
 minSize: 2
 role: Node
 subnets:
  - us-east-1a
```

In this case, change machineType to t2.small, and maxSize/minSize to the 1 and then save it. After that, run the kops update command to apply settings:

```
$ kops update cluster --name my-cluster.k8s-devops.net --state=s3://k8s-
devops --yes
I0820 00:57:17.900874    2837 executor.go:91] Tasks: 0 done / 94 total; 38
can run
I0820 00:57:19.064626    2837 executor.go:91] Tasks: 38 done / 94 total; 20
can run
...
Kops has set your kubectl context to my-cluster.k8s-devops.net
Cluster changes have been applied to the cloud.
Changes may require instances to restart: kops rolling-update cluster
```

As you see in the preceding message, you need to run the `kops rolling-update cluster` command to reflect to the existing instances. It may take a few minutes to replace the existing instance to the new instance:

```
$ kops rolling-update cluster --name my-cluster.k8s-devops.net --
state=s3://k8s-devops --yes
NAME              STATUS        NEEDUPDATE   READY MIN   MAX   NODES
bastions          Ready         0            1     1     1     0
master-us-east-1a Ready         0            1     1     1     1
nodes             NeedsUpdate 1              0     1     1     1
I0820 01:00:01.086564    2844 instancegroups.go:350] Stopping instance
"i-07e55394ef3a09064", node "ip-10-0-40-170.ec2.internal", in AWS ASG
"nodes.my-cluster.k8s-devops.net".
```

Now the Kubernetes node instance has been decreased from 2 to 1 as follows:

```
$ kubectl get nodes
NAME                        STATUS         AGE    VERSION
ip-10-0-36-157.ec2.internal Ready,master   1h     v1.7.0
ip-10-0-58-135.ec2.internal Ready,node     34s    v1.7.0
```

Summary

In this chapter, we have discussed public cloud. AWS is the most popular public cloud service and it gives the API to control AWS infrastructure programmatically. We can achieve automation and infrastructure as code easily. Especially, kops brings us to ultra-fast AWS and Kubernetes setup from scratch. Both Kubernetes and kops development are quite active. Please keep monitoring those projects, which will have more functionality and configuration in the near future.

The next chapter will introduce **Google Cloud Platform** (**GCP**), which is another popular public cloud service. **Google Container Engine** (**GKE**) is the hosted Kubernetes service that makes using Kubernetes much easier.

10
Kubernetes on GCP

Google Cloud Platform (**GCP**) is getting popular in the public cloud industry that is provided by Google. GCP has similar concepts as AWS such as VPC, Compute Engine, Persistent Disk, Load Balancing, and several managed services. In this chapter, you will learn about GCP and how to set up Kubernetes on GCP through the following topics:

- Understanding GCP
- Using and understanding GCP components
- Using **Google Container Engine** (**GKE**), the hosted Kubernetes service

Introduction to GCP

GCP was officially launched in 2011. But not like AWS; at the beginning, GCP provided **PaaS** (**Platform as a Service**) first. So you can deploy your application directly, instead of launching VM. After that, keep enhance functionality that supports a variety of services.

The most important service for Kubernetes users is GKE, which is a hosted Kubernetes service. So you can get some relief from Kubernetes installation, upgrade, and management. It has a pay–as–you–go style approach to use the Kubernetes cluster. GKE is also a very active service that keeps providing new versions of Kubernetes in a timely manner, and also keeps coming up with new features and management tools for Kubernetes as well.

Let's take a look at what kind of foundation and services are provided by GCP and then explore GKE.

GCP components

GCP provides a web console and **command-line interface** (**CLI**). Both are easy and straightforward to control GCP infrastructure, but Google accounts (such as Gmail) are required. Once you have a Google account, go to the GCP sign up page (https://cloud.google.com/free/) to set up your GCP account creation.

If you want to control via CLI, you need to install Cloud SDK (https://cloud.google.com/sdk/gcloud/), which is similar to AWS CLI that you can use to list, create, update, and delete GCP resources. After installing Cloud SDK, you need to configure it with the following command to associate it to a GCP account:

```
$ gcloud init
```

VPC

VPC in GCP is quite a different policy compared with AWS. First of all, you don't need to set CIDR prefix to VPC, in other words, you cannot set CIDR to VPC. Instead, you just add one or some subnets to the VPC. Because subnet is always coming with certain CIDR blocks, therefore, GCP VPC is identified as a logical group of subnets, and subnets within VPC can communicate with each other.

Note that GCP VPC has two modes, either **auto** or **custom**. If you choose auto, it will create some subnets on each region with predefined CIDR blocks. For example, if you type the following command:

```
$ gcloud compute networks create my-auto-network --mode auto
```

It will create 11 subnets as shown in the following screenshot (because, as of August, 2017, GCP has 11 regions):

my-auto-network	11	Auto ▾		
us-central1	my-auto-network		10.128.0.0/20	10.128.0.1
europe-west1	my-auto-network		10.132.0.0/20	10.132.0.1
us-west1	my-auto-network		10.138.0.0/20	10.138.0.1
asia-east1	my-auto-network		10.140.0.0/20	10.140.0.1
us-east1	my-auto-network		10.142.0.0/20	10.142.0.1
asia-northeast1	my-auto-network		10.146.0.0/20	10.146.0.1
asia-southeast1	my-auto-network		10.148.0.0/20	10.148.0.1
us-east4	my-auto-network		10.150.0.0/20	10.150.0.1
australia-southeast1	my-auto-network		10.152.0.0/20	10.152.0.1
europe-west2	my-auto-network		10.154.0.0/20	10.154.0.1
europe-west3	my-auto-network		10.156.0.0/20	10.156.0.1

Auto mode VPC is probably good to start with. However, in auto mode, you can't specify CIDR prefix and 11 subnets from all regions might not fit with your use case. For example, if you want to integrate to your on–premise data center via VPN, or want to create subnets from a particular region only.

In this case, choose custom mode VPC, then you can create subnets with desired CIDR prefix manually. Type the following command to create custom mode VPC:

```
//create custom mode VPC which is named my-custom-network
$ gcloud compute networks create my-custom-network --mode custom
```

Because custom mode VPC won't create any subnets as shown in the following screenshot, let's add subnets onto this custom mode VPC:

my-custom-network	0	Custom	0

Subnets

Subnet in GCP, its always across multiple zones (availability zone) within region. In other words, you can't create subnets on a single zone like AWS. You always need to specify entire regions when creating a subnet.

In addition, there are no significant concepts of public and private subnets such as AWS (combination of route and internet gateway or NAT gateway to determine as a public or private subnet). This is because all subnets in GCP have a route to internet gateway.

Instead of subnet level access control, GCP uses host (instance) level access control using **network tags** to ensure the network security. It will be described in more detail in the following section.

It might make network administrators nervous, however, GCP best practice brings you much more simplified and scalable VPC administration, because you can add subnets anytime to expand entire network blocks.

 Technically, you can launch VM instance to set up as a NAT gateway or HTTP proxy, and then create a custom priority route for the private subnet that points to the NAT/proxy instance to achieve an AWS–like private subnet.
Please refer to the following online document for details:
`https://cloud.google.com/compute/docs/vpc/special-configurations`

One more thing, an interesting and unique concept of GCP VPC is that you can add different CIDR prefix network blocks to the single VPC. For example, if you have custom mode VPC then add the following three subnets:

- `subnet-a` (`10.0.1.0/24`) from `us-west1`
- `subnet-b` (`172.16.1.0/24`) from `us-east1`
- `subnet-c` (`192.168.1.0/24`) from `asia-northeast1`

The following commands will create three subnets from three different regions with different CIDR prefix:

```
$ gcloud compute networks subnets create subnet-a --network=my-custom-
network --range=10.0.1.0/24 --region=us-west1
$ gcloud compute networks subnets create subnet-b --network=my-custom-
network --range=172.16.1.0/24 --region=us-east1
$ gcloud compute networks subnets create subnet-c --network=my-custom-
network --range=192.168.1.0/24 --region=asia-northeast1
```

The result will be the following web console. If you are familiar with AWS VPC, you won't believe these combinations of CIDR prefixes within a single VPC! This means that, whenever you need to expand a network, you can feel free to assign another CIDR prefix to add to the VPC.

my-custom-network	3	Custom		0
us-west1	**subnet-a**	10.0.1.0/24	10.0.1.1	
us-east1	**subnet-b**	172.16.1.0/24	172.16.1.1	
asia-northeast1	**subnet-c**	192.168.1.0/24	192.168.1.1	

Firewall rules

As mentioned previously, GCP firewall rule is important to achieve network security. But GCP firewall is more simple and flexible than AWS **security group** (**SG**). For example, in AWS, when you launch an EC2 instance, you have to assign at least one SG that is tight coupling with EC2 and SG. On the other hand, in GCP, you can't assign any firewall rules directly. Instead, firewall rule and VM instance are loosely coupled via **network tag**. Therefore, there is no direct association between firewall rule and VM instance. The following diagram is a comparison between AWS security group and GCP firewall rule. EC2 requires security group, on the other hand, GCP VM instance just sets a tag. This is regardless of whether the corresponding firewall has the same tag or not.

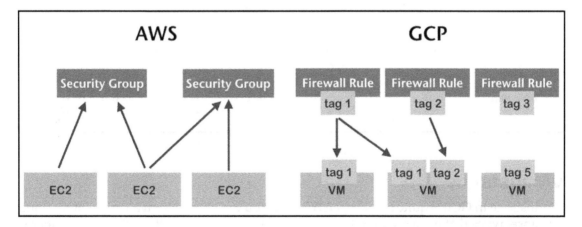

For example, create a firewall rule for public host (use network tag `public`) and private host (use network tag `private`) as given in the following command:

```
//create ssh access for public host
$ gcloud compute firewall-rules create public-ssh --network=my-custom-
network --allow="tcp:22" --source-ranges="0.0.0.0/0" --target-tags="public"

//create http access (80/tcp for public host)
$ gcloud compute firewall-rules create public-http --network=my-custom-
network --allow="tcp:80" --source-ranges="0.0.0.0/0" --target-tags="public"

//create ssh access for private host (allow from host which has "public"
tag)
$ gcloud compute firewall-rules create private-ssh --network=my-custom-
network --allow="tcp:22" --source-tags="public" --target-tags="private"

//create icmp access for internal each other (allow from host which has
either "public" or "private")
$ gcloud compute firewall-rules create internal-icmp --network=my-custom-
network --allow="icmp" --source-tags="public,private"
```

It creates four firewall rules as shown in the following screenshot. Let's create VM instances to use either the `public` or `private` network tag to see how it works:

Name	Targets	Source filters	Protocols / ports	Action	Priority	Network ⌄
internal-icmp	public, 1 more ▾	Tags: public, 1 more ▾	icmp	Allow	1000	my-custom-network
private-ssh	private	Tags: public	tcp:22	Allow	1000	my-custom-network
public-http	public	IP ranges: 0.0.0.0/0	tcp:80	Allow	1000	my-custom-network
public-ssh	public	IP ranges: 0.0.0.0/0	tcp:22	Allow	1000	my-custom-network

VM instance

VM instance in GCP is quite similar to AWS EC2. You can choose from a variety of machine (instance) types that have different hardware configurations. As well as OS images that are Linux or Windows–based OS or your customized OS, you can choose.

As mentioned when talking about firewall rules, you can specify zero or more network tags. A tag is not necessary to be created beforehand. This means you can launch VM instances with network tags first, even though a firewall rule is not created. It is still valid, but no firewall rule is applied in this case. Then create a firewall rule to have a network tag. Eventually a firewall rule will be applied to the VM instances afterwards. This is why VM instances and firewall rules are loosely coupled, which provides flexibility to the user.

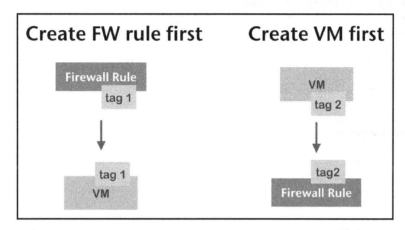

Before launching a VM instance, you need to create a ssh public key first, the same as AWS EC2. The easiest way to do this is to run the following command to create and register a new key:

```
//this command create new ssh key pair
$ gcloud compute config-ssh

//key will be stored as ~/.ssh/google_compute_engine(.pub)
$ cd ~/.ssh
$ ls -l google_compute_engine*
-rw-------  1 saito  admin  1766 Aug 23 22:58 google_compute_engine
-rw-r--r--  1 saito  admin   417 Aug 23 22:58 google_compute_engine.pub
```

Now let's get started to launch a VM instance on GCP.

Deploy two instances on both `subnet-a` and `subnet-b` as public instances (use the `public` network tag) and then launch another instance on the `subnet-a` as private instance (with a `private` network tag):

```
//create public instance ("public" tag) on subnet-a
$ gcloud compute instances create public-on-subnet-a --machine-type=f1-
micro --network=my-custom-network --subnet=subnet-a --zone=us-west1-a --
tags=public
```

```
//create public instance ("public" tag) on subnet-b
$ gcloud compute instances create public-on-subnet-b --machine-type=f1-
micro --network=my-custom-network --subnet=subnet-b --zone=us-east1-c --
tags=public

//create private instance ("private" tag) on subnet-a with larger size (g1-
small)
$ gcloud compute instances create private-on-subnet-a --machine-type=g1-
small --network=my-custom-network --subnet=subnet-a --zone=us-west1-a --
tags=private

//Overall, there are 3 VM instances has been created in this example as
below
$ gcloud compute instances list
NAME                                             ZONE           MACHINE_TYPE
PREEMPTIBLE    INTERNAL_IP    EXTERNAL_IP       STATUS
public-on-subnet-b                               us-east1-c     f1-micro
172.16.1.2    35.196.228.40    RUNNING
private-on-subnet-a                              us-west1-a     g1-small
10.0.1.2      104.199.121.234  RUNNING
public-on-subnet-a                               us-west1-a     f1-micro
10.0.1.3      35.199.171.31    RUNNING
```

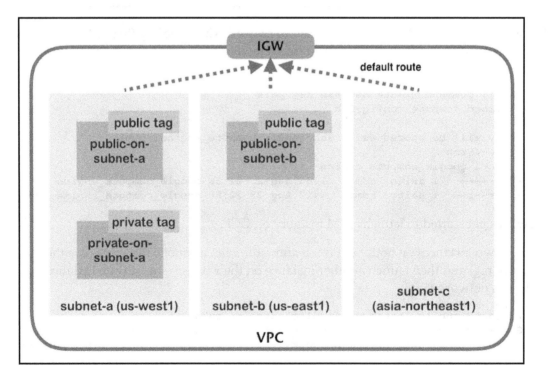

You can log in to those machines to check whether a firewall rule works as expected. First of all, you need to add a ssh key to the ssh-agent on your machine:

```
$ ssh-add ~/.ssh/google_compute_engine
Enter passphrase for /Users/saito/.ssh/google_compute_engine:
Identity added: /Users/saito/.ssh/google_compute_engine
(/Users/saito/.ssh/google_compute_engine)
```

Then check whether an ICMP firewall rule can reject from external, because ICMP allows only public or private tagged hosts, so it must not allow ping from your machine as shown in the following screenshot:

```
$ ping -c 3 35.196.228.40
PING 35.196.228.40 (35.196.228.40): 56 data bytes
Request timeout for icmp_seq 0
Request timeout for icmp_seq 1

--- 35.196.228.40 ping statistics ---
3 packets transmitted, 0 packets received, 100.0% packet loss
$
```

On the other hand, the public host allows ssh from your machine, because public-ssh rule allows any (0.0.0.0/0).

```
$ ssh -A 35.196.228.40
The authenticity of host '35.196.228.40 (35.196.228.40)' can't be established.
ECDSA key fingerprint is SHA256:plGeb+dE1X0rANB4GklVeM0z835KE8FHGSCdSCdXCn4.
Are you sure you want to continue connecting (yes/no)? yes
Warning: Permanently added '35.196.228.40' (ECDSA) to the list of known hosts.
Linux public-on-subnet-b 4.9.0-3-amd64 #1 SMP Debian 4.9.30-2+deb9u3 (2017-08-06) x86_64

The programs included with the Debian GNU/Linux system are free software;
the exact distribution terms for each program are described in the
individual files in /usr/share/doc/*/copyright.

Debian GNU/Linux comes with ABSOLUTELY NO WARRANTY, to the extent
permitted by applicable law.
Last login: Thu Aug 24 06:27:21 2017 from 107.196.102.199
saito@public-on-subnet-b:~$
```

Of course, this host can ping and ssh to private hosts on `subnet-a` (`10.0.1.2`) through a private IP address, because of the `internal-icmp` rule and `private-ssh` rule.

Let's ssh to a private host and then install `tomcat8` and `tomcat8-examples` package (it will install the `/examples/` application to Tomcat).

```
● ● ●                    saito — saito@private-on-subnet-a: ~ — ssh -A 35.196.228.40 — 101×22
                              saito@private-on-subnet-a: ~ — ssh -A 35.196.228.40
saito@public-on-subnet-b:~$ ping -c 3 10.0.1.2
PING 10.0.1.2 (10.0.1.2) 56(84) bytes of data.
64 bytes from 10.0.1.2: icmp_seq=1 ttl=64 time=67.6 ms
64 bytes from 10.0.1.2: icmp_seq=2 ttl=64 time=66.5 ms
64 bytes from 10.0.1.2: icmp_seq=3 ttl=64 time=66.5 ms

--- 10.0.1.2 ping statistics ---
3 packets transmitted, 3 received, 0% packet loss, time 2003ms
rtt min/avg/max/mdev = 66.564/66.921/67.630/0.543 ms
saito@public-on-subnet-b:~$
saito@public-on-subnet-b:~$ ssh 10.0.1.2
Linux private-on-subnet-a 4.9.0-3-amd64 #1 SMP Debian 4.9.30-2+deb9u3 (2017-08-06) x86_64

The programs included with the Debian GNU/Linux system are free software;
the exact distribution terms for each program are described in the
individual files in /usr/share/doc/*/copyright.

Debian GNU/Linux comes with ABSOLUTELY NO WARRANTY, to the extent
permitted by applicable law.
Last login: Sun Aug 27 01:28:37 2017 from 172.16.1.2
saito@private-on-subnet-a:~$ sudo su
root@private-on-subnet-a:/home/saito# apt-get -y update; apt-get -y install tomcat8 tomcat8-examples
```

Remember that `subnet-a` is `10.0.1.0/24` CIDR prefix, but `subnet-b` is `172.16.1.0/24` CIDR prefix. But within the same VPC, there is connectivity with each other. This is a great benefit and advantage of using GCP whereby you can expand a network address block whenever you need.

Now, install nginx to public hosts (`public-on-subnet-a` and `public-on-subnet-b`):

```
//logout from VM instance, then back to your machine
$ exit

//install nginx from your machine via ssh
$ ssh 35.196.228.40 "sudo apt-get -y install nginx"
$ ssh 35.199.171.31 "sudo apt-get -y install nginx"

//check whether firewall rule (public-http) work or not
$ curl -I http://35.196.228.40/
HTTP/1.1 200 OK
Server: nginx/1.10.3
Date: Sun, 27 Aug 2017 07:07:01 GMT
Content-Type: text/html
```

```
Content-Length: 612
Last-Modified: Fri, 25 Aug 2017 05:48:28 GMT
Connection: keep-alive
ETag: "599fba2c-264"
Accept-Ranges: bytes
```

However, at this moment, you can't access Tomcat on a private host. Even if it has a public IP address. This is because a private host doesn't have any firewall rule that allows 8080/tcp yet:

```
$ curl http://104.199.121.234:8080/examples/
curl: (7) Failed to connect to 104.199.121.234 port 8080: Operation timed
out
```

Moving forward, not to just creating a firewall rule for Tomcat but will also be setting up a LoadBalancer to configure both nginx and Tomcat access from a single LoadBalancer.

Load balancing

GCP provides several types of load balancers as follows:

- Layer 4 TCP LoadBalancer
- Layer 4 UDP LoadBalancer
- Layer 7 HTTP(S) LoadBalancer

Layer 4, both TCP and UDP, LoadBalancers are similar to AWS Classic ELB. On the other hand, Layer 7 HTTP(S) LoadBalancer has content (context) based routing. For example, URL /img will forward to instance-a, everything else will forward to instance-b. So, it is more like an application level LoadBalancer.

 AWS also provides **Application Load Balancer** (**ALB** or **ELBv2**), which is quite similar to GCP Layer 7 HTTP(S) LoadBalancer. For details, please visit https://aws.amazon.com/blogs/aws/new-aws-application-load-balancer/.

In order to set up LoadBalancer, unlike AWS ELB, there are several steps needed to configure some items beforehand:

Configuration item	Purpose
Instance group	Determine group of VM instances or VM template (OS image).
Health check	Set health threshold (interval, timeout, and so on) to determine instance group health status.

Backend service	Set load threshold (maximum CPU or request per second) and session affinity (sticky session) to the instance group and also associate to health check.
url-maps (LoadBalancer)	This is an actual place holder to represent an L7 LoadBalancer that associates backend services and target HTTP(S) proxy
Target HTTP(S) proxy	This is a connector that makes relationships between frontend forwarding rules to LoadBalancer
Frontend forwarding rule	Associate IP address (ephemeral or static), port number to the target HTTP proxy
External IP (static)	(Optional) Allocate static external IP address for LoadBalancer

The following diagram is for all the preceding components' association that constructs L7 LoadBalancer:

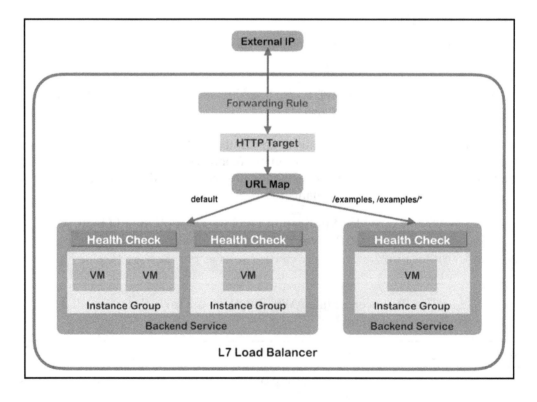

Let's set up an instance group first. In this example, there are three instance groups to create. One for private host Tomcat instance (8080/tcp) and another two instance groups for public HTTP instances per zones.

To do that, execute the following command to group three of them:

```
//create instance groups for HTTP instances and tomcat instance
$ gcloud compute instance-groups unmanaged create http-ig-us-west --zone
us-west1-a
$ gcloud compute instance-groups unmanaged create http-ig-us-east --zone
us-east1-c
$ gcloud compute instance-groups unmanaged create tomcat-ig-us-west --zone
us-west1-a

//because tomcat uses 8080/tcp, create a new named port as tomcat:8080
$ gcloud compute instance-groups unmanaged set-named-ports tomcat-ig-us-
west --zone us-west1-a --named-ports tomcat:8080

//register an existing VM instance to correspond instance group
$ gcloud compute instance-groups unmanaged add-instances http-ig-us-west --
instances public-on-subnet-a --zone us-west1-a
$ gcloud compute instance-groups unmanaged add-instances http-ig-us-east --
instances public-on-subnet-b --zone us-east1-c
$ gcloud compute instance-groups unmanaged add-instances tomcat-ig-us-west
--instances private-on-subnet-a --zone us-west1-a
```

Health check

Let's set standard settings by executing the following commands:

```
//create health check for http (80/tcp) for "/"
$ gcloud compute health-checks create http my-http-health-check --check-
interval 5 --healthy-threshold 2 --unhealthy-threshold 3 --timeout 5 --port
80 --request-path /

//create health check for Tomcat (8080/tcp) for "/examples/"
$ gcloud compute health-checks create http my-tomcat-health-check --check-
interval 5 --healthy-threshold 2 --unhealthy-threshold 3 --timeout 5 --port
8080 --request-path /examples/
```

Backend service

First of all, we need to create a backend service that specifies health check. And then add each instance group with threshold with CPU utilization that utilizes up to 80% and max capacity as 100% for both HTTP and Tomcat:

```
//create backend service for http (default) and named port tomcat
(8080/tcp)
$ gcloud compute backend-services create my-http-backend-service --health-
checks my-http-health-check --protocol HTTP --global
$ gcloud compute backend-services create my-tomcat-backend-service --
health-checks my-tomcat-health-check --protocol HTTP --port-name tomcat --
global


//add http instance groups (both us-west1 and us-east1) to http backend
service
$ gcloud compute backend-services add-backend my-http-backend-service --
instance-group http-ig-us-west --instance-group-zone us-west1-a --
balancing-mode UTILIZATION --max-utilization 0.8 --capacity-scaler 1 --
global
$ gcloud compute backend-services add-backend my-http-backend-service --
instance-group http-ig-us-east --instance-group-zone us-east1-c --
balancing-mode UTILIZATION --max-utilization 0.8 --capacity-scaler 1 --
global

//also add tomcat instance group to tomcat backend service
$ gcloud compute backend-services add-backend my-tomcat-backend-service --
instance-group tomcat-ig-us-west --instance-group-zone us-west1-a --
balancing-mode UTILIZATION --max-utilization 0.8 --capacity-scaler 1 --
global
```

Creating a LoadBalancer

The LoadBalancer needs to bind both `my-http-backend-service` and `my-tomcat-backend-service`. In this scenario, only `/examples` and `/examples/*` will be the forwarded traffic to `my-tomcat-backend-service`. Other than that, every URI forwards traffic to `my-http-backend-service`:

```
//create load balancer(url-map) to associate my-http-backend-service as
default
$ gcloud compute url-maps create my-loadbalancer --default-service my-http-
backend-service

//add /examples and /examples/* mapping to my-tomcat-backend-service
$ gcloud compute url-maps add-path-matcher my-loadbalancer --default-
service my-http-backend-service --path-matcher-name tomcat-map --path-rules
/examples=my-tomcat-backend-service,/examples/*=my-tomcat-backend-service

//create target-http-proxy that associate to load balancer(url-map)
$ gcloud compute target-http-proxies create my-target-http-proxy --url-
map=my-loadbalancer
```

```
//allocate static global ip address and check assigned address
$ gcloud compute addresses create my-loadbalancer-ip --global
$ gcloud compute addresses describe my-loadbalancer-ip --global
address: 35.186.192.6

//create forwarding rule that associate static IP to target-http-proxy
$ gcloud compute forwarding-rules create my-frontend-rule --global --
target-http-proxy my-target-http-proxy --address 35.186.192.6 --ports 80
```

If you don't specify an `--address` option, it will create and assign an ephemeral external IP address.

Finally, LoadBalancer has been created. However, one missing configuration is remaining. Private hosts don't have any firewall rules to allow Tomcat traffic (8080/tcp). This is why when you see LoadBalancer status, healthy status of `my-tomcat-backend-service` is kept down (0).

Backend

Backend services

1. my-http-backend-service

Endpoint protocol: **HTTP**   Named port: **http**   Timeout: **30 seconds**   Health check: my-http-health-check

Cloud CDN: **disabled**

⌄ Advanced configurations

Instance group ⌃	Zone	Healthy	Autoscaling	Balancing mode ⌃	Capacity
http-ig-us-east	us-east1-c	1 / 1	Off	Max CPU: 80%	100%
http-ig-us-west	us-west1-a	1 / 1	Off	Max CPU: 80%	100%

2. my-tomcat-backend-service

Endpoint protocol: **HTTP**   Named port: **tomcat**   Timeout: **30 seconds**   Health check: my-tomcat-health-check

Cloud CDN: **disabled**

⌄ Advanced configurations

Instance group ⌃	Zone	Healthy	Autoscaling	Balancing mode	Capacity
tomcat-ig-us-west	us-west1-a	0 / 1	Off	Max CPU: 80%	100%

In this case, you need to add one more firewall rule that allows connection from LoadBalancer to a private subnet (use the `private` network tag). According to GCP documentation (https://cloud.google.com/compute/docs/load-balancing/health-checks#https_ssl_proxy_tcp_proxy_and_internal_load_balancing), health check heart beat will come from address range `130.211.0.0/22` and `35.191.0.0/16`:

```
//add one more Firewall Rule that allow Load Balancer to Tomcat (8080/tcp)
$ gcloud compute firewall-rules create private-tomcat --network=my-custom-
network --source-ranges 130.211.0.0/22,35.191.0.0/16 --target-tags private
--allow tcp:8080
```

After a few minutes, `my-tomcat-backend-service` healthy status will be up (1); now you can access LoadBalancer from a web browser. When access to / it should route to `my-http-backend-service`, which has nginx application on public hosts:

On the other hand, if you access `/examples/` URL with the same LoadBalancer IP address, it will route to `my-tomcat-backend-service`, which is a Tomcat application on a private host, as shown in the following screenshot:

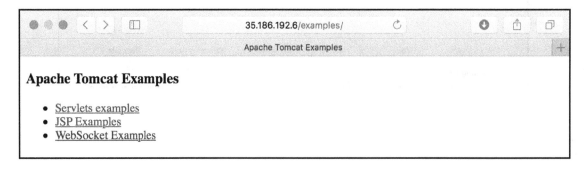

Overall, there are some steps needed to be performed to set up LoadBalancer, but it is useful to integrate different HTTP applications onto a single LoadBalancer to deliver your service efficiently with minimum resources.

Persistent Disk

GCE also has a storage service called **Persistent Disk** (**PD**) that is quite similar to AWS EBS. You can allocate desired size and types (either standard or SSD) on each zone and attach/detach to VM instances anytime.

Let's create one PD and then attach to the VM instance. Note that when attaching PD to the VM instance, both must be sat in the same zones. This limitation is the same as AWS EBS. So before creating PD, check the VM instance location once again:

```
$ gcloud compute instances list
NAME                                            ZONE          MACHINE_TYPE
PREEMPTIBLE   INTERNAL_IP   EXTERNAL_IP     STATUS
public-on-subnet-b                              us-east1-c    f1-micro
172.16.1.2    35.196.228.40    RUNNING
private-on-subnet-a                             us-west1-a    g1-small
10.0.1.2      104.199.121.234  RUNNING
public-on-subnet-a                              us-west1-a    f1-micro
10.0.1.3      35.199.171.31    RUNNING
```

Let's choose us-west1-a and then attach it to public-on-subnet-a:

```
//create 20GB PD on us-west1-a with standard type
$ gcloud compute disks create my-disk-us-west1-a --zone us-west1-a --type
pd-standard --size 20

//after a few seconds, check status, you can see existing boot disks as
well
$ gcloud compute disks list
NAME                                            ZONE          SIZE_GB  TYPE
STATUS
public-on-subnet-b                              us-east1-c    10       pd-
standard  READY
my-disk-us-west1-a                              us-west1-a    20       pd-
standard  READY
private-on-subnet-a                             us-west1-a    10       pd-
standard  READY
public-on-subnet-a                              us-west1-a    10       pd-
standard  READY

//attach PD(my-disk-us-west1-a) to the VM instance(public-on-subnet-a)
$ gcloud compute instances attach-disk public-on-subnet-a --disk my-disk-
```

```
us-west1-a --zone us-west1-a


//login to public-on-subnet-a to see the status
$ ssh 35.199.171.31
Linux public-on-subnet-a 4.9.0-3-amd64 #1 SMP Debian 4.9.30-2+deb9u3
(2017-08-06) x86_64
The programs included with the Debian GNU/Linux system are free software;
the exact distribution terms for each program are described in the
individual files in /usr/share/doc/*/copyright.
Debian GNU/Linux comes with ABSOLUTELY NO WARRANTY, to the extent
permitted by applicable law.
Last login: Fri Aug 25 03:53:24 2017 from 107.196.102.199
saito@public-on-subnet-a:~$ sudo su
root@public-on-subnet-a:/home/saito# dmesg | tail
[ 7377.421190] systemd[1]: apt-daily-upgrade.timer: Adding 25min 4.773609s
random time.
[ 7379.202172] systemd[1]: apt-daily-upgrade.timer: Adding 6min 37.770637s
random time.
[243070.866384] scsi 0:0:2:0: Direct-Access     Google    PersistentDisk   1
PQ: 0 ANSI: 6
[243070.875665] sd 0:0:2:0: [sdb] 41943040 512-byte logical blocks: (21.5
GB/20.0 GiB)
[243070.883461] sd 0:0:2:0: [sdb] 4096-byte physical blocks
[243070.889914] sd 0:0:2:0: Attached scsi generic sg1 type 0
[243070.900603] sd 0:0:2:0: [sdb] Write Protect is off
[243070.905834] sd 0:0:2:0: [sdb] Mode Sense: 1f 00 00 08
[243070.905938] sd 0:0:2:0: [sdb] Write cache: enabled, read cache:
enabled, doesn't support DPO or FUA
[243070.925713] sd 0:0:2:0: [sdb] Attached SCSI disk
```

You may see PD has been attached at /dev/sdb. Similar to AWS EBS, you have to format this disk. Because this is a Linux OS operation, the steps are exactly the same as described in Chapter 9, *Kubernetes on AWS*.

Google Container Engine (GKE)

Overall, there are some GCP components that have been introduced in previous sections. Now you can start to set up Kubernetes on GCP VM instances using those components. You can even use kops that was also introduced in Chapter 9, *Kubernetes on AWS* too.

However, GCP has a managed Kubernetes service called GKE. Underneath, it uses some GCP components such as VPC, VM instances, PD, firewall rules, and LoadBalancers.

Of course, as usual, you can use the `kubectl` command to control your Kubernetes cluster on GKE, which is included Cloud SDK. If you don't install the `kubectl` command on your machine yet, type the following command to install `kubectl` via Cloud SDK:

```
//install kubectl command
$ gcloud components install kubectl
```

Setting up your first Kubernetes cluster on GKE

You can set up a Kubernetes cluster on GKE using the `gcloud` command. It needs to specify several parameters to determine some configurations. One of the important parameters is network. You have to specify which VPC and subnet you will deploy. Although GKE supports multiple zones to deploy, you need to specify at least one zone for Kubernetes master node. This time, it uses the following parameters to launch a GKE cluster:

Parameter	Description	Value
`--cluster-version`	Specify Kubernetes version	`1.6.7`
`--machine-type`	VM instance type for Kubernetes Node	`f1-micro`
`--num-nodes`	Initial number size of Kubernetes nodes	`3`
`--network`	Specify GCP VPC	`my-custom-network`
`--subnetwork`	Specify GCP Subnet if VPC is custom mode	`subnet-c`
`--zone`	Specify single zone	`asia-northeast1-a`
`--tags`	Network tags that will be assigned to Kubernetes nodes	`private`

In this scenario, you need to type the following command to launch a Kubernetes cluster on GCP. It may take a few minutes to complete because, behind the scenes, it will launch several VM instances and set up Kubernetes master and nodes. Note that Kubernetes master and etcd will be fully managed by GCP. This means master node and etcd don't consume your VM instances:

```
$ gcloud container clusters create my-k8s-cluster --cluster-version 1.6.7 -
-machine-type f1-micro --num-nodes 3 --network my-custom-network --
subnetwork subnet-c --zone asia-northeast1-a --tags private
Creating cluster my-k8s-cluster...done.
Created
[https://container.googleapis.com/v1/projects/devops-with-kubernetes/zones/
asia-northeast1-a/clusters/my-k8s-cluster].
kubeconfig entry generated for my-k8s-cluster.
NAME            ZONE              MASTER_VERSION   MASTER_IP
MACHINE_TYPE  NODE_VERSION  NUM_NODES  STATUS
my-k8s-cluster asia-northeast1-a  1.6.7            35.189.135.13  f1-micro
1.6.7         3             RUNNING

//check node status
$ kubectl get nodes
NAME                                                  STATUS   AGE    VERSION
gke-my-k8s-cluster-default-pool-ae180f53-47h5         Ready    1m     v1.6.7
gke-my-k8s-cluster-default-pool-ae180f53-6prb         Ready    1m     v1.6.7
gke-my-k8s-cluster-default-pool-ae180f53-z611         Ready    1m     v1.6.7
```

Note that we specify the `--tags private` option, so Kubernetes node VM instance has a network tag as `private`. Therefore, it behaves the same as other regular VM instances that have `private` tags. Therefore you can't ssh from public Internet and you can't HTTP from internet either. But you can ping and ssh from another VM instance which has a `public` network tag.

Once all nodes are ready, let's access Kubernetes UI, which is installed by default. To do that, use the `kubectl proxy` command to connect to your machine as a proxy. Then access the UI via proxy:

```
//run kubectl proxy on your machine, that will bind to 127.0.0.1:8001
$ kubectl proxy
Starting to serve on 127.0.0.1:8001

//use Web browser on your machine to access to 127.0.0.1:8001/ui/
http://127.0.0.1:8001/ui/
```

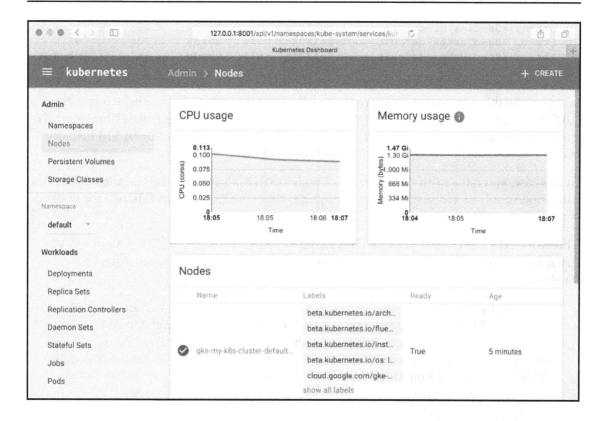

Node pool

When launching the Kubernetes cluster, you can specify the number of nodes using the `--num-nodes` option. GKE manages a Kubernetes node as node pool. Which means you can manage one or more node pools that attach to your Kubernetes cluster.

What if you need to add more nodes or delete some nodes? GKE provides a functionality to resize the node pool by following the command to change Kubernetes node from 3 to 5:

```
//run resize command to change number of nodes to 5
$ gcloud container clusters resize my-k8s-cluster --size 5 --zone asia-northeast1-a

//after a few minutes later, you may see additional nodes
$ kubectl get nodes
NAME                                              STATUS   AGE   VERSION
gke-my-k8s-cluster-default-pool-ae180f53-47h5     Ready    5m    v1.6.7
gke-my-k8s-cluster-default-pool-ae180f53-6prb     Ready    5m    v1.6.7
```

```
gke-my-k8s-cluster-default-pool-ae180f53-f8ps    Ready    30s    v1.6.7
gke-my-k8s-cluster-default-pool-ae180f53-qzxz    Ready    30s    v1.6.7
gke-my-k8s-cluster-default-pool-ae180f53-z611    Ready    5m     v1.6.7
```

Increasing the number of nodes will help if you need to scale out your node capacity. However, in this scenario, it still uses the smallest instance type (f1-micro, which has only 0.6 GB memory). It might not help if a single container needs more than 0.6 GB memory. In this case you need to scale up, which means you need to add a larger size of VM instance type.

In this case, you have to add another set of node pools onto your cluster. Because within the same node pool, all VM instances are configured the same. So you can't change the instance type in the same node pool.

Therefore, add a new node pool that has two new sets of g1-small (1.7 GB memory) VM instance type to the cluster. Then you can expand Kubernetes nodes with different hardware configuration.

 By default, there are some quotas that you can create a number limit of VM instances within one region (for example, up to eight cpu cores on us-west1). If you wish to increase this quota, you must change your account to be a paid account. Then request quota change to GCP. For more details, please read online documentation from https://cloud.google.com/compute/quotas and https://cloud.google.com/free/docs/frequently-asked-questions#how-to-upgrade.

Run the following command that adds an additional node pool that has two instances of g1-small instance:

```
//create and add node pool which is named "large-mem-pool"
$ gcloud container node-pools create large-mem-pool --cluster my-k8s-
cluster --machine-type g1-small --num-nodes 2 --tags private --zone asia-
northeast1-a

//after a few minustes, large-mem-pool instances has been added
$ kubectl get nodes
NAME                                                STATUS    AGE
VERSION
gke-my-k8s-cluster-default-pool-ae180f53-47h5       Ready     13m
v1.6.7
gke-my-k8s-cluster-default-pool-ae180f53-6prb       Ready     13m
v1.6.7
gke-my-k8s-cluster-default-pool-ae180f53-f8ps       Ready     8m
v1.6.7
gke-my-k8s-cluster-default-pool-ae180f53-qzxz       Ready     8m
```

```
v1.6.7
gke-my-k8s-cluster-default-pool-ae180f53-z611        Ready        13m
v1.6.7
gke-my-k8s-cluster-large-mem-pool-f87dd00d-9v5t      Ready        5m
v1.6.7
gke-my-k8s-cluster-large-mem-pool-f87dd00d-fhpn      Ready        5m
v1.6.7
```

Now you have a total of seven CPU cores and 6.4 GB memory in your cluster that has more capacity. However, due to larger hardware types, Kubernetes scheduler will probably assign to deploy pod to the `large-mem-pool` first, because it has enough memory capacity.

However, you may want to preserve `large-mem-pool` node in case a big application needs large heap memory size (for example, Java application). Therefore, you may want to differentiate `default-pool` and `large-mem-pool`.

In this case, Kubernetes label `beta.kubernetes.io/instance-type` helps to distinguish instance type of node. Therefore, use `nodeSelector` to specify a desired node to the pod. For example, following `nodeSelector` parameter will force to use `f1-micro` node for nginx application:

```
//nodeSelector specifies f1-micro
$ cat nginx-pod-selector.yml
apiVersion: v1
kind: Pod
metadata:
 name: nginx
spec:
 containers:
 - name: nginx
   image: nginx
 nodeSelector:
   beta.kubernetes.io/instance-type: f1-micro

//deploy pod
$ kubectl create -f nginx-pod-selector.yml
pod "nginx" created

//it uses default pool
$ kubectl get pods nginx -o wide
NAME       READY     STATUS      RESTARTS    AGE       IP              NODE
nginx      1/1       Running     0           7s        10.56.1.13      gke-my-k8s-
cluster-default-pool-ae180f53-6prb
```

If you want to specify a particular label instead of
`beta.kubernetes.io/instance-type`, use `--node-labels` option to
create a node pool. That assigns your desired label for the node pool.
For more details, please read the following online document:
`https://cloud.google.com/sdk/gcloud/reference/container/node-pools/create`.

Of course, you can feel free to remove a node pool if you no longer need it. To do that, run
the following command to delete `default-pool` (`f1-micro` x 5 instances). This operation
will involve pod migration (terminate pod on `default-pool` and re-launch on `large-mem-pool`) automatically, if there are some pods running at `default-pool`:

```
//list Node Pool
$ gcloud container node-pools list --cluster my-k8s-cluster --zone asia-northeast1-a
NAME            MACHINE_TYPE   DISK_SIZE_GB   NODE_VERSION
default-pool    f1-micro       100            1.6.7
large-mem-pool  g1-small       100            1.6.7

//delete default-pool
$ gcloud container node-pools delete default-pool --cluster my-k8s-cluster
--zone asia-northeast1-a

//after a few minutes, default-pool nodes x 5 has been deleted
$ kubectl get nodes
NAME                                                STATUS   AGE
VERSION
gke-my-k8s-cluster-large-mem-pool-f87dd00d-9v5t     Ready    16m
v1.6.7
gke-my-k8s-cluster-large-mem-pool-f87dd00d-fhpn     Ready    16m
v1.6.7
```

You may have noticed that all of the preceding operations happened in a single zone
(`asia-northeast1-a`). Therefore, if `asia-northeast1-a` zone gets an outage, your
cluster will be down. In order to avoid zone failure, you may consider setting up a multi
zone cluster.

Multi zone cluster

GKE supports multi zone cluster that allows you to launch Kubernetes nodes on multiple
zones, but limits within the same region. In previous examples, it has been provisioned at
`asia-northeast1-a` only, so let's re-provision a cluster that has `asia-northeast1-a`,
`asia-northeast1-b` and `asia-northeast1-c` in a total of three zones.

It is very simple; you just append an `--additional-zones` parameter when creating a new cluster.

As of August, 2017, there is a beta feature that supports to update existing clusters from single zones to multi zones. Use a beta command as follows:
`$ gcloud beta container clusters update my-k8s-cluster --additional-zones=asia-northeast1-b,asia-northeast1-c.`
To change an existing cluster to multi zone, it may need an additional SDK tool installation, but out of SLA.

Let's delete the previous cluster, and create a new cluster with an `--additional-zones` option:

```
//delete cluster first
$ gcloud container clusters delete my-k8s-cluster --zone asia-northeast1-a

//create a new cluster with --additional-zones option but 2 nodes only
$ gcloud container clusters create my-k8s-cluster --cluster-version 1.6.7 --machine-type f1-micro --num-nodes 2 --network my-custom-network --subnetwork subnet-c --zone asia-northeast1-a --tags private --additional-zones asia-northeast1-b,asia-northeast1-c
```

In this example, it will create two nodes per zones (`asia-northeast1-a`, b and c); therefore, a total of six nodes will be added:

```
$ kubectl get nodes
NAME                                               STATUS   AGE   VERSION
gke-my-k8s-cluster-default-pool-0c4fcdf3-3n6d      Ready    44s   v1.6.7
gke-my-k8s-cluster-default-pool-0c4fcdf3-dtjj      Ready    48s   v1.6.7
gke-my-k8s-cluster-default-pool-2407af06-5d28      Ready    41s   v1.6.7
gke-my-k8s-cluster-default-pool-2407af06-tnpj      Ready    45s   v1.6.7
gke-my-k8s-cluster-default-pool-4c20ec6b-395h      Ready    49s   v1.6.7
gke-my-k8s-cluster-default-pool-4c20ec6b-rrvz      Ready    49s   v1.6.7
```

You may also distinguish node zone by Kubernetes label `failure-domain.beta.kubernetes.io/zone` so that you can specify desired zones to deploy a pod.

Cluster upgrade

Once you start to manage Kubernetes, you may encounter some difficulty when upgrading Kubernetes clusters. Because the Kubernetes project is very aggressive, around every three months, there is a new release, such as 1.6.0 (released on March 28th 2017) to 1.7.0 (released on June 29th 2017).

GKE also keeps adding new version support in a timely manner. It allows us to upgrade both master and nodes via the `gcloud` command. You can run the following command to see which Kubernetes version is supported by GKE:

```
$ gcloud container get-server-config
Fetching server config for us-east4-b
defaultClusterVersion: 1.6.7
defaultImageType: COS
validImageTypes:
- CONTAINER_VM
- COS
- UBUNTU
validMasterVersions:
- 1.7.3
- 1.6.8
- 1.6.7
validNodeVersions:
- 1.7.3
- 1.7.2
- 1.7.1
- 1.6.8
- 1.6.7
- 1.6.6
- 1.6.4
- 1.5.7
- 1.4.9
```

So, you may see the latest supported version is 1.7.3 on both master and node at this moment. Since the previous example installed is version 1.6.7, let's update to 1.7.3. First of all, you need to upgrade master first:

```
//upgrade master using --master option
$ gcloud container clusters upgrade my-k8s-cluster --zone asia-northeast1-a
--cluster-version 1.7.3 --master
Master of cluster [my-k8s-cluster] will be upgraded from version
[1.6.7] to version [1.7.3]. This operation is long-running and will
block other operations on the cluster (including delete) until it has
run to completion.
Do you want to continue (Y/n)?  y
Upgrading my-k8s-cluster...done.
```

```
Updated
[https://container.googleapis.com/v1/projects/devops-with-kubernetes/zones/
asia-northeast1-a/clusters/my-k8s-cluster].
```

It takes around 10 minutes depending on environment, after that you can verify via the following command:

```
//master upgrade has been successfully to done
$ gcloud container clusters list --zone asia-northeast1-a
NAME            ZONE                 MASTER_VERSION  MASTER_IP
MACHINE_TYPE  NODE_VERSION  NUM_NODES  STATUS
my-k8s-cluster  asia-northeast1-a  1.7.3            35.189.141.251  f1-micro
1.6.7 *        6              RUNNING
```

Now you can upgrade all nodes to version 1.7.3. Because GKE tries to perform rolling upgrade, it will perform the following steps per node one by one:

1. Deregister a target node from the cluster.
2. Delete old VM instance.
3. Provision a new VM instance.
4. Set up the node with the 1.7.3 version.
5. Register to master.

Therefore, it takes much longer than a master upgrade:

```
//node upgrade (not specify --master)
$ gcloud container clusters upgrade my-k8s-cluster --zone asia-northeast1-a
--cluster-version 1.7.3
All nodes (6 nodes) of cluster [my-k8s-cluster] will be upgraded from
version [1.6.7] to version [1.7.3]. This operation is long-running and will
block other operations on the cluster (including delete) until it has run
to completion.
Do you want to continue (Y/n)?  y
```

During rolling upgrade, you can see node status as follows and it shows a mid process of rolling update (two nodes have upgraded to 1.7.3, one node is upgrading, three nodes are pending):

```
NAME                                                 STATUS
AGE        VERSION
gke-my-k8s-cluster-default-pool-0c4fcdf3-3n6d  Ready
37m        v1.6.7
gke-my-k8s-cluster-default-pool-0c4fcdf3-dtjj  Ready
37m        v1.6.7
gke-my-k8s-cluster-default-pool-2407af06-5d28  NotReady,SchedulingDisabled
37m        v1.6.7
```

```
gke-my-k8s-cluster-default-pool-2407af06-tnpj    Ready
37m        v1.6.7
gke-my-k8s-cluster-default-pool-4c20ec6b-395h    Ready
5m         v1.7.3
gke-my-k8s-cluster-default-pool-4c20ec6b-rrvz    Ready
1m         v1.7.3
```

Kubernetes cloud provider

GKE also integrates Kubernetes cloud provider out of box that deep integrate to GCP infrastructure; for example overlay network by VPC route, StorageClass by Persistent Disk, and Service by L4 LoadBalancer. The best part is ingress by L7 LoadBalancer. Let's take a look at how it works.

StorageClass

As per as kops on AWS, GKE also sets up StorageClass by default, which uses Persistent Disk:

```
$ kubectl get storageclass
NAME                  TYPE
standard (default)    kubernetes.io/gce-pd

$ kubectl describe storageclass standard
Name:           standard
IsDefaultClass:    Yes
Annotations:        storageclass.beta.kubernetes.io/is-default-class=true
Provisioner:        kubernetes.io/gce-pd
Parameters: type=pd-standard
Events:            <none>
```

Therefore, when creating Persistent Volume Claim, it will allocate GCP Persistent Disk as Kubernetes Persistent Volume automatically. Regarding Persistent Volume Claim and Dynamic Provisioning, please refer to Chapter 4, *Working with Storage and Resources*:

```
$ cat pvc-gke.yml
apiVersion: v1
kind: PersistentVolumeClaim
metadata:
    name: pvc-gke-1
spec:
  storageClassName: "standard"
  accessModes:
    - ReadWriteOnce
```

```
    resources:
      requests:
        storage: 10Gi

//create Persistent Volume Claim
$ kubectl create -f pvc-gke.yml
persistentvolumeclaim "pvc-gke-1" created

//check Persistent Volume
$ kubectl get pv
NAME                                      CAPACITY   ACCESSMODES
RECLAIMPOLICY    STATUS    CLAIM           STORAGECLASS   REASON    AGE
pvc-bc04e717-8c82-11e7-968d-42010a920fc3  10Gi       RWO                   Delete
Bound      default/pvc-gke-1    standard              2s

//check via gcloud command
$ gcloud compute disks list
NAME                                                         ZONE
SIZE_GB   TYPE            STATUS
gke-my-k8s-cluster-d2e-pvc-bc04e717-8c82-11e7-968d-42010a920fc3  asia-
northeast1-a  10          pd-standard  READY
```

L4 LoadBalancer

Similar to AWS cloud provider, GKE also supports using L4 LoadBalancer for Kubernetes
Service. Just specify `Service.spec.type` as LoadBalancer, and then GKE will set up and
configure L4 LoadBalancer automatically.

Note that the corresponding firewall rule between L4 LoadBalancer to Kubernetes node can
be created by cloud provider automatically. It is simple but powerful enough if you want to
expose your application to the internet quickly:

```
$ cat grafana.yml
apiVersion: apps/v1beta1
kind: Deployment
metadata:
  name: grafana
spec:
  replicas: 1
  template:
    metadata:
      labels:
        run: grafana
    spec:
      containers:
        - image: grafana/grafana
```

```
          name: grafana
          ports:
            - containerPort: 3000
---
apiVersion: v1
kind: Service
metadata:
  name: grafana
spec:
  ports:
    - port: 80
      targetPort: 3000
  type: LoadBalancer
  selector:
    run: grafana

//deploy grafana with Load Balancer service
$ kubectl create -f grafana.yml
deployment "grafana" created
service "grafana" created

//check L4 Load balancer IP address
$ kubectl get svc grafana
NAME       CLUSTER-IP     EXTERNAL-IP     PORT(S)        AGE
grafana    10.59.249.34   35.189.128.32   80:30584/TCP   5m

//can reach via GCP L4 Load Balancer
$ curl -I 35.189.128.32
HTTP/1.1 302 Found
Location: /login
Set-Cookie: grafana_sess=f92407d7b266aab8; Path=/; HttpOnly
Set-Cookie: redirect_to=%252F; Path=/
Date: Wed, 30 Aug 2017 07:05:20 GMT
Content-Type: text/plain; charset=utf-8
```

L7 LoadBalancer (ingress)

GKE also supports Kubernetes ingress that can set up GCP L7 LoadBalancer to dispatch HTTP requests to the target service based on URL. You just need to set up one or more NodePort services and then create ingress rules to point to services. Behind the scenes, Kubernetes creates and configures firewall rules, health check, backend service, forwarding rules, and URL maps automatically.

Let's create same examples that use nginx and Tomcat to deploy to the Kubernetes cluster first. These are using Kubernetes Services that bind to NodePort instead of LoadBalancer:

```
● ● ●                    📄 chapter10 — -bash — 73×19
                              -bash                                    +
$ kubectl create -f nginx.yml
deployment "nginx" created
service "nginx" created
$
$ kubectl create -f tomcat.yml
deployment "tomcat" created
service "tomcat" created
$
$ kubectl get pods
NAME                      READY     STATUS     RESTARTS    AGE
nginx-158599303-vk6cs     1/1       Running    0           46s
tomcat-670632475-l6h8q    1/1       Running    0           40s
$
$ kubectl get svc
NAME          CLUSTER-IP      EXTERNAL-IP    PORT(S)           AGE
kubernetes    10.59.240.1     <none>         443/TCP           19h
nginx         10.59.253.114   <nodes>        80:30339/TCP      53s
tomcat        10.59.248.76    <nodes>        8080:30813/TCP    47s
$ ▊
```

At this moment, you cannot access service, because there are no firewall rules that allow access to the Kubernetes node from the internet yet. So, let's create Kubernetes ingress that points to these services.

You can use `kubectl port-forward <pod name> <your machine available port><: service port number>` to access via the Kubernetes API server. For the preceding case, use `kubectl port-forward tomcat-670632475-l6h8q 10080:8080..`
After that, open your web browser to `http://localhost:10080/` and then you can access Tomcat pod directly.

Kubernetes ingress definition is quite similar to GCP backend service definition as it needs to specify a combination of URL path, Kubernetes service name, and service port number. So in this scenario, URL `/` and `/*` point to nginx service, also URL `/examples` and `/examples/*` point to the Tomcat service as follows:

```
$ cat nginx-tomcat-ingress.yaml
apiVersion: extensions/v1beta1
kind: Ingress
metadata:
  name: nginx-tomcat-ingress
spec:
  rules:
  - http:
      paths:
      - path: /
```

```
      backend:
        serviceName: nginx
        servicePort: 80
   - path: /examples
      backend:
        serviceName: tomcat
        servicePort: 8080
   - path: /examples/*
      backend:
        serviceName: tomcat
        servicePort: 8080
```

```
$ kubectl create -f nginx-tomcat-ingress.yaml
ingress "nginx-tomcat-ingress" created
```

It takes around 10 minutes to fully configure GCP components such as health check, forwarding rule, backend services, and url-maps:

```
$ kubectl get ing
NAME                    HOSTS    ADDRESS           PORTS    AGE
nginx-tomcat-ingress    *        107.178.253.174   80       1m
```

You can also check the status on the web console as follows:

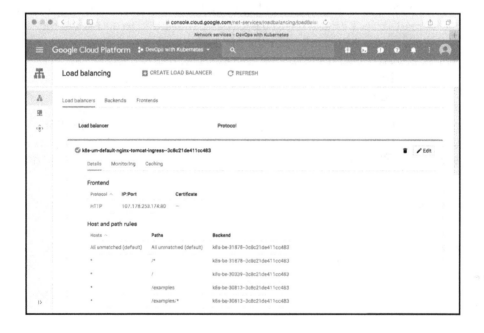

Once you have completed the setup of L7 LoadBalancer, you can access the public IP address of LoadBalancer (`http://107.178.253.174/`) to see the nginx page. As well as access to `http://107.178.253.174/examples/` then you can see `tomcat example` page.

In the preceding steps, we created and assigned an ephemeral IP address for L7 LoadBalancer. However, the best practice to use L7 LoadBalancer is to assign a static IP address instead, because you can also associate DNS (FQDN) to the static IP address.

To do that, update ingress setting to add an annotation `kubernetes.io/ingress.global-static-ip-name` to associate a GCP static IP address name as follows:

```
//allocate static IP as my-nginx-tomcat
$ gcloud compute addresses create my-nginx-tomcat --global

//check assigned IP address
$ gcloud compute addresses list
NAME               REGION  ADDRESS          STATUS
my-nginx-tomcat            35.186.227.252   IN_USE

//add annotations definition
$ cat nginx-tomcat-static-ip-ingress.yaml
apiVersion: extensions/v1beta1
kind: Ingress
metadata:
  name: nginx-tomcat-ingress
  annotations:
    kubernetes.io/ingress.global-static-ip-name: my-nginx-
tomcat
spec:
  rules:
  - http:
      paths:
      - path: /
        backend:
          serviceName: nginx
          servicePort: 80
      - path: /examples
        backend:
          serviceName: tomcat
          servicePort: 8080
      - path: /examples/*
        backend:
          serviceName: tomcat
          servicePort: 8080
```

```
//apply command to update Ingress
$ kubectl apply -f nginx-tomcat-static-ip-ingress.yaml

//check Ingress address that associate to static IP
$ kubectl get ing
NAME                      HOSTS      ADDRESS           PORTS     AGE
nginx-tomcat-ingress      *          35.186.227.252    80        48m
```

So, now you can access ingress via a static IP address as `http://35.186.227.252/` (nginx) and `http://35.186.227.252/examples/` (Tomcat) instead.

Summary

In this chapter, we discussed Google Cloud Platform. The basic concept is similar to AWS, but some of the policies and concepts are different. Especially Google Container Engine, as it is a very powerful service to use Kubernetes as production grade. Kubernetes cluster and node management are quite easy, not only the installation, but also upgrade. Cloud provider is also fully integrated to GCP, especially Ingress as it can configure L7 LoadBalancer with one command. Therefore, it is highly recommended to try GKE if you plan to use Kubernetes on the public cloud.

The next chapter will provide a sneak preview to some new features and alternative services to against Kubernetes.

11
What's Next

So far we have gone through topics around carrying out DevOps' tasks on Kubernetes across the board. Nevertheless, it's always challenging to implement knowledge under real-world circumstances, hence you may wonder whether Kubernetes is able to solve particular problems that you are currently facing. In this chapter, we'll learn the following topics to work out with challenges:

- Advanced Kubernetes features
- Kubernetes communities
- Other container orchestrator frameworks

Exploring the possibilities of Kubernetes

Kubernetes is evolving day by day, and it's at a pace where it is publishing one major version quarterly. Aside from the built-in functions that come with every new Kubernetes distribution, contributions from the community also play an important role in the ecosystem, and we'll have a tour around them in this section.

Mastering Kubernetes

Kubernetes' objects and resources are categorized into three API tracks, namely, alpha, beta, and stable to denote their maturity. The `apiVersion` field at the head of every resource indicates their level. If a feature has a versioning such as v1alpha1, it belongs to alpha-level API, and beta API is named in the same way. An alpha-level API is disabled by default and is subject to change without notice.

The beta-level API is enabled by default; it's well tested and considered to be stable, but the schema or object semantics could be changed as well. The rest of the parts are the stable, generally available ones. Once an API enters a stable stage, it's unlikely to be changed anymore.

Even though we've discussed concepts and practices about Kubernetes extensively, there are still considerable features that we haven't mentioned, that deal with a variety of workload as well as scenarios, and make Kubernetes extremely flexible. They may or may not apply to everyone's needs and are not stable enough in particular cases. Let's take a brief look at the popular ones.

Job and CronJob

They are also high-level pod controllers, that allow us to run containers that will eventually terminate. A job ensures a certain number of pods run to completion with success; a CronJob ensures that a job is invoked at given times. If we have the need to run batch workloads or scheduled tasks, we'd know that there are built-in controllers that come into play. Related information can be found at:
`https://kubernetes.io/docs/concepts/workloads/controllers/jobs-run-to-completion/`.

Affinity and anti-affinity between pods and nodes

We know a pod can be manually assigned to some nodes with the node selector, and a node can reject pods with taints. However, when it comes to more flexible circumstances, say, maybe we want some pods to be co-located, or we want pods to be distributed equally across availability zones, arranging our pods either by node selectors or by node taints may take a great effort. Thus, the affinity is designed to solve the case:
`https://kubernetes.io/docs/concepts/configuration/assign-pod-node/#affinity-and-anti-affinity`.

Auto-scaling of pods

Almost all modern infrastructure supports auto-scaling an instance group that runs the application, so does Kubernetes. The pod horizontal scaler (`PodHorizontalScaler`) is able to scale pod replicas with CPU/memory metrics in a controller such as Deployment. Starting from Kubernetes 1.6, the scaler formally supports scaling based on custom metrics, say transactions-per-second. More information can be found at
`https://kubernetes.io/docs/tasks/run-application/horizontal-pod-autoscale/`.

Prevention and mitigation of pod disruptions

We know pods are volatile, and they'd be terminated and relaunched across nodes as the cluster scales in and out. If too many pods of an application are destroyed simultaneously, it could result in lowering the service level or even the application fails. Especially when the application is stateful or quorum-based, it might barely tolerate, pod disruptions. To mitigate the disruption, we could leverage `PodDisruptionBudget` to inform Kubernetes of how many unavailable pods at any given time our application can tolerate so that Kubernetes is able to take proper actions with the knowledge of the applications on top of it. For more information, refer to `https://kubernetes.io/docs/concepts/workloads/pods/disruptions/`.

On the other hand, since `PodDisruptionBudget` is a managed object, it still cannot preclude disruptions caused by factors outside Kubernetes, such as hardware failures of a node, or node components being killed by the system due to insufficient memory. As such, we can incorporate tools such as node-problem-detector into our monitoring stack and properly configure the threshold on the resources of a node, to notify Kubernetes which begins to drain the node or evict excessive pods to prevent situations getting worse. For more detailed guides on node-problem-detector and resource thresholds, refer to the following topics:

- `https://kubernetes.io/docs/tasks/debug-application-cluster/monitor-node-health/`
- `https://kubernetes.io/docs/tasks/administer-cluster/out-of-resource/`

Kubernetes federation

A federation is a cluster of clusters. In other words, it's formed by multiple Kubernetes clusters and is accessible from a single control plane. The resources that are created on a federation will be synchronized across all connected clusters. As of Kubernetes 1.7, resources that can be federated include Namespace, ConfigMap, Secret, Deployment, DaemonSet, Service, and Ingress.

Capabilities of the federation to build a hybrid platform bring us another level of flexibility when architecting our software. For instance, we can federate clusters deployed in on-premise data centers and various public clouds together, to distribute workloads by cost, and utilize platform-specific features while keeping the elasticity to move around. Another typical use case is federating clusters scattered in different geographical locations to lower the edge latency to customers across the globe. Moreover, a single Kubernetes cluster backed by etcd3 supports 5,000 nodes while keeping the p99 of API response time less than 1 second (on version 1.6). If there is a need to have a cluster with thousands of nodes or beyond, we can surely federate clusters to get there.

The guide for a federation can be found at the following link: `https://kubernetes.io/docs/tasks/federation/set-up-cluster-federation-kubefed/`.

Cluster add-ons

Cluster add-ons are programs, that are designed or configured to enhance a Kubernetes cluster, and they are considered to be inherent parts of Kubernetes. For instance, Heapster, which we used in `Chapter 6`, *Monitoring and Logging*, is one of the add-on components, and so is the node-problem-detector we mentioned earlier.

As cluster add-ons may be used in some critical functions, some hosted Kubernetes services such as GKE deploy the add-on manager to safeguard the state of the add-ons from being modified or deleted. Managed add-ons will be deployed with a label, `addonmanager.kubernetes.io/mode`, on the pod controller. If the mode is `Reconcile`, any modification to the specification will be rolled back to its initial state; the `EnsureExists` mode only checks whether the controller exists, but doesn't check whether its specification is modified. For instance, the following Deployments are deployed on a 1.7.3 GKE cluster by default, and all of them are protected in the `Reconcile` mode:

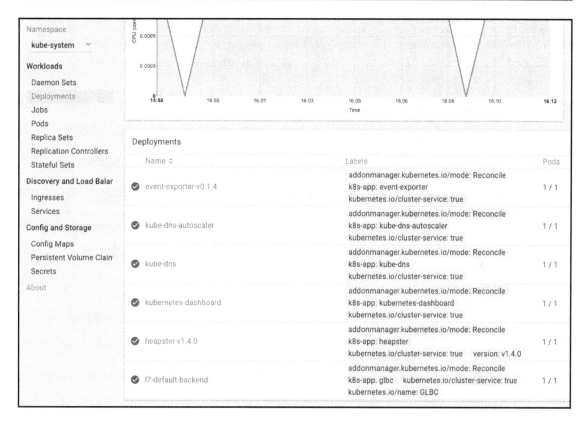

If you'd like to deploy add-ons in your own cluster, they can be found at: `https://github.com/kubernetes/kubernetes/tree/master/cluster/addons`.

Kubernetes and communities

When choosing an open source tool to use, we definitely wonder how supportiveness it is after we begin to use it. The supportiveness includes factors such as who is leading the project, whether the project is opinionated, how is the project's popularity, and so on.

Kubernetes originated from Google, and it's now backed by the **Cloud Native Computing Foundation** (**CNCF**, `https://www.cncf.io`). At the time when Kubernetes 1.0 was released, Google partnered with the Linux Foundation to form the CNCF, and donated Kubernetes as the seed project. The CNCF is meant to promote the development of containerized, dynamic orchestrated, and microservices-oriented applications.

Since all projects under the CNCF is container-based, they certainly could work fluently with Kubernetes. Prometheus, Fluentd, and OpenTracing, which we demonstrated and mentioned in `Chapter 6`, *Monitoring and Logging*, are all member projects of the CNCF.

Kubernetes incubator

Kubernetes incubator is a process to support projects for Kubernetes:

`https://github.com/kubernetes/community/blob/master/incubator.md.`

Graduated projects might become a core function of Kubernetes, a cluster add-on, or an independent tool for Kubernetes. Throughout the book, we have already seen and used many of them, including the Heapster, cAdvisor, dashboard, minikube, kops, kube-state-metrics, and kube-problem-detector, whatever makes Kubernetes better and better. You can explore these projects under Kubernetes (`https://github.com/kubernetes`), or the Incubator (`https://github.com/kubernetes-incubator`).

Helm and charts

Helm (`https://github.com/kubernetes/helm`) is a package manager, that simplifies the day-0 through day-n operations of running software on Kubernetes. It's also a graduated project from the incubator.

As what we've learned in `Chapter 7`, *Continuous Delivery*, deploying a containerized software to Kubernetes is basically writing manifests. Nonetheless, an application may be built with dozens of Kubernetes resources. If we're going to deploy such an application many times, the task to rename the conflict parts could be cumbersome. If we introduce the idea of template engines to solve the renaming hell, we will soon realize that we should have a place to store the templates as well as the rendered manifests. Hence, the Helm is meant to solve such annoying chores.

A package in Helm is called a chart, and it's a collection of configurations, definitions, and manifests to run an application. Charts contributed by the communities are published here: `https://github.com/kubernetes/charts`. Even if we are not going to use it, we can still find verified manifests for a certain package there.

Using Helm is quite simple. First get the Helm by running the official installation script here: `https://raw.githubusercontent.com/kubernetes/helm/master/scripts/get`.

After getting the Helm binary working, it fetches our kubectl configurations to connect to the cluster. We'd need to have a manager `Tiller` inside our Kubernetes cluster to manage every deployment task from Helm:

```
$ helm init
$HELM_HOME has been configured at /Users/myuser/.helm.
Tiller (the Helm server-side component) has been installed into your
Kubernetes Cluster.
Happy Helming!
```

> If we'd like to initialize the Helm client without installing the Tiller to our Kubernetes cluster, we can add the `--client-only` flag to `helm init`. Furthermore, using the `--skip-refresh` flag together allows us to initialize the client offline.

The Helm client is able to search the available charts from the command line:

```
$ helm search
NAME                         VERSION     DESCRIPTION
stable/aws-cluster-autoscaler 0.2.1      Scales worker nodes within
autoscaling groups.
stable/chaoskube             0.5.0       Chaoskube periodically kills
random pods in you...
...
stable/uchiwa                0.2.1       Dashboard for the Sensu
monitoring framework
stable/wordpress             0.6.3       Web publishing platform for
building blogs and ...
```

Let's install a chart from the repository, say the last one, `wordpress`:

```
$ helm install stable/wordpress
NAME:   plinking-billygoat
LAST DEPLOYED: Wed Sep  6 01:09:20 2017
NAMESPACE: default
STATUS: DEPLOYED
...
```

The deployed chart in Helm is a release. Here, we have a release, `plinking-billygoat`, installed. Once the pods and the services are ready, we can connect to our site and check the result:

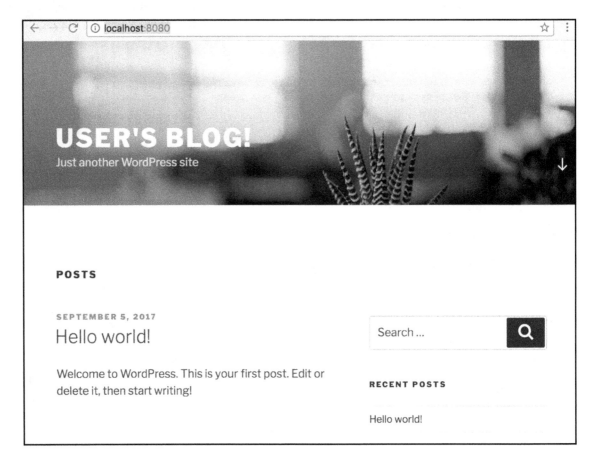

The teardown of a release also takes only one line of command:

```
$ helm delete plinking-billygoat
release "plinking-billygoat" deleted
```

 Helm leverages ConfigMap to store the metadata of a release, but deleting a release with `helm delete` won't delete its metadata. To wholly clear these metadata, we could either manually delete these ConfigMaps or add the `--purge` flag when executing `helm delete`.

In addition to managing packages in our cluster, another value brought by Helm is it is established as a standard to share packages and so it allows us to install popular software directly, such as the Wordpress we installed, rather than rewriting manifests for every software we used.

Gravitating towards a future infrastructure

It's always hard to tell whether a tool is a right fit or not, especially on opting for a cluster management software to underpin business missions, because the difficulties and challenges with which everyone is confronted varies. Apart from objective concerns such as performance, stability, availability, scalability, and usability, real circumstances also account for a significant portion of the decision. For instance, perspective on choosing a stack for developing greenfield projects and for building additional layers on top of bulky legacy systems could be diverse. Likewise, operating services by a highly cohesive DevOps team and by an organization working in the old day styles could also lead to distinct choices.

In addition to Kubernetes, there are still other platforms, which also feature orchestrating containers, and they all provide some easy ways to getting started. Let's step back and take an overview over them to find out the best fit.

Docker swarm mode

Swarm mode (`https://docs.docker.com/engine/swarm/`) is Docker's native orchestrator integrated in the Docker engine since version 1.12. As such, it shares the same API and user interface with Docker itself, including the use of Docker Compose files. Such degrees of integration are considered to be advantages as well as disadvantages depending on if one is comfortable with working on a stack, where all the components are from the same vendor.

A swarm cluster consists of managers and workers, where the managers are part of a consensus group to maintain the state of a cluster while keeping high availability. Enabling the swarm mode is quite easy. Roughly speaking, it's only two steps here: creating a cluster with `docker swarm init` and joining other managers and workers with `docker swarm join`. Additionally, Docker Cloud (`https://cloud.docker.com/swarm`) provided by Docker helps us bootstrap a swam cluster on various cloud providers.

Features that come with the swarm mode are the ones we'd expect to have in a container platform, that is to say, container lifecycle managements, two scheduling strategies (replicated and global, which resemble to Deployment and DaemonSet in Kubernetes respectively), service discovery, secret managements, and so on. There is also an ingress network that works like the NodePort type service in Kubernetes, but we'll have to bring up something such as nginx or Traefik if we need a L7 layer LoadBalancer.

All in all, the swarm mode proffers an option to orchestrate containerized applications that works out of the box once one begins to use Docker. Meanwhile, as it speaks the same language with Docker and simple architecture, it's also considered to be the easiest platform among all choices. Therefore, it's indeed reasonable to choose the swarm mode to get something done quickly. However, its simplicity sometimes leads to lack of flexibility. For example, in Kubernetes we are able to employ Blue/Green deployment strategy by merely manipulating selector and labels, but there is no easy way to do so in the swarm mode. Since the swarm mode is still under active development, such as the function to store configuration data, which is analogous to ConfigMap in Kubernetes is introduced in version 17.06, we definitely could look forward to the swarm mode becoming more powerful in the future while retaining its simplicity.

Amazon EC2 container service

EC2 container service (ECS, `https://aws.amazon.com/ecs/`) is AWS' answer to the Docker upsurge. Unlike Google Cloud Platform and Microsoft Azure, which provides open source cluster managers such as Kubernetes, Docker Swarm, and DC/OS, AWS sticks to its own way in response to the need of container services.

ECS takes its Docker as its container runtime, and it also accepts Docker Compose files in syntax version 2. Moreover, terminologies of ECS and Docker Swarm mode are pretty much the same thing, such as the idea of task and service. Yet the similarities stop here. Although the core functions of ECS is simple and even rudimentary, as a part of AWS, ECS fully utilizes other AWS products to enhance itself such as VPC for container networking, CloudWatch, and CloudWatch Logs for monitoring and logging, Application LoadBalancer and Network LoadBalancer with Target Groups for service discovering, Lambda with Route 53 for DNS-based service discovering, CloudWatch Events for CronJob, EBS and EFS for data persistence, ECR for docker registry, Parameter Store and KMS for storing configuration files and secrets, CodePipeline for CI/CD, and so forth. There is another AWS product, AWS Batch (https://aws.amazon.com/batch/) that is built on top of ECS for processing batch workloads. Furthermore, an open source tool from AWS ECS team, Blox (https://blox.github.io), augments the capabilities to customize the scheduling that are not shipped with ECS, such as the DaemonSet-like strategy, by wiring couples of AWS products up. From another perspective, if we take AWS as an integral whole to evaluate ECS, it's truly mighty.

Setting up an ECS cluster is easy: create an ECS cluster via the AWS console or API and join EC2 nodes with the ECS agent to the cluster. The good thing is that the master side is managed by AWS so that we are free from keeping wary eye on the master.

Overall, ECS is easy to getting started, especially for people who are familiar with Docker as well as AWS products. On the other hand, if we aren't satisfied with the primitives currently provided, we have to do some handworks either with other AWS services mentioned earlier or third-party solutions to get things done, and this could result in undesired costs on those services and efforts on configurations and maintenances to make sure every component works together nicely. Besides, ECS is only available on AWS, which could also be one concern that people would take it seriously.

Apache Mesos

Mesos (http://mesos.apache.org/) had been created long before Docker set off the trend of containers, and its goal is to solve the difficulties regarding management of resources in a cluster comprising general hardware while supporting diverse workloads. To build such a general platform, Mesos makes use of a two-tier architecture to divide the resource allocation and the task execution. As such, the execution part can theoretically extend to any kind of task, including orchestrating Docker containers.

Even though we talked about only the name Mesos here, it is basically in charge of one tier of jobs as a matter of fact, and the execution part is done by other components called Mesos frameworks. For example, Marathon (`https://mesosphere.github.io/marathon/`) and Chronos (`https://mesos.github.io/chronos/`) were two popular frameworks to deploy long-running and batch-job tasks respectively, and both of them support the Docker container. In this way, when it comes to the term Mesos, it's referring to a stack such as Mesos/Marathon/Chronos or Mesos/Aurora. In fact, under Mesos' two-tier architecture, it's viable to run Kubernetes as a Mesos framework as well.

Frankly speaking, a properly organized Mesos stack and Kubernetes are pretty much the same in terms of capabilities except that Kubernetes requires that everything that is run on it should be containerized regardless of Docker, rkt, or a hypervisor container. On the other hand, as Mesos focuses on its generic scheduling and tends to keep its core small, some essential functions should be installed, tested, and operated separately, which could bring about extra efforts.

DC/OS (`https://dcos.io/`) published by Mesosphere takes advantages of Mesos to build a full-stack cluster management platform, which is more comparable to Kubernetes with respect to capabilities. As a one-stop-shop for every solution built atop Mesos, it bundles couples of components to drive the whole system, Marathon for common workloads, Metronome for scheduled jobs, Mesos-DNS for service discovery, and so forth. Though these building blocks seem to be complicated, DC/OS greatly simplified the works on installations and configurations by CloudFormation/Terraform templates, and its package management system, Mesosphere Universe. Since DC/OS 1.10, Kubernetes is officially integrated into DC/OS, and it can be installed via the Universe. Hosted DC/OS is also available on some cloud providers such as Microsoft Azure.

The following screenshot is the web console interface of DC/OS, which aggregates information from every component:

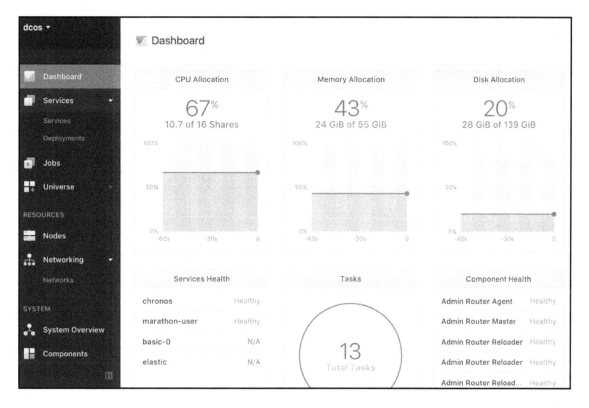

So far we have discussed the community version of DC/OS, but some features are only available in the enterprise edition. They are mostly on security and compliance, and the list can be found at `https://mesosphere.com/pricing/`.

Summary

In this chapter, we have briefly discussed Kubernetes features that applies to certain more specific use cases, and guided where and how to leverage the strong communities, including the Kubernetes incubator and the package manager Helm.

In the end, we went back to the start and gave overview to three other popular alternatives for the same goal: orchestrating containers, so as to leave the conclusion in your mind for choosing your next generation infrastructure.

Index

R

RBAC (role-based access control) 195
readiness probe 237
Remote Method Invocation (RMI) 18
remoting 19
ReplicaSet (RS) 70, 88
ReplicationController (RC) 70, 88
Resource QoS (Quality of Service) 156
Resource Quotas
    reference link 330
resources
    DaemonSet, updating 226
    rollouts, managing 224
    StatefulSet, updating 226
    updates, triggering 222
    updating 221
RESTful design 20
rkt
    reference link 41
RMI compiler (rmic) 18
rollouts
    managing 224
Route 53 291
RubyGems
    URL 15

S

security group (SG) 284, 313
Sendmail 22
service-loadbalancer
    reference link 188
shell form 55
SIGTERM
    container process, forwarding issue 241
    handling 241
    termination handler, invoking issue 243
Simple Queue Service (SQS) 276
Simple Storage Service (S3) 276, 295
Slack
    URL 31
SOAP 19
Software as a Service (SaaS) 23
Software Defined Network (SDN) 10, 276
software delivery challenges

about 7
    agile models 8
    Continuous Delivery (CD) 11
    Continuous Integration (CI) 10
    physical delivery 7
    software delivery, on cloud 9
    waterfall 7
Software Development Life Cycle (SDLC) 7
Spring Boot
    reference link 21
SpringMVC
    reference link 17
Standard Operation Procedure (SOP) 13
StatefulSet
    about 228
    updating 226
steps, continuous delivery pipeline
    after_success 232
    deploy 233
    script 231
Storage Area Network (SAN) 276
Struts
    URL 17
subnet 278, 312

T

TeamCity
    reference link 23
Tomcat 129
tools, continuous delivery pipeline
    steps explained 230
tools
    about 22
    communication tools 30
    Continuous Delivery tool 24
    Continuous Integration tool 22
    logging 27
    monitoring 27
    Public Cloud 31
    selecting 229
Travis CI
    about 229
    URL 23

www.ingramcontent.com/pod-product-compliance
Lightning Source LLC
Chambersburg PA
CBHW080611060326
40690CB00021B/4656